NEWMAN'S
BIRDS
BY COLOUR

*This book is dedicated
to all fledgling birders*

NEWMAN'S
BIRDS
BY COLOUR

Text and illustrations by
KENNETH NEWMAN

Original concept
Irene Bredenkamp and Phoebus Perdikis
UPDATED BY VANESSA NEWMAN

Struik Publishers

(a division of New Holland Publishing (South Africa) (Pty) Ltd)

Cornelis Struik House, 80 McKenzie Street, Cape Town, 8001

New Holland Publishing is a member of Johnnic Communications Ltd.

Visit us at **www.struik.co.za**

Log on to our photographic website

www.imagesofafrica.co.za for an African experience

First published 2000

Second edition 2008

First impression

Copyright © in text: Ken Newman 2000, 2008

Copyright © in photographs (unless otherwise indicated)

and illustrations: Ken Newman 2000, 2008

Copyright © in published edition:

Struik New Holland Publishing (Pty) Ltd 2000, 2008

Publishing manager: Pippa Parker

Editor: Pearson Editorial

Designer: Lyndall du Toit

Design update: Louise Topping

Cover Design: Janice Evans, Louise Topping

Proofreader and Indexer: Glynne Newlands

Concept: Irene Bredenkamp and Phoebus Perdikis

Reproduction by Hirt & Carter Cape (Pty) Ltd, Cape Town

Printed and bound by Kyodo Printing Co (Singapore) Pte Ltd

ISBN 978 1 77007 179 7

CONTENTS

INTRODUCTION 6

How to use this book 7

What is a bird? 8

The classification of birds 8

The anatomy of a bird 10

What is a passerine? 11

Birds' legs and feet 12

Beaks and bills 14

Feather structure and arrangement 19

Colour in feathers 21

The flying bird 24

Bird migration 25

Methods of feeding 27

Display in courtship, aggression and fear 30

The nests they build 32

What do I need to go birding? 35

Where to look for birds 37

When to look for birds 39

How to look at birds 39

Jizz 41

Finding your way around
    'Newman's field guide' 42

DESCRIBING BIRDS BY COLOUR 46–297

Colour key 45

Glossary 298

Index 299

INTRODUCTION

This book has been designed primarily as a guide for beginner birdwatchers and all those, a little higher up the birding ladder, who continue to struggle with getting to know some common birds. Time and again I am told, 'It flew away before I could get a better look at it, but it was *red*' (or blue, or green or yellow). Invariably others who saw the bird will argue about its colour or exactly where on the bird the colour was. Much time will be spent paging through the field guide, from albatrosses to canaries, but to no avail. Rather than accepting the motto 'A bird flown is seldom known', the disgruntled birder will suffer a restless night. What can be done?

There is little doubt that the features memorised by most novice birders in the above circumstances are the bird's approximate size and its colour, or the colour that made an impression. There is no doubt whatsoever that colour, no matter how briefly glimpsed, remains in the memory. If one is to assume that the bird seen was indeed red, then the list of possible species will be very short indeed. However, when you delve a little deeper into the problem, it usually transpires that, on second thoughts, it was only its beak, head or tail that was red (or was it green?). In retrospect the observer is never quite certain. At this point the 'expert' is expected to produce the correct answer and put everyone out of their misery.

My co-authors experienced these identification problems on many occasions and so the germ of an idea was born. After many months and much homework, Irene had cut to pieces numerous copies of *Newman's Birds of Southern Africa* to assemble a weighty paste-up collection of birds by colour. This eventually arrived on my publisher's desk. And so the idea began to take shape.

Birds by Colour focuses on birds that have a dominant colour in their plumage, beaks or legs. It is not a field guide and was never intended to be, but should be regarded as a companion to my field guide *Newman's Birds of Southern Africa.*

KENNETH NEWMAN

How to use this book

This book has been planned with a dual purpose. The first section gives aspirant birders a broad overview of what makes a bird a 'bird' as opposed to other animals, and a glimpse of the way birds live. The section touches on flight, migration, feeding, display, nests and bird habitats. It is written without scientific jargon, to introduce the novice to birds as fascinating living beings. This is followed by notes on identifying birds: how to start, what you need, and where to look for them.

The second section is designed to help the beginner identify 'the one that got away'; a briefly seen, tantalising feathered creature that flew before you

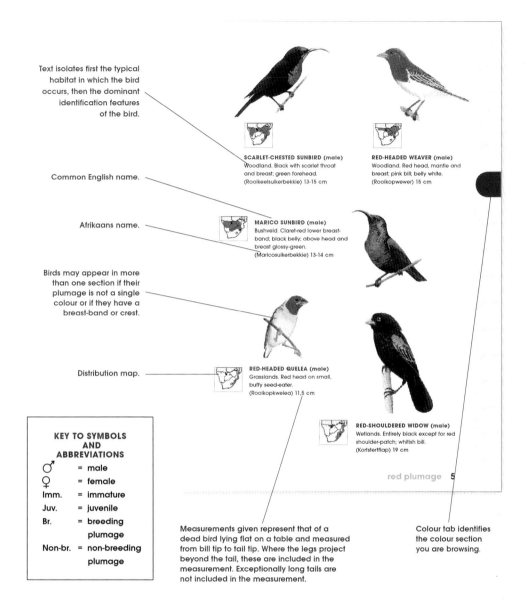

Text isolates first the typical habitat in which the bird occurs, then the dominant identification features of the bird.

SCARLET-CHESTED SUNBIRD (male)
Woodland. Black with scarlet throat and breast; green forehead.
(Rooikeelsuikerbekkie) 13-15 cm

RED-HEADED WEAVER (male)
Woodland. Red head, mantle and breast; pink bill; belly white.
(Rooikopwewer) 15 cm

Common English name.

Afrikaans name.

MARICO SUNBIRD (male)
Bushveld. Claret-red lower breast-band; black belly; above head and breast glossy-green.
(Maricosuikerbekkie) 13-14 cm

Birds may appear in more than one section if their plumage is not a single colour or if they have a breast-band or crest.

Distribution map.

RED-HEADED QUELEA (male)
Grasslands. Red head on small, buffy seed-eater.
(Rooikopkwelea) 11,5 cm

RED-SHOULDERED WIDOW (male)
Wetlands. Entirely black except for red shoulder-patch; whitish bill.
(Kortstertflap) 19 cm

red plumage 5

KEY TO SYMBOLS AND ABBREVIATIONS

♂	=	male
♀	=	female
Imm.	=	immature
Juv.	=	juvenile
Br.	=	breeding plumage
Non-br.	=	non-breeding plumage

Measurements given represent that of a dead bird lying flat on a table and measured from bill tip to tail tip. Where the legs project beyond the tail, these are included in the measurement. Exceptionally long tails are not included in the measurement.

Colour tab identifies the colour section you are browsing.

could focus but left a lasting colour impression. Let's say you've seen an un-identified bird and retained an impression of its predominant colour, say red. You can now page to the section dealing with red birds and see if you can find the bird there. Once the bird has been 'found' in this book by its colour, refer to *Newman's Birds of Southern Africa* to confirm your identification. Once you have located the bird in the index of Newman's field guide, ascertain from the distribution map on the relevant page that the bird you think you saw occurs in the region and that it is present at the appropriate time of the year, plus all the other information about the species that will help confirm the accuracy of your identification.

What is a bird?

It is not enough simply to say a bird is a creature that flies. In fact, not all birds can fly, whereas some reptiles, fish and even mammals do fly. Certain lizards have thin membranes stretched between their legs which act as simple wings, while some frogs have enlarged feet with webs between their toes. These simple 'air foils' merely enable the creatures to descend through the air slowly. In other words, they are gliders; they cannot flap their 'air foils' to fly higher. We all know about flying fish with their significantly enlarged fins that resemble wings, but once the fish has jumped out of the water its flight is merely a delayed descent back again. An important exception to these delayed descents is one group of mammals: the bats. Like birds, bats are able to fly and manoeuvre at great speed, the membranes between their front and rear legs being well developed and stiffened by bones. This modification enables these membranes to be flapped like wings to propel the bat over long distances.

The one important structural difference that characterises a bird is its unique covering of feathers, which are believed to be an evolutionary modification of reptilian scales. The earliest and most primitive known avian fossil, named Archaeopteryx, was discovered in Germany and lived in the late Jurassic period (150–155 million years ago). Archaeopteryx was a creature somewhere between a reptile and a bird, with feathers all over its body to facilitate flight. However, it had teeth, three sharp claws on its wings and a bony, reptilian tail. It lacked the shoulder joint mobility to lift its wings above its back like modern birds and its feathers were large and not very well aligned, so the aerial mobility of Archaeopteryx is unclear.

Feathers take various forms, from contour feathers to the very important flight feathers. Read about them in the section entitled 'feather structure'.

Archaeopteryx, the earliest known bird-like creature, lived 150–155 million years ago.

The classification of birds

Although we do not use scientific names for birds in this book, every bird (as well as all other known creatures and plants) has a scientific name in addition to the common names that we use in the various languages. When common names are used internationally they often cause confusion, since names used elsewhere can be quite different from those used in individual countries. For example, in southern

Africa we are familiar with birds such as louries, mousebirds and dikkops, but in much of the rest of Africa, and even in the rest of the world, these birds are known as turacos, colies and thick-knees! The same sort of local naming takes place in other countries too, and there are no rules to prevent it. It is therefore important to have a standardised set of names for all living things to prevent any possibility of confusion. The international system for scientific names is used by all countries whatever their home language. Under this system all living things are given two-part names using a neutral language: Latin or Ancient Greek. No two birds (or any other living things) can have the same scientific name and, once the name has been allocated, it cannot easily be changed.

Birds are grouped into families, and within the families are one or more genera (genus in the singular). Each genus has within it one or more species. A species can be further divided into subspecies. For example, the common House Sparrow belongs to the family Ploceidae. Within that family we find the genus *Passer*, and within that genus the House Sparrow has been given the specific name *domesticus*. The House Sparrow's official name is *Passer domesticus* throughout the world and it is always written in italic type. This particular sparrow originated in Europe but, over the years, its range spread into Asia, Africa and even farther afield. Some of these far-flung populations of the House Sparrow developed changes in size and plumage details. Ultimately they came to be regarded as subspecies of the original or nominate European race and were given an additional subspecific name. As a result, the Indian race of the House Sparrow is known as *Passer domesticus indicus* and it is this subspecies that was introduced, and eventually became dominant, in South Africa. There are three other sparrows in South Africa, all belonging to the genus *Passer*. They are the Cape Sparrow *P. melanurus*, the Great Sparrow *P. motitensis* and the Southern Grey-headed Sparrow *P. diffusus*. While all scientific bird names are written in italic type, only the first or generic name is given a capital initial.

What is a species?

A species is best defined as a type of bird that can only reproduce with other members of its kind. For example, we have discussed four species of sparrow that live in southern Africa. Although all four belong to the genus *Passer,* under normal circumstances the four species will not interbreed.

During courtship, species are prevented from interbreeding in various natural ways. Voice certainly plays an important role. Although we may not detect any great difference between the voice of, say, the Cape Sparrow and the Great Sparrow, there are in fact many subtle differences in structure and pitch that are quite clear to the birds themselves. Another important factor is plumage colour. The marks and colours seen in birds play an important role in courtship and territorial defence. For example, the black markings on the heads and breasts of both the male Cape and Great sparrows each have a different pattern and these are important recognition features for the female, as is the distribution of the chestnut plumage colouring in the males. Voice, plumage and the male's unique courtship behaviour all combine to ensure specific isolation.

The anatomy of a bird

Getting to know the names of the various parts of a bird is necessary if you are to understand the terminology used in discussing birds in your field guide. You may wonder, for instance, why the White-fronted Bee-eater is so called when it obviously doesn't have a white breast, but if you check the anatomy diagram you will see that the 'front' of a bird is not its chest but its forehead. Likewise, terms such as secondaries, primaries, coverts, tarsus and orbital ring need to be understood. I recommend that you give yourself 15 minutes to study the external 'Anatomy of a Bird' chart below and thereafter refer to it from time to time just to refresh your memory.

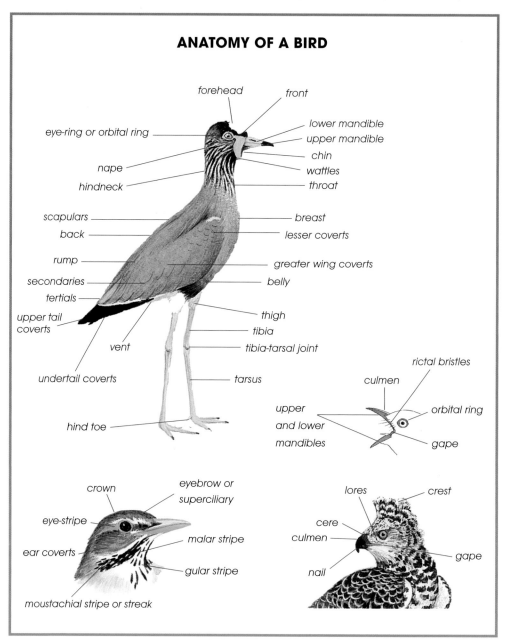

ANATOMY OF A BIRD

What is a passerine?

Passerines, also known as songbirds or perching birds, consist of about 5 200 species and make up more than 50% of the roughly 9 000 bird species found in the world. Passerines are land birds and typical members of this group are the robins, thrushes, white-eyes and wagtails that frequent our gardens. They are all small- to medium-sized birds, the largest passerines being the crow family. The most important external feature of a passerine bird is its four toes, all set at the same level: three toes facing forwards and one toe directed backwards, all unwebbed. This standard foot arrangement of passerines is crucial to their perching ability. Have you ever wondered why these little birds don't get blown off their perches while roosting on a windy night? It's because their feet actually lock onto the perch while the bird is crouched sleeping, and only relax and unlock when the bird flexes its legs by standing (see the diagram below).

The passerine foot typically has all four toes joined at the same level: three face forwards and one backwards.

SONGBIRDS

The term 'songbird' when applied to passerines is not entirely accurate. Although most of the world's finest songsters are passerines, there are also some very pleasant sounds uttered by non-passerines, such as the pleasant duet of Black-collared Barbets or the soft cooing of a Laughing Dove.

A SIMPLIFIED DIAGRAM OF A PERCHING FOOT

To settle securely on a small branch or slender wire, the bird's flexion leg-tendons are automatically tightened as the leg is folded.

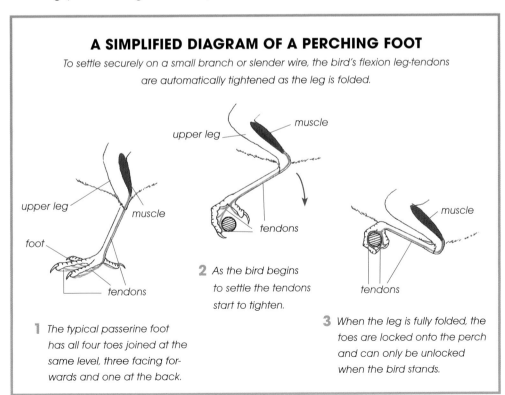

muscle

upper leg

upper leg

muscle

foot

tendons

tendons

tendons

muscle

1 The typical passerine foot has all four toes joined at the same level, three facing forwards and one at the back.

2 As the bird begins to settle the tendons start to tighten.

3 When the leg is fully folded, the toes are locked onto the perch and can only be unlocked when the bird stands.

Non-passerines

The remaining feathered creatures are ocean birds, inland waterbirds, bustards, francolins, raptors, sandgrouse, doves and pigeons, cuckoos, coucals, parrots, nightjars, swifts, bee-eaters, kingfishers, barbets, honeyguides, woodpeckers, rollers, hoopoes and hornbills. These birds do not have locking feet like passerines, but you will notice that some have long legs (inland waterbirds and grassland birds) while others have very short legs (terns, swifts, nightjars, wood-hoopoes). A closer look will reveal the great variety of leg lengths and foot shapes shared by this group. Some plovers, dikkops, coursers, oystercatchers and bustards have no hind toe. In those that do, the hind toe is often small and may be placed higher up the leg than the front toes. Another variable feature of non-passerines is the great variety of beak shapes and lengths seen in this group, from the very long beaks of some waterbirds to the heavy appearance of those carried by hornbills.

Birds' legs and feet

We see very little of the true leg in most birds because the upper sections, the bird's 'knee' and tibia, are covered by feathers. What we see as the backwards-bending 'knee' is equivalent to our ankle joint, while the lower 'leg' is actually the ankle. Technically then, a bird's foot extends from what we see as the 'knee' (the tibio-tarsal joint) down to the toes.

In some long-legged non-passerine birds, for example, storks and flamingoes, quite a lot of the 'upper leg' or tibia is exposed, but in the majority of passerines it is either fully or partially covered by feathers. Again the total leg length of a bird varies enormously in relation to its body size, from the very long legs of the Secretarybird to the extremely short legs of a swift or a nightjar. Birds that need to run at speed, such as the Common Ostrich and other terrestrial species, need long legs, whereas aerial feeders, which have little need to walk, have the shortest legs.

PADDLE-FEET

Ducks have webbed, paddle-like feet as an aid to swimming, but cormorants and many other waterbirds also have webbed feet. The Dabchick, Red-knobbed Coot and African Finfoot have semi-webbed or lobed feet that serve a similar purpose. Some webbed or semi-webbed feet, as found in flamingoes, storks and avocets, serve a dual purpose, allowing the bird to walk on soft mud and to swim.

In birds' feet we again see great variation. Birds of prey have very powerful feet, especially the inner and rear toes, which are used for grasping and holding. Their talons are also large, well curved and very sharp. A similar foot with short toes and sharp claws is found in parrots, but in their case the foot is used for clinging and scrambling along branches, often in strange attitudes, to reach fruit. The foot is then used as a hand for feeding.

Certain waterbirds that need to walk on floating vegetation have long toes to enable them to do so by spreading their weight over a greater area. The African Jacana has the longest toes of all, plus greatly elongated claws. In contrast, swifts have very small feet with all four toes facing forwards – an arrangement

An African Jacana showing a long-toed foot as it approaches its nest with eggs.

W. Tarboton

that, coupled with their sharp needle-like claws, enables them to cling to the rough surfaces of rocky cliffs (or buildings) where they roost and nest. Swifts cannot perch on trees or telephone wires like swallows.

A highly specialised foot is that of the flightless Common Ostrich, with only two toes, one large and the other small, designed for fast running. Perhaps the strangest foot of all also has the strangest name: the zygodactyl or yoke-toed foot found in woodpeckers, barbets, cuckoos, parrots and others. In this foot the toes are permanently paired, two in front and two behind, the first and fourth toes pointing backwards to ensure a very firm grip. Adaptations of the zygodactyl foot are found in kingfishers, hornbills and rollers, where the third and fourth toes are joined: the syndactyl foot.

THE LEGS OF A SWIFT

The legs of swifts are so short that they can barely walk on a flat surface. If they were to settle on the ground by accident they could only shuffle and, with their combination of short legs and enormously long wings, would be unable to flap sufficiently to fly away unless a strong wind was blowing. Because of this, swifts spend their lives flying, unless they are roosting or nesting. They cannot perch.

An Alpine Swift

EXAMPLES OF SPECIALISED FEET

The typical raptor foot of the African Crowned Eagle. The powerful talons are adapted for gripping.

The Cape Shoveller, in common with most ducks, has the front three toes joined by webs.

The Common Ostrich has only two toes, an adaption for fast running.

The Red-knobbed Coot has a lobed foot in contrast with the webbed feet of ducks.

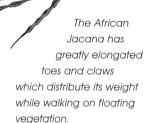

The African Jacana has greatly elongated toes and claws which distribute its weight while walking on floating vegetation.

Woodpeckers have two toes facing backwards, a good arrangement for climbing on trees.

Swifts have all four toes facing forwards for clinging to rough surfaces. They cannot perch.

BEAK OR BILL?

The words 'beak' and 'bill' are synonymous. This author uses both as a personal choice: beak for the smaller ones and bill for the larger. In fact, there are no rules unless you wish to get technical, in which case we refer to the bird's 'rostrum'.

Beaks and bills

In general usage we refer to a bird's bill (or beak) as being two separate extensions of its jaw: the upper and lower 'mandibles' (see 'Anatomy of a Bird' on page 10). The upper ridge of the upper mandible, extending from the tip to the bird's forehead, is called the 'culmen'. The region where the two mandibles join (the corner of the mouth) is known as the 'gape'. The young of many small birds that are still dependent on their parents for food have the soft gape coloured creamy, yellow or orange.

In birds of prey, parrots and pigeons the base of the upper mandible, surrounding the nostrils, is soft and thickened, forming a 'cere'. In birds of prey the

MASTERS OF THE AIR

Swifts are by far the most aerial of birds; so much so that at least one species remains airborne for a year or more. This is the European or Northern Swift *Apus apus*, which visits southern Africa during the northern winter, when the birds are not breeding.

When at home in their northern breeding grounds these swifts tend to breed in church towers, houses and other buildings where they are able to fly directly into the nest site. At worst they will alight on the wall or parapet, where they cling briefly before shuffling to the nest on their minute legs. Their nesting period, egg-laying, incubation and young-rearing lasts approximately seven weeks, after which the parents take to the air again where they probably remain until the following breeding period some 10 months later. Once the young bird has left its nest it does not return to it but joins its parents' flock. If by the following breeding season the young bird is not ready to breed, it will probably remain airborne for another year. It seems that at night these swifts rise to a great height and are able to sleep, or 'cat-nap', on the wing.

In parrots and some raptors the cere is grey, but in the Feral Pigeon (left) it is whitish and swollen in appearance. On the right is a Wahlberg's Eagle, showing its yellow cere.

cere is often yellow in colour, while in parrots and pigeons it is usually grey. Many seabirds have long, tubular nostrils, either paired or singular, that extend along the culmen. These extended nostrils, or 'nares', serve to conduct the excretion of surplus salt and seawater, ingested with their food, from the seabird's system.

Soft swellings or knobs are seen on the upper mandible of the male Knob-billed Duck and, to a lesser extent, on

THE FEEDING ACTION OF THE GREATER FLAMINGO

Flamingoes are filter-feeders on microscopic blue algae found in soda lakes and salt lagoons. The brilliant pink plumage of flamingoes is derived from this diet. To feed, the peculiar bill with its very small, lid-like upper mandible is held inverted beneath the surface.

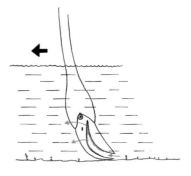

Fine, brush-like projections called 'lamellae' fringe the inside of the of the flamingo's upper and lower mandibles, and act as sieves to catch the microscopic algae on which the bird feeds. Water is taken into the bill by a pumping action of the tongue and sieved through the lamellae to retain the algae before being expelled.

SOME SPECIALISED BILLS

The Trumpeter Hornbill has a hollow casque on its bill for amplifying sound.

Insectivorous birds often have short, slender bills.

Parrots' powerful bills are designed for cracking large, hard-shelled seeds and extracting the kernels.

Many insectivorous birds have long, curved bills for probing into soft ground.

Kingfishers have sharp, dagger-like bills for catching and holding fish.

A skimmer uses its longer lower mandible to plough through surface-water while flying. On contact with a fish, the bill snaps shut.

The huge, hooked bill of a large vulture is a tool for tearing the tough hide of animals killed by four-legged predators.

The slender, curved bill of sunbirds, coupled with their long tongues, enables them to probe deep into flowers to reach the nectar.

Short, stout bills are for crushing seeds.

Rollers feed on large grasshoppers, beetles, scorpions, lizards and small frogs.

Many ocean birds have external, tubular nostrils through which excess sea salt is expelled.

The huge Saddle-billed Stork has an equally large and colourful bill with a yellow 'saddle' which gives this bird its name.

The Great White Pelican has an extendible pouch below its bill that is used as a scoop for catching fish.

The African Spoonbill moves its partially open bill through the water in a sideways, sweeping motion to catch small aquatic creatures.

The Lesser Moorhen, in common with many of its relatives, has a colourful 'frontal shield' on its forehead.

The Pied Avocet uses its recurved bill to sweep the water's surface for small organisms.

The powerful hooked bills of raptors are used for tearing the flesh of their prey.

BEE-EATERS

The colourful bee-eaters are, as their name implies, adept at catching and eating bees, although they also eat many other flying insects. Bees are caught in flight in the bird's long, decurved bill and taken immediately to a suitable branch where they are killed by being rubbed against the perch. If this fails to remove the sting, the victim's rear body is squeezed and the venom ejected before the bee is eaten.

the bill of the male Spur-winged Goose. The function of these knobs is not known. Others have functional additions to their culmens, such as the horny casques carried by many hornbills and well demonstrated in the bill of the Trumpeter Hornbill. These lightweight casques are hollow and probably act as 'resonance' boxes to increase the volume and carrying power of the bird's voice. They are usually largest in the male bird.

Whether a bird has a small beak or a large bill, the reason for its size and shape will be found in the bird's food and feeding habits. Knowing this is a sure guide to the type of bird it is.

There are many birds that feed only while flying; these are the swifts, swallows, nightjars and bee-eaters. Swifts are powerful flyers and are able to cover great distances on their long, scimitar-shaped wings to avoid bad weather. They feed on airborne insects and spiders, often called 'aerial plankton', which they catch in their wide mouths while flying. Swallows feed in much the same way as swifts, but they are entirely unrelated: swallows are passerines while swifts are non-passerines. Swallows' legs, though fairly short, enable them to walk when necessary, as they must do when collecting mud for nest-building. Swallows, and their close relatives the martins, are not as rapid on the wing as swifts, their flight action being more leisurely. Nightjars are strictly nocturnal aerial feeders, lying up by day among leaves on the

ground, or on a branch or rock according to their specific behaviour. Nightjars also have very wide gapes, but have, in addition, stiff 'rictal' bristles surrounding them, which serve as a sort of catching net for moths and other night-flying insects that make up their diet.

This close-up of a nightjar's head shows its short, soft bill, wide gape and the stiff rictal bristles. The large eye is typical of a nocturnal bird.

Feather structure and arrangement

A feather is made up of a main shaft, from which vanes project. Each vane has barbs and interlocking barbules; when the barbules become unlocked the bird relocks them by drawing them through its bill while preening. The body of a bird is covered with an underlying layer of soft down feathers that have no interlocking barbules, and they in turn are covered by contour feathers that cover all regions except the beak and the scaled parts of the legs and feet. This double feather layer serves to both insulate and streamline the body, to keep it waterproof and to protect the skin from abrasive wind-borne particles.

The main feathers of the wing are the flight feathers, made up of:
- outer primary feathers, attached to the 'hand'
- secondary feathers, attached to the 'forearm'
- tertiary feathers, attached to the humerus or 'upper arm'
- the small bastard wing or alula.

THE UPPER WING OF A BIRD

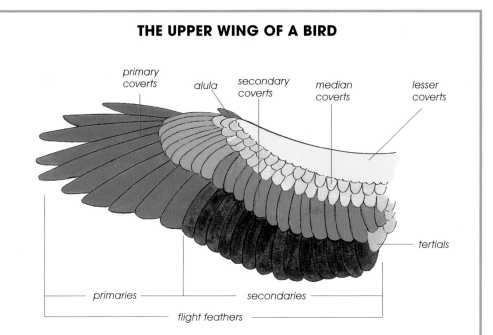

The shape of a bird's wing varies: it is short and rounded in birds that fly little, or long and tapering in fast-flying birds. The primary feathers are the most important in a bird's wing and can be likened to the fingers of a human hand. Most birds have nine primary feathers, but some have as many as 12. Between the primary feathers and the bird's body are the secondary feathers, and these can number from 10 to 12 in passerines or as many as 32 in the larger albatrosses.

The bases of these major wing feathers, where they join the bone within the wing, are covered by overlaying contour feathers called 'coverts'. The base of the primary feathers are covered by the primary coverts, the secondaries by the secondary coverts and so on, each successive row of coverts getting smaller than the preceding one to produce a smooth wing surface.

P. Steyn

W. Tarboton

Above: *The Long-crested Eagle is the most easily recognised large raptor; note its wide, yellow gape.*

Above centre: *A Cattle Egret displaying its nuptial plumes plus red bill and leg colouring.*

Above right: *The head crest of an African Red-eyed Bulbul can be erected at will.*

Right: *The African Crowned Eagle with raised crest is an intimidating sight.*

Far right: *The tail of an incubating male African Paradise Flycatcher almost negates the purpose of its inconspicuous nest.*

MOULTING

All birds moult their feathers once a year, usually after breeding: the post-nuptial moult. The moulting process is normally gradual, especially in the wing feathers, where opposing feathers in each wing are shed simultaneously. In some ducks and geese the flight feathers are all shed simultaneously, rendering the birds flightless for several weeks. For safety in these circumstances the birds retreat to moult on large waters where they remain until they are able to fly again.

This Fork-tailed Drongo is regrowing its outer tail feathers following its moult.

G. Lockwood

The flight feathers (remiges) and tail feathers (rectrices) are stiffened to provide a strong, smooth surface that can be manipulated by the bird for maximum flight efficiency. Looking at a bird's upper wing surface, we see that the bases of the primaries are covered by contour feathers, called primary coverts, while the bases of the secondaries are similarly covered by the secondary coverts. Further forward, the bases of these coverts are covered in turn by the median coverts, then the lesser coverts, and finally the small marginal coverts on the leading edge of the wing. A similar arrangement is seen on the underwing. This succession of contour feathers provides the wing with a smooth surface and an unimpeded airflow. The alula consists of small quill feathers attached to the base of the first primary. They prevent the wing from stalling at slow flying speeds.

Many bird species have specialised or ornate feathers that may be used in display, particularly in courtship. Such feathers may have extended shafts, as seen in the long tails of male widows, whydahs and the African Paradise Flycatcher. Others have extendible head crests, as in mousebirds, louries or the Long-crested Eagle, while many herons and egrets develop filamentous plumes on their heads, breasts or backs during the breeding season.

When birds preen each other, like these White-faced Ducks, it is called 'allopreening', a mutual comfort-action.

G. Lockwood

A female Cape Sparrow preening its shoulder.

PREENING

Because a bird's feathers are so important they are given regular care and maintenance by preening. Dirty or disarranged feathers are cleaned or rearranged mostly by being pulled through the bird's bill, but its feet are also used for certain functions, such as scratching to loosen dust, old feather particles and parasitic mites. Many birds have a gland on their rump near the base of the tail, which secretes oil when the bill or head rubs on it. The oil is then distributed over the feather surfaces, especially the flight feathers, and probably serves to condition them. In addition to these activities, birds will also bathe in water or in dust. Even gulls that spend much time in seawater fly to freshwater ponds or lagoons to bathe and preen.

Colour in feathers

Humans are mainly attracted to colourful birds and pay much less attention to the plainly coloured ones, or LBJs (little brown jobs) as they are called. However, within the bird's world, dull colours are as important and as functional as bright ones, and may make the difference between the survival or extinction of a species.

In species with sexually different plumages (sexual dimorphism), the difference is often only marked for a short duration. The male Southern Red Bishop, for example, wears its bright plumage only during the breeding season, after which it assumes a drab plumage similar to the female's.

Bright colours or bold markings in a bird serve to advertise the individual's presence in different situations, aid species or mate recognition, and are functional in territorial display and courtship. The male Southern Red Bishop patrols the region surrounding the females and their nests in regular territorial flights or by perching conspicuously, always with plumage fluffed out to exaggerate the impact of its colour. This activity transmits a message to other males of its kind: this area is occupied, enter at your own risk. Such signals are clear and reduce the risk of confrontation. The fact that birds, especially when defending a territory, react strongly to colour has been well demonstrated. In an experiment carried out in Europe, a stuffed robin was placed in the territory of a resident robin. The territorial bird immediately attacked the stuffed bird so violently and persistently that it literally knocked the stuffing out of it. The resident robin was reacting to the orange breast of the stuffed bird.

The Southern Masked Weaver male, assuming the brightest or boldest breeding plumage in spring and building the first acceptable nest on which to display both his colours and his handiwork, is likely to be the most successful in attracting females.

The breast-bands on birds, often black, not only serve as clear territorial signals but may also function as recognition features and as an aid when feeding their young. When the well-known Cattle Egret has nestlings, its bill assumes a bright orange-red colour, and the sight of this causes the chicks to open their bills and beg for food. Experiments have shown that when artificial bills of different colours are shown to the chicks they do not respond until a 'bill' of the correct colour is used. The Orange-throated Longclaw has a bright orange-red throat surrounded by a black border, which is at its most brilliant during breeding. The nestlings of this species have identical orange-red mouth interiors. When the parent bird comes to the nest with food the chicks, on seeing the brightly coloured throat, are stimulated into opening their gapes to receive the food. The parent, in turn,

Above left: *A male Southern Red Bishop in full display.*
Above right: *A male Southern Red Bishop moulting into breeding plumage.*

Above and below right: *An Orange-throated Longclaw at its nest in the grass. Note how the colour of its throat matches that of its chick's gape in the nest behind it.*

*A Cattle Egret nestling will only accept food presented by the orange bill of its parents **(left)**.*
*When offered a bill of another colour the chick shows no interest **(right)**.*

on seeing the chicks' bright gapes, is stimulated into delivering the meal. These reactions are inbred and involve no thought process on the part of either parent or chick. We assume that if the longclaw's throat were to be painted another colour, then the chicks would not be fed.

We have discussed the conspicuous breeding plumages of the male Southern Red Bishop and the Southern Masked Weaver, but why do the females remain comparatively dull at this time? The answer lies in their need to be inconspicuous. The females take no part in territorial defence and do not display but go about the job of incubating their eggs and raising their young; a time when the avoidance of predators has its advantages.

Many species maintain dull colouring in both sexes at all times, especially warblers and others that prefer a secretive way of life in their chosen reed or thicket habitats.

Cryptic colours, by which certain birds, their nests, eggs and young blend with their surroundings, demonstrate well the art of camouflage. Nightjars have the most cryptic plumage, while among plovers and other ground nesters both eggs and young are remarkably well camouflaged to avoid detection.

CONCEALING THE COLOURS

Birds that wear vivid plumage at all times, such as rollers, bee-eaters, barbets and hornbills, are invariably hole-nesters. Once inside their nest chamber they are not visible to predators; even their eggs are conspicuously white.

Both the newly hatched chick and egg of the ground-nesting Crowned Plover are cryptically coloured.

The flying bird

The sight of a bird flapping through the air is such an everyday experience that it is seldom given a second thought. However, getting into a mere flap gets no-one anywhere, let alone the bird. The flapping wing may get the bird into the air vertically but it needs more than this to get it moving. Propulsion is achieved by the bird lifting its wings and thrusting them downwards and backwards in an oar-like movement. It is difficult for us to see the backwards thrust unless shown in slow-action photography.

Heavy-bodied birds with their greater wing-loading, such as guineafowl, need to flap vigorously to remain airborne; otherwise, like vultures, eagles and storks, they must seek less exhausting ways of remaining aloft. These soaring birds do so by seeking rising warm air. On sunny days, ploughed fields, buildings and warm, sheltered valleys cause bubbles of warm air to rise. Since they are warmer than the surrounding air, these bubbles rise quickly, sometimes to a great height. By circling in these warm air bubbles or thermals, large birds are able not only to gain height without flapping their wings but to travel cross-country.

HOW SOARING BIRDS TRAVEL WITHOUT EXPENDING ENERGY

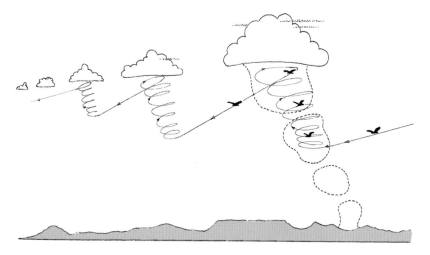

Warm, moist air, heated by the sun, accumulates in valleys, over towns and in rocky places. When the air becomes warmer than its surroundings, it breaks away to rise in large 'bubbles' or warm columns called thermals. (In Africa, thermals are often visible as 'dust devils'.) As the thermal reaches cooler altitudes, the moisture within it condenses and forms a cumulus cloud which continues to grow as more heat and moisture reaches it. Large birds, such as storks, eagles and buzzards, seek these thermals and circle within them to gain height without needing to flap their wings. Once the bird has reached the base of the cumulus cloud, usually between 1 000 and 2 000 m above ground, it sets course again and glides, gradually losing height as it goes, until it encounters the next thermal and regains the height lost in the glide. During a typical sunny day, a soaring bird can travel cross-country for at least seven hours in this way with the minimum exertion.

Because gravity is at all times trying to pull the bird back to earth, the use of a thermal to gain height is akin to a person walking slowly down an ascending escalator; the escalator will get you to the top although you have been walking down.

To remain airborne when gliding, a bird must maintain a certain minimum airspeed. The heavier the bird, the faster its airspeed when gliding. Should its airspeed fall below the minimum, its wings will stall and the bird will fall unless it flaps its wings. If, say, a bird's normal gliding speed, with no wing-flapping, is 20 kilometres an hour (km/h) in relation to the air, and if it is facing into a wind blowing at 20 km/h, then the bird will remain motionless in relation to the ground. If the wind increased to 30 km/h the bird would move backwards at 10 km/h in relation to the ground, but the airspeed over its wings would remain at 20 km/h. When a Black-breasted Snake Eagle or a Black-shouldered Kite is seen to hover on motionless wings it has merely adjusted its forward speed to that of the approaching wind.

Bird migration

Migrations may be long-distance, as seen in the millions of birds that arrive in Africa from Europe and the Arctic Circle every year in our early summer, or they may be within Africa, the so-called intra-Africa migrants. Another form of local migration is a comparatively short-distance, altitudinal one in which many birds move annually at the onset of the cold season from high ground to lower, coastal regions.

Birds that migrate into Africa from the northern hemisphere (the Palaearctic region) do so at the onset of the northern winter. At this time temperatures, especially within the Arctic Circle, drop to well below freezing. With waters frozen over and the land deep in snow there is little food for birds. The great southward movement to warmer, food-rich regions involves countless millions of birds of every description, large and small. This migration takes place over a wide front and, while millions move into Africa, others move into India, China and even Australia. At the same time a similar movement occurs between North America and South America in the great worldwide trek for survival.

In Africa, birds arrive in September-October and return north again in March-April, just before the onset of our winter. As they arrive in the northern regions some weeks later, the ice and snow of the north are starting to thaw. Suddenly there is a great hatching of flies, mosquitoes and many other insects, in addition to the birth of countless small mammals. An inhospitable land becomes the land of plenty for a few short summer months. In these ideal conditions birds breed and feed their young; smaller birds take advantage of the insect glut or the spawning fish, while raptors exploit newly born rodents and other birds.

Yellow-billed Stork

How do birds find their way?

Navigation for day-flying migrants is based on inherent instinct and a visual memory of well-used routes. Many smaller birds navigate by observing the position of the sun. There are three major migratory routes into Africa. In the first and most used route, the birds converge on the Bosporus in the eastern Mediterranean and continue south through Turkey and Israel into Egypt, so avoiding a lengthy sea crossing. The second route converges on Gibraltar, where the birds have a short sea crossing into Morocco. The third and least used route carries them down Italy and to various Mediterranean islands. Although it involves crossing both sea and the Sahara Desert, this route is nevertheless preferred by certain species.

Once in Africa, the eastern migrants follow the Nile River and physical features of the land, such as mountain ranges and the African lakes of the Rift Valley, before finally fanning out to their various eventual destinations. In the west, those from the Gibraltar crossing tend to follow the West African coastline before entering the tropics.

Perhaps the most remarkable long-distance migrants are the warblers. These diminutive birds travel some 12 000 km, flying at night and navigating by the stars. Although they rest by day there is little opportunity for feeding; instead they rely on their own fat reserves, often arriving in southern Africa having lost a third of their original body weight. Shorebirds and seabirds tend to follow coastlines or rivers and lakes. They fly fast and non-stop day and night; then, on sighting a convenient shoreline or estuary, may spend several days feeding before continuing their journey.

PRINCIPAL MIGRATION ROUTES BETWEEN EUROPE AND AFRICA

Most birds on migration avoid lengthy ocean crossings whenever possible. The map shows the main migration routes between the Palearctic region (Europe, Scandinavia and Western Russia) and Africa. The popular Bosporus and Gibraltar routes avoid lengthy sea and desert crossings, yet many small birds do take a direct route across the Mediterranean and the Sahara Desert.

A Garden Warbler, typical of the many small Palearctic migrants that arrive in southern Africa in our summer.

G. Lockwood

BIRD RINGING

Bird ringing is a research tool used by trained members of bird clubs to determine bird movements, longevity and certain other aspects of their lives. The birds are caught in very fine 'mist nets' that capture them without injury. Each bird's leg is then fitted with a small, lightweight metal ring carrying a distinct number and the address of the national bird-ringing unit that issued the ring. All the details of the bird are recorded before it is released so that, when it is eventually recovered, dead or alive, its age and the distance it has travelled in the interim can be ascertained.

A mist net being used to catch birds near a water reservoir.

How long do birds spend migrating?

It is difficult to know when many birds leave on migration, or exactly when they arrive, but bird ringing has provided some answers. The majority of birds seem to take about six weeks for the journey, depending on their method of travel and weather conditions *en route*. The record holder is a European Swallow that, along with many others, was ringed and released in Germiston, South Africa, and recaptured in Moscow, Russia, 32 days later.

Methods of feeding

Birds as a whole feed on almost anything that lives on this earth, be it animal or vegetable. The ways in which many birds go about obtaining their food, however, are fascinating and often unique.

Most herons and egrets stalk their fish with stealth and great patience, but the Black Egret makes fish-spotting easier by mantling its wings to cut out surface reflection. The Green-backed Heron has shown a remarkable instance of tool usage by a bird. This heron sometimes uses 'bait' to attract fish within reach of its bill. It will seize a small insect or spider and place it on the water, watching carefully for a fish to rise. If the 'bait' should begin to float away, the heron will replace it within reach until an unsuspecting fish responds.

Both Eastern White and Pink-backed Pelicans will sometimes indulge in co-operative fishing, a dozen or more birds herding a fish shoal into the shallows while swimming in close formation and repeatedly plunging their bills in unison. This is followed by a feeding frenzy, each bird plunging and replunging its bill into the fish shoal and scooping them up in its net-like pouch.

At sea, especially, fish hunting also takes place from the air. This is well demonstrated by the Cape Gannet and its tropical cousins, the boobies. Both gannets

A Black Egret, with its wings mantled, has a quick look around between bouts of fishing.

The Squacco Heron feeds on small fishes and insects, hunting them with stealth.

and boobies plunge-dive from a height of 20-30 metres to catch fish, while Brown- and Red-footed Boobies pursue and overtake flying fish, which are often disturbed by the bows of a moving ship. A gannet's breast is protected by a number of air sacs beneath the skin that cushion its impact with the water when plunge-diving.

Wilson's, Red-necked and Grey phalaropes are rare visitors to our shores, and can be described as long-legged sandpipers that spend many months of the year feeding at sea. Their unique method of feeding has the bird swimming rapidly in a tight circle that creates a miniature whirlpool. The resultant vortex action of the water brings small insects and plankton towards the surface where they are snapped up by the phalarope.

The aerial pirates of the sea are undoubtedly skuas and frigatebirds. Skuas are dark brown, gull-like seabirds from the cooler oceans, that obtain their fish by chasing and harrying other seabirds to make them disgorge. Frigatebirds are huge, long-winged, fork-tailed, blackish birds that perform much the same action in the tropics. Even the larger species, with a 2-metre wingspan, are highly manoeuvrable in flight. Although frigatebirds feed at sea they seldom enter the water.

The African Skimmer's bill has an elongated lower mandible. The bird flies just above the surface of the water with its lower mandible immersed, skimming the surface in a sort of blind hit-and-miss forage. On striking a small fish, the jaw is snapped shut and the prey is swallowed, either in flight or after the bird settles.

A flock of Eastern White Pelicans herding a shoal of fish.

Inland birds also have interesting feeding habits. Woodpeckers seek the grubs of ants, termites and woodboring beetles, which are often unseen, deep in their feeding tunnels within trees. To reach them, woodpeckers are equipped with either a sticky or a barbed tongue. The very long, extensible tongue is inserted deep into the grub's tunnel to locate and extract the prey.

Some of the most interesting feeding behaviour is seen in our birds of prey. The Bearded Vulture is partial to bones and bone marrow. When the bones are too large to be swallowed, they are taken into the air in the bird's feet and dropped from a height onto rocks to break them. Usually the vulture has a favourite dropping area, and it may require several drops to shatter large bones. Another vulture with a strange diet is the Palm-nut Vulture. Fairly catholic in its tastes, the Palm-nut Vulture will eat a variety of fruit and small animals in addition to

The majestic Frigatebird, a pirate of the tropical seas.

stranded fish and carrion found on the sea and river shores. But its name derives from its habit of feeding on the fruits of raffia palms, and it seldom moves far from these trees.

Another example of an odd diet for a large bird is that of the Steppe Eagle, a summer visitor from Eastern Europe and Asia. The Steppe Eagle is related to our resident Tawny Eagle, but is somewhat larger. While in Africa, the preferred diet of these eagles is termite alates, commonly called 'flying ants'. To collect them, the eagles congregate at the point where the termites emerge. They are seldom alone. Tawny Eagles, Lesser Spotted Eagles and even Bateleurs will join in the feast.

The Gymnogene forages for lizards, amphibians, small mammals, insects, young birds and birds' eggs. This large-winged hawk has long legs that are able to bend in three directions from the tarsal joint. It raids the nests of weavers, swallows, swifts, woodpeckers and others, hanging on with one foot while the other is inserted into the nest of its victim. Not unnaturally, the Gymnogene is unpopular among small birds, which will mob it whenever they have the chance.

Small owls prey on insects, birds and small rodents, while large owls obviously feed on larger prey. What is surprising is that many owls prey on other owls. The Giant Eagle Owl will kill others as large as the Spotted Eagle Owl. In one reported observation, a Giant Eagle Owl was found feeding on a Pel's Fishing Owl, a bird equal in size to its predator.

A Cardinal Woodpecker using its long, barbed tongue to extract a woodborer beetle grub from its burrow deep in a tree.

A Gymnogene investigating the interior of a woodpecker's nest-hole in a tree.

Many owls, such as this Spotted Eagle Owl, are known to prey on other owls.

Display in courtship, aggression and fear

As discussed under '*Colour in Feathers*', birds will display themselves to con-specifics (others of the same species) in defence of their territory through plumage colours or patterns. However, many other forms of display are used in courtship and pair bonding. These include the use of plumage colours, plumage manipulations, posturing or a combination of these and others. Many displays are highly ritualised and it is often difficult to detect the narrow margin between courtship and aggressive displays. A posture that can commonly be seen in the garden is that adopted during the breeding season by the Olive Thrush. The male thrush, when courting a female, will strut about with its wings drooped and its fanned tail scraping the ground. However, should another male approach too closely, it will use the same posture to drive it away. Another easily seen courtship display is that used by many ducks, in which the male will swim towards the female while bobbing its head. In some species both sexes bob or shake their heads as a form of pair bonding (strengthening their relationship).

W. Tarboton

The conspicuous territorial display of the Long-tailed Widow.

Egyptian Geese pairs form long-term relationships and, should the pairs become temporarily separated, the return of the missing individual involves a noisy and highly ritualised pair bonding. The two geese approach each other with outstretched necks and much loud calling, and then rub their necks together.

In that colourful garden bird, the Bokmakierie, courtship involves both sexes facing each other on the ground and shuffling around in a circle, alternatively bowing to the ground and 'sky-pointing' with their bills while making scarcely discernible sounds.

Some bustards and korhaans are noted for their extravagant displays during courtship, and the Kori Bustard is no exception. The male struts with its head thrown back and breast feathers splayed outwards to expose the white underfeathers, while the tail is thrown upwards and forwards to display the white feathers beneath. These and similar plumage transformations are used in several large species. The only time that the brick-red crest of the male Red-crested Korhaan is exposed is during its courtship display. The male circles around the female in a sort of hop-and-jump action while making soft calls.

During courtship, cranes indulge in elegant dances, each member of the pair leaping and twisting around with wings outspread, uttering bugling calls. Single birds within a flock can be seen doing this silently from time to time, probably in an attempt to stimulate others to reciprocate.

In mild aggression, such as during territorial or feeding encounters, birds will spread their wings and those with head-crests will raise them, while many others will merely raise their head feathers or their body contour feathers or both. These actions serve to intimidate the opposition by making the bird appear larger.

With many plovers, and ducks too, the incubating bird will flush from the nest at the last moment in the face of disturbance, and flop away with one wing outstretched as though disabled – a display termed 'injury feigning'. It serves to draw the intruder away from the nest in pursuit of the apparently injured bird. In such cases the displaying bird stays just ahead of its pursuer and flies off at the last moment, only to return to its eggs when the danger has been averted.

Egyptian Geese engaged in a greeting ritual.

A Kori Bustard displaying.

W. Tarboton
The 'bubble display' of the male Maccoa Duck.

Above: *As its ground nest is approached by a potential predator, a Crowned Plover assumes an aggressive posture with its wings fully extended and calling loudly.*

Above right: *When the aggressor continues to approach the nest, the plover becomes undecided between aggression and retreat, and so directs its aggression in a neutral direction while still calling.*

Right: *As a final strategy, the plover feigns injury, running away in the 'broken-wing' posture to encourage the predator to follow it and so move away from the nest.*

The nests they build

Birds build nests primarily as a place in which to lay their eggs and to raise their young, but many small birds build them for roosting purposes outside the breeding season. The nests chosen as roosts are usually of the domed type, where many individuals may crowd together for shared bodily warmth.

The term 'nest' brings to mind an intricate construction, as is certainly made by numerous birds, but in most terrestrial species the eggs are laid on the bare ground, or at best in a shallow depression scraped out by the bird's feet. Coursers, pratincoles, dikkops, plovers, bustards and nightjars all lay their clutches on open ground. In many cases ground-nesters will lay their eggs close to some obstacle, such as a stone, a dried mammal dropping or a fallen branch, a disruptive ploy that serves to render both the eggs and the incubating bird less obvious to potential predators. Others, such as the African Black Oystercatcher which lays its eggs on the seashore, do so among dried seaweed at the high tide mark, while the White-fronted Plover and others may allow the sand to almost obscure the eggs.

Perhaps the most widely used nest type is the conventional cup-shaped nest of thrushes, robins, wagtails, flycatchers, shrikes and many others. The basic materials of these nests are grasses, rootlets, bark strips, leaves and hair, often with a softer lining. In contrast, the Olive Thrush and others line the nest with mud. Many flycatchers and members of the shrike family decorate the outside of the nest with lichens and then bind it with spider web for added strength.

Largest of the cup-shaped nests are those of eagles and some storks. Eagles use dry sticks to build the nest, adding to it in successive years until it may become 3 to 4 metres in height. Most eagles practise a form of nest hygiene by lining the bowl of the nest daily with fresh green leaves.

Some birds gather small feathers to line their nests, especially sparrows and others that construct an enclosed nest. Many ducks actually pluck soft down from their own breasts to create a thick, warm layer for the eggs. Eiderdown comes from the breast of the female Eider Duck of the northern hemisphere, and is collected commercially in Iceland.

Weaver nests are as variable as the materials used to build them. The Spectacled Weaver constructs a long tunnel entrance to its nest, which may serve to deter predators; the Thick-billed Weaver's nest is made of the finest materials; and the Red-headed Weaver builds a nest of pliable, hairy twigs. The hairy covering of the twigs causes them to lock firmly together but, since the twigs are brown in colour, the nest appears to be old from the outset. Sociable Weavers, a species from the drier western regions, carry gregariousness to the extreme. Their massive nest structures, with 50 or more separate nest chambers, are added to constantly and may eventually break under their own weight.

The most intricate ball-type nests are those of Cape and Grey Penduline tits. Their nests are soft, oval balls of tightly felted plant and animal wool and spider webs. The entrance is a protruding spout near to the top on one side, but immediately below it there is a false entrance. When the bird leaves the nest it stands on the rim of the false entrance

A male Southern Masked Weaver building its nest.

The African Black Oystercatcher, a ground-nester on our coastline, lays its eggs among dried kelp at the high tide mark as a disruptive ploy.

W. Tarboton

A female Chin-spot Batis on its small, cup-shaped nest.

G. Lockwood

A male Thick-billed Weaver at its nest of fine grasses and tendrils.

and closes the real entrance by pushing upwards with its head. On returning it stands on the rim of the false entrance and pulls the real entrance open with its beak or foot, closing it again once it has entered.

Swallows build nests of mud gathered from puddles. Their nests may be cup-shaped or enclosed, and are fastened firmly under a rock, a branch or a building overhang. The inverted retort-shaped mud nests of striped swallows and others are similar to the nests used by burrow-nesters and hole-nesters. Some swallows and their relatives, the martins, nest in deep burrows in riverbanks or road cuttings, the nest chambers being at the end of a half-metre tunnel.

Falcons, kestrels and owls make no nest at all. They either lay their eggs on a rock ledge or, as often happens, in the disused nest of another raptor, adding no extra material to the chosen site.

The communal nest of Sociable Weavers may reach massive dimensions.

A Lanner Falcon attending its chicks in a Martial Eagle's nest.

The White-throated Swallow, in common with many other swallows, builds a bowl of mud pellets and grass which is attached to a rock or wall.

The Cape Penduline Tit's remarkable nest of plant down and animal fur showing both the entrance spout and the false entrance below it.

P. Steyn

34 introduction

What do I need to go birding?

The answer is 'very little'. The most expensive and necessary piece of equipment is a pair of binoculars. You can't look at distant or small birds without them. Today the choice of makes and models is so wide that it really depends on how much you are prepared to spend. Although the upper limits are in the thousands, there are many very usable binoculars in the R1 000 to R1 500 price range. Spend as much as you can afford – it will be a worthwhile investment. When choosing binoculars, there are a few golden rules to bear in mind. Cheap binoculars have poor lenses that may damage your eyes and the lenses themselves are glued into place. If the binoculars receive a knock, the lenses are likely to fall out of alignment. Binoculars should feel comfortable in the hands and should not be so heavy that you cannot hold them steady. They should also feel light and comfortable when hanging around your neck, otherwise you may discover that a few hours of birding can literally become a pain in the neck! If you wear spectacles, get binoculars that have roll-back rubber eyepieces.

For birdwatching I recommend roof-prism binoculars rather than barrel-type binoculars because they are more compact and easier to hold (see illustrations). The best binoculars for birdwatching are within the range of 7,5 x 30, 8 x 35 and 10 x 40-50. The first number is the magnification, which means that 8 x binoculars will enlarge the bird eight times. The second number is the millimetre diameter of the large front lens. Thus in 8 x 35 binoculars the front lenses each have a diameter of 35 mm. The larger the diameter of the front lenses, the wider the field of view and the brighter the image, because a wide lens gathers more light. Image brightness is particularly important when viewing birds in poor light, and a wide field of view facilitates locating the bird, especially in flight, through the binoculars. My personal preference is 10 x 40 or 10 x 50 roof-prism binoculars.

Roof-prism binoculars.

Don't hurry your purchase of binoculars. Examine and handle many before you finally decide. First be sure that the lenses are adjusted to your eyes; the salesperson will show you how to do this. Test the binoculars by going to the shop door and focusing on some object at a distance. The image must be sharp and clear without any colour aberration. Should the image be surrounded by a colour outline, the lenses are inferior and possibly harmful to your eyes.

Compact roof-prism binoculars, suitable for the pocket or handbag, are popular and particularly useful when travelling. They are very small and usually come in 8 x 20, 10 x 22 or thereabouts. However, as the front lenses are small, their light gathering capability is low and the field of view is very narrow, but as a second pair for travel or emergencies they are handy. While I do not recommend that you buy a telescope initially, there will probably come a time that

Barrel-type binoculars.

you feel the need. This is especially true when looking at distant shorebirds. The guidelines for purchasing a scope are much the same as for binoculars, but of course you will also need a tripod.

The second thing you need when birdwatching is a bird book, better known as a field guide. It is necessary to have a field guide that illustrates the birds clearly, describes each bird and provides a map of its distribution. The best of these books are fairly small and easy to carry. The type of field guide you choose will depend on the layout and style of illustration that most appeals to you. Some field guides use photographs to illustrate the birds while others use paintings. Even when good photographs are used there are shortcomings, in that each bird is usually illustrated by only one picture. Also, with some of the rarer, difficult-to-photograph species, the author often needs to rely on second-rate photographs or resort to a painting.

The advantage of hand-painted illustrations is that there is no limit to the number of pictures that can be used for each bird. Species that have different adult and immature plumages, and those that have plumage variations, can all be shown in addition to flight pictures. In my own field guide, *Newman's Birds of Southern Africa,* it has been possible in some instances to show six or more illustrations of one species.

Another advantage of hand-painted illustrations is that birds can be consistently depicted in their most characteristic attitudes and with their most useful field features highlighted, something not usually possible in photographs.

So much for expenses. The next and final piece of equipment you should arm yourself with is a small notebook and a pencil or ballpoint pen. Cultivate the habit of making notes of the birds you have seen, particularly when you are not sure what you've spotted. A simple sketch, no matter how crude, with notes about beak shape, leg colour, habitat, etc. will prove essential when you page through your field guide that evening, trying to identify 'the one that got away' or 'the bird that isn't in Newman's book'.

I cannot over-emphasise the advantage of going into the field with helpful, more experienced birders; it's the quickest way to learn. Bird clubs, with their weekend and day outings, provide this essential service. So, if there's a club near you, why not go along? You'll also find that your local bird club offers evening lectures about birds by their more experienced members, usually accompanied by slides or films, and may provide a quarterly coloured bird magazine and a newsletter about forthcoming club activities.

T. Camacho/ Images of Africa

Roof-prism rather than barrel-type binoculars are recommended for birdwatching.

Where to look for birds

The best place to begin looking for birds is in your own garden or local park. You are likely to find at least 20 species with which to familiarise yourself, and they provide a good starting point for searches farther afield. Away from the garden, birds can be found almost anywhere. You may be surprised to know that the Karoo is rich in birds. Even deserts have their special bird inhabitants. Some regions certainly have a richer avifauna than others, and it is wise to become familiar with their locations.

A typical wetland with a flock of White-winged Terns.

Wetlands

This name is applied to a wide variety of inland waterways and other moist situations. Unspoilt wetlands are highly productive for the birder and I recommend them as a very good habitat in which to enjoy your early birdwatching. The birds in a wetland are, for the most part, fairly large, easy to see and reasonably easily identified. Of course, in summer, there are often a number of little grey shorebirds and they may initially prove difficult to correctly identify; leave them for later, when you have gained more experience.

Most waterbirds belong to the non-passerine group, so many will have long legs or long beaks, even striking plumages. In wetlands you may discover various herons, ibises, ducks and geese, flamingoes, storks and others that may be quite new to you. Having started at a productive wetland you may come away having identified 10 or more new birds, and that gives great confidence.

Near the coast, the best wetlands are river estuaries, backwaters and lagoons. Inland farm dams or marshes can be very productive, with sewage disposal pans top of the waterbird list. Bird clubs have prearranged access to many such locations. Many wetlands, especially within municipal boundaries or nature reserves, have hides that make it possible to sit and watch the birds without them seeing you. Otherwise it's a good idea to watch them from a car. Remember that most birds are wary of human beings but are tolerant of cars.

Bushveld

This is a term sometimes applied loosely to any indigenous wooded region, whether the vegetation be bushes, trees or a mixture of both. Whatever its composition, it is likely to be a very productive bird habitat. Bushveld covers vast areas of the land both within reserves and without, and it falls into the two broad categories of thornveld and broad-leaved woodland.

Thornveld is a habitat of predominantly thorn bushes, and is highly attractive to many birds, both those that feed in the thorny canopies and on the ground. In bushveld you should watch the ground for francolins, guineafowls, sandgrouse, larks and waxbills. Check the lower stratum of the bushes for tchagra shrikes, boubous and prinias, and within the canopies for bush shrikes, eremomelas and other warblers. At higher levels watch for flycatchers, drongos, starlings, weavers, barbets and sunbirds, while some taller trees may harbour woodpeckers and birds of prey.

Broad-leaved woodland, in which the grassy understorey is fairly open and the trees are well spaced, supports a number of canopy-feeding birds. These can include birds of prey, flycatchers, bush shrikes, woodpeckers and tits. The main difference between this and other habitats is that bird inhabitants of woodland normally occur in mixed groups called 'bird parties'. You may walk for, say, 10 minutes without seeing birds; then, suddenly, you encounter a bird party and are hard put to record them all before they have passed on.

Riverine bush or forest

Also called riparian woodland or forest. As its name indicates this is the well-treed woodland of many river banks where, better watered than the surrounding bush, the trees tend to be larger and evergreen. It is invariably good for birds of all kinds, including louries, flycatchers, cuckooshrikes, birds of prey and, during summer, cuckoos and kingfishers.

Grasslands

Don't ignore grasslands; they harbour numerous interesting birds, from larks, pipits, widows, korhaans and cisticolas to francolins and cranes. Grasslands are particularly active during summer when many of the widows and bishops adopt their colourful breeding plumages, and others are making their presence known by calling.

Evergreen forests

Evergreen forests include a great variety of indigenous trees and are found in regions of good rainfall, from the kloofs of the Drakensberg escarpment eastwards to the coastal regions and south to the Eastern Cape. These beautiful forests are home to a variety of special birds. The forest robins and thrushes, the African Emerald Cuckoo, Knysna Lourie and African Crowned Eagle are all there for the finding, but be warned that locating them is no easy task. They can certainly be heard as they call from high in the forest canopies, but seeing them calls for great patience, neck-stretching and perseverance.

When to look for birds

The majority of birds are with us all year round, but a few are seasonal migrants that arrive here in our spring and depart again in late summer. Birds generally are most active during the morning, from dawn until about 10h30, and in the evening, from about 16h30 till last light. During the middle of the day they tend to rest, or at least be less active, especially in hot weather. Exceptions are the high-flying eagles and vultures, but even these are most active during the first half of the day. Nocturnal birds – owls, nightjars and dikkops – are most active between dusk and midnight, and longer when the moon is bright. Nightjars do much of their feeding during the first few hours of darkness and can often be seen flying at dusk.

When reading about a bird in your field guide, check whether it is a resident or migrant. If the latter, it is unlikely to be seen between mid-April and mid-September.

How to look at birds

When looking at an unfamiliar bird, make a habit of mentally noting its important features so that you will remember them once it has flown. The following simple system should prove helpful. There are six stages that, after a little practice, will be remembered subconsciously:

THE MAGIC ID FORMULA

1. Note the bird's approximate size.
2. Check its beak.
3. Check its legs.
4. Note bold markings or colours.
5. Note its habitat.
6. Note what it is doing.

Tiny coloured birds on the edge of the track are often waxbills or finches.

1 *What was its size?*

A good way to memorise a bird's size is to compare it with three common birds that you know. Is it smaller or larger than a sparrow (mossie)? If larger, is it smaller or larger than a city pigeon? If larger, is the bird smaller or larger than a guineafowl? Try to establish this in your mind while you are looking at the bird.

Sparrow   Pigeon   Guineafowl

2 Beak shape and colour

This is important. The beak may be long and slender as in some shorebirds. It may be curved downwards like that of a bee-eater or sunbird, or curved upwards as in the Avocet. It may be short and stout as seen in the seed-eating sparrows, weavers and canaries, or hooked as in birds of prey and parrots. Some birds have coloured beaks. These points need to be memorised or noted.

3 Leg length and colour

Legs are also important identity clues. Are the bird's legs of 'normal' length in proportion to its body size, as seen for example in sparrows or thrushes? The legs may be long, even very long, as in many waterbirds, or very short, as seen in swallows and swifts. If they are long, what colour are they?

4 Plumage colours and markings

The colours or plumage markings that first strike you should be memorised. Note whether the bird has colour on its head, breast, tail or wings, or if it has any bold markings, such as a white wing-bar or black band across its breast. These are important clues for identification.

5 What habitat was it in?

The habitat in which you see the bird is also an important clue to its identity, as certain look-alikes are found in totally different habitats.

6 What was the bird doing?

The bird's behaviour is another important clue to its identity. It might be swimming, wading, flying or merely walking. If the bird is in a tree, then what is it doing in the tree? It could be feeding in the outer leaves of the canopy (warbler) or perched on top of the tree (flycatcher, shrike or drongo) or on one side of the tree (roller or kingfisher). The bird could be pecking at the tree trunk or a branch (woodpecker or barbet).

Malachite Sunbird (male) on an aloe.

P. Pickford/ Images of Africa

Jizz

This strange word refers to a bird's general shape and size, or the impression it makes when you first see it. It is a good thing to learn the 'jizz' of the various bird families. When we look, for example, at the common Cattle Egret, we know that it belongs to the heron family (as do bitterns), not only because it has long legs and a longish neck (many other bird families have these things) but because of the specific posture of this group of birds: their jizz. Likewise, we all know what a wagtail looks like and how it walks. If you were to see a similar bird with bright blue or pink colouring you would recognise it as a wagtail of sorts because of its strutting walk and bobbing tail: its jizz.

There are often many species of birds within a family. In southern Africa we have 13 robins and 18 related chats and their allies, all of which have a similar jizz.

There are 13 different starlings, and they too have a distinctive family jizz, as do sunbirds, bee-eaters, woodpeckers, etc. I cannot stress too strongly the importance of becoming familiar with the jizz of the different bird families as soon as possible. This can be done by studying the birds in your Newman's field guide. Look carefully at the robins, chats and their allies, the rockjumpers and wheatears. They are all quite closely related and share not only similar body shapes and sizes, but also postures such as the tail-up stance and jerky, alert movements.

Study ducks and note how most of them stand with their bodies in the horizontal position. At your local dam, or even at a zoo, you can see how ducks waddle as they walk; this is because their legs are widely spaced and placed in the middle of their bodies. No other waterbirds walk in this fashion. These things plus the duck's bill shape all add up to its familiar jizz. In contrast, the whistling ducks, represented by White-faced and Fulvous Ducks, being more closely related to geese, have an erect stance and walk without waddling. This is because their legs are less widely spaced and are placed further back on their bodies.

Robin   Chat   Thrush   Starling   Woodpecker

Dabbling duck   Whistling duck   Sunbird   Bee-eater

Shrike   *Bush shrike*   *Tchagra*   *Helmet shrike*

Get to know the jizz of the shrikes. Notice their rather bulky bodies, heavy-headed appearance and strong, hooked beaks. Shrikes can also be divided into four distinct groups. True Shrikes, plus the Fiscal Shrike and Souza's Shrike (refer to *Newman's Birds of Southern Africa*) habitually perch in an exposed position, maybe on a tree or a telephone wire, from where they seize insects on the ground. (This behaviour is known as still-hunting.)

Boubous and bush shrikes tend to seek their food from within the canopies of trees and bushes. Tchagra shrikes mostly forage on the ground or in the lower strata while helmet shrikes flutter in groups from tree to tree. In these cases the birds' identities can be established by a combination of plumage colouring, jizz and habits.

Identify these colourful kingfishers by their beaks. They can be found in Newman's Birds of Southern Africa.

Newman's Birds of Southern Africa

You will avoid endless page turning if you spend some time familiarising yourself with the layout of your Newman's field guide. For instance, if you don't live near the coast you will have little use for the pages showing seabirds, therefore isolate these pages (colour code: dark green) by putting an elastic band around them. This will reduce the number of pages in your field guide until your next holiday at the coast.

The next section covers many inland waterbirds (colour code: yellow), the birds you are likely to see at any dam, lake, river or pond. Spend a little time studying these bird pictures and descriptions before your first wetland visit, then you will have an idea of what to expect.

The next section includes many birds that are water-associated (colour code: red), that is to say they feed on the shorelines or close to water. Some of the species in this section, which includes shorebirds (sometimes called 'waders'), are very difficult for the beginner to identify because they are either rare, secretive or just very similar to each other. Best leave them until you have gained more experience. The birds covered in the rest of this section, including plovers, oystercatchers and stilts, are easily seen and identified.

The terrestrial birds are featured in the next section (colour code: light blue), all those you are likely to encounter in grasslands or bush. Some of them will give cause for a little head-scratching unless you get a good look at them; others are quite easy to identify.

Birds of prey, or raptors (colour code: grey) come next. These birds, from vultures to kestrels, can be both fascinating and very confusing. Get to know them first in the field guide before tackling them in the field. They sometimes confuse even experienced birders, so don't be downhearted!

The next three sections cover various birds from sandgrouse and the pigeon family (colour code: purple) through a variety of colourful birds such as owls (colour code: pink), cuckoos, coucals, louries, rollers, kingfishers, bee-eaters, woodpeckers and barbets (colour code: blue). Also included are some difficult families such as nightjars, swallows and swifts. When tackling these last two groups, do remember that swallows are mostly dark blue above and white underneath, sometimes with some streaking or orange colouring. Swifts are blackish, some with a little white on them. Most important, remember that swallows can perch, but swifts cannot perch and are always seen flying.

All the sections so far discussed have covered non-passerines, with the exception of swallows and one or two others. The rest of the book describes passerines. This section contains the larks and pipits (colour code: orange), which are difficult birds for the beginner, plus all the small- to medium-sized bush birds (colour code: dark pink), the largest among the passerines being the crows. When looking at passerines, remember to examine beak shapes and colours, and plumage details. If the bird has a stout, conical beak it will be a seed-eater (colour code: light green).

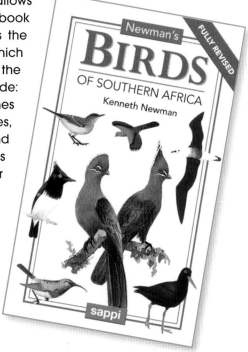

An additional section at the end of the species descriptions describes very rare vagrant visitors. Because they are seldom seen they are of interest mostly to very advanced birders.

It is a good idea to memorise the colour code of each section and the groups of birds covered in it. This will facilitate speedy access to the section you want to study.

DESCRIBING BIRDS BY COLOUR

Crimson-breasted Shrike

Cape Penduline Tit

Magpie Shrike

Knysna Turaco

European Roller

African Fish Eagle

African Snipe

KEY TO IDENTIFICATION

●	Black plumage	46-59
◑	Black-and-white plumage	60-79
●	Grey plumage	80-97
○	White plumage	98-101
●	Blue plumage	102-115
●	Red plumage	116-127
●	Red bills, facial skins and legs	128-145
●	Orange plumage	146-153
●	Yellow colouring	154-173
●	Green plumage	174-185
●	Purple, violet or lilac plumage	186-191
●	Rufous plumage	192-213
●	Dark brown plumage	214-241
●	Light brown plumage	242-255
●	Speckled plumage	256-263
●	Collars and breast-bands	264-275
●	Crests and head-plumes	276-285
⌇	Flight patterns	286-297

birds with
black
plumage

White-rumped Swift

Black plumage in birds probably serves various functions, according to species. It is certainly true that black birds have distasteful flesh and are therefore not sought after by predators. This may be why black drongos can afford to be so brazen when pestering eagles and other large raptors, even pecking them in flight.

In some species black colouring is a camouflage in their chosen environment. The Black Oystercatcher is difficult to see when feeding on mussel-covered rocks and, when it is incubating its eggs, is almost invisible among dried kelp at the high tide mark, provided it doesn't move.

Black waterbirds, either at the coast or on inland waters, may not be much sought after as tasty meals and are difficult to detect from the air on the dark background of water. Dark plumage also serves many smaller birds since they are difficult to detect in the dark interiors of dense bushes, trees and rocks.

Large black birds have little need for camouflage and can take advantage of their dark plumage in other ways. The Black Eagle, for example, nests during the cold months on the shadow side of mountain cliffs. In such exposed, cold situations the colour black is a good heat retainer.

Swifts, being high-speed, airborne feeders, and hole-nesters, also have little need for camouflage.

Black Sunbird

The birds you will find in this chapter

(African) Black Eagle 51
African Black Oystercatcher 50
(African) Pied Starling 57
Bank Cormorant 48
Bat Hawk 52
Bateleur 51
Black Crake 50
Black Crow 55
Black Cuckoo 52
Black Cuckooshrike 54
Black Egret 49
Black Harrier 52
Black Saw-wing 54
Black Sparrowhawk 52
Black Sunbird 58
Black Widow Finch 59
Boulder Chat 56
Cape Cormorant 48
Carp's Tit 55
(Common) Scimitarbill 53
Crested Guineafowl 51
Crowned Cormorant 48
(Eastern) Paradise Whydah 59
European Starling 57
Fork-tailed Drongo 53
Gabar Goshawk 52
Helmeted Guineafowl 51
House Crow 55
Jacobin Cuckoo 52
Lesser Moorhen 50
Little Swift 54
Long-crested Eagle 51
Long-tailed Shrike 56
Long-tailed Widow 59

Mocking Chat 56
Moorhen 50
Mountain Chat 56
Open-billed Stork 49
Pale-winged Starling 57
Red-billed Buffalo
   Weaver 58
Red-billed Helmet Shrike 57
Red-billed Woodhoopoe 53
Red-collared Widow 58
Red-knobbed Coot 50
Red-shouldered Widow 58
Red-winged Starling 57
Reed Cormorant 48
Rufous-bellied Heron 49
Scarlet-chested Sunbird 58
Slaty Egret 49
(Southern) Ant-eating Chat 56
(Southern) Black Flycatcher 54
Southern Black Tit 55
Southern Ground Hornbill 53
Southern Violet Woodhoopoe 53
Spur-winged Goose 49
Square-tailed Drongo 53
Thick-billed Weaver 58
White-necked Raven 55
White-rumped Swift 54
White-winged Widow 59
Yellow-backed Widow 59
Yellow-rumped Widow 59

Crested Guineafowl

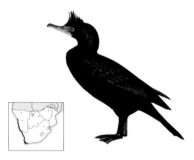

CROWNED CORMORANT
Cape west coast. Like a short-tailed Reed Cormorant with permanent crest.
(Kuifkopduiker) **54 cm**

CAPE CORMORANT
Cape and Namibian coasts. Flocks fly over the sea in long, undulating lines.
(Trekduiker) **64 cm**

BANK CORMORANT
Cape west coast. Small groups on islands and rocks.
(Bankduiker) **75 cm**

REED CORMORANT
Inland and coastal waters. Brown-speckled wings.
(Rietduiker) **60 cm**

48 black plumage

RUFOUS-BELLIED HERON
Inland waters. Yellow legs, bill and facial skin. Appears all black.
(Rooipensreier) 58 cm

OPEN-BILLED STORK
Uncommon on inland waters. Tawny bill with gap between mandibles.
(Oopbekooievaar) 94 cm

BLACK EGRET
Inland waters. Differs from Slaty Egret in yellow feet only. Mantles its wings when feeding.
(Swartreier) 66 cm

SLATY EGRET
Okavango. Lagoons and backwaters. Told by yellow legs and feet plus tawny throat.
(Rooikeelreier) 60 cm

SPUR-WINGED GOOSE
Inland waters. Pink bill and variable amount of white.
(Wildemakou) 102 cm

black plumage **49**

RED-KNOBBED COOT
Inland waters. Told by white
bill and frontal shield.
(Bleshoender) 43 cm

BLACK CRAKE
Inland waters. Small size,
yellow bill and red legs. Walks
on floating vegetation.
(Swartriethaan) 20-23 cm

MOORHEN
Inland waters. White flank marks;
red frontal shield and bill; bill-tip
and legs yellow.
(Waterhoender) 30-36 cm

AFRICAN BLACK OYSTERCATCHER
Coastal bird on rocky shores.
Red bill and legs.
(Swarttobie) 51 cm

LESSER MOORHEN
Secluded inland waters. Small
shield and culmen red; rest of
bill yellow.
(Kleinwaterhoender) 23 cm

HELMETED GUINEAFOWL
Bushveld and grassland.
Looks black at distance.
(Gewone tarentaal) 53-58 cm

(AFRICAN) BLACK EAGLE
Mountains, cliffs. White 'V'
mark on its back; cere
and feet yellow.
(Witkruisarend) 84 cm

CRESTED GUINEAFOWL
Riverine forests and dense
woodland. Pale beak; black
tufted head and neck.
(Kuifkoptarentaal) 50 cm

BATELEUR
Game parks. Told by red face
and legs, short tail and rocking
flight action.
(Berghaan) 55-70 cm

LONG-CRESTED EAGLE
Lowland, hilly regions. Long
crest unmistakable.
(Langkuifarend) 53-58 cm

GABAR GOSHAWK
Woodland. Black form uncommon.
All black; cere and legs bright red.
Small, fast flying.
(Witkruissperwer) 30-34 cm

BAT HAWK
Well-wooded rivers. Whitish eyes,
legs and chin. Flies at dusk.
(Vlermuisvalk) 45 cm

BLACK SPARROWHAWK
Black form uncommon. Often
found in gum trees.
(Swartsperwer) 45-58 cm

JACOBIN CUCKOO
Woodland in summer. All black
form has white in wings only.
Noisy and active.
(Bontnuwejaarsvoël) 33-34 cm

BLACK HARRIER
Grasslands. Cere, eyes and legs
yellow. Underwing shows white
when hovering.
(Witkruisvleivalk) 48-53 cm

BLACK CUCKOO
Perches and calls in same
tree for long periods.
Diagnostic call 'I'm so SICK'.
(Swartkoekoek) 30 cm

SOUTHERN VIOLET WOODHOOPOE
Woodland. Dark violet-blue and black plumage; black bill and legs.
(Perskakelaar) 40-42 cm

RED-BILLED WOODHOOPOE
Small flocks in woodland. Curved red bill and long tail. Loud, cackling call.
(Gewone kakelaar) 30-36 cm

SOUTHERN GROUND HORNBILL
Large black hornbill with red facial and neck skin. White in wings when flying.
(Bromvoël) 90 cm

(COMMON) SCIMITARBILL
Woodland. Told by very curved black beak.
(Swartbekkakelaar) 24-28 cm

SQUARE-TAILED DRONGO
Forest fringes. Tail has shallow fork only. Wine-red eyes. Noisy.
(Kleinbyvanger) 19 cm

FORK-TAILED DRONGO
Bushveld. Forked tail diagnostic.
(Mikstertbyvanger) 25 cm

(SOUTHERN) BLACK FLYCATCHER
Woodland. Dark eyes. Tail with small indentation. Quiet bird.
(Swartvlieëvanger) 19-22 cm

WHITE-RUMPED SWIFT
Fork-tailed with white crescent shape on lower back. Fast flyer.
(Witkruiswindswael) 15 cm

BLACK CUCKOOSHRIKE
Woodland in summer. Rounded tail and orange-yellow gape. Sometimes with yellow shoulder spot.
(Swartkatakoeroe) 22 cm

LITTLE SWIFT
Square tail. Large white patch on rump visible from side.
(Kleinwindswael) 14 cm

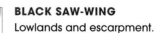

BLACK SAW-WING
Lowlands and escarpment. Slow, low flight.
(Swartsaagvlerkswael) 15 cm

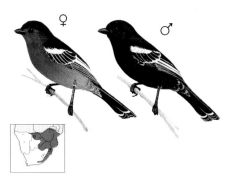

SOUTHERN BLACK TIT

Woodland. Female has greyer underparts. Both sexes have much white in wings.
(Gewone swartmees) 16 cm

CARP'S TIT
Northern Namibia. Like Southern Black Tit but smaller.
(Ovamboswartmees) 14 cm

WHITE-NECKED RAVEN
Eastern, hilly regions. White patch on hind-neck. Heavy bill.
(Withalskraai) 50-54 cm

HOUSE CROW

Durban. Introduced. Has grey mantle and breast but looks all black.
(Huiskraai) 43 cm

BLACK CROW

Farmlands, open country, often on telephone poles. Entirely black.
(Swartkraai) 48-53 cm

MOCKING CHAT
Rocky regions. Female has dull
red underparts but seems black.
(Dassievoël) 20-23 cm

LONG-TAILED SHRIKE
Woodland. Tail shorter in
female. Both sexes have
white wing-stripe.
(Langstertlaksman) 40-50 cm

BOULDER CHAT
Rocky regions. Zimbabwe
and Botswana. White spots
on upper wing and tail tip.
(Swartberglyster) 23-27 cm

MOUNTAIN CHAT (female)
Rocky hills. Male all grey, in some
areas plumage varies from dark
grey or even black, with white
shoulder and vent; in dry areas
may have white belly; wings black.
(Bergwagter) 17-20 cm

(SOUTHERN) ANT-EATING CHAT
Well-grazed grasslands. Male
darkest. Flutters up showing
pale wing feathers.
(Swartpiek) 18 cm

PALE-WINGED STARLING
Rocky regions in the west. Has
orange eyes and white wing-
panels with an orange tinge.
Often in small flocks.
(Bleekvlerkspreeu) 26 cm

RED-BILLED HELMET SHRIKE
Riverine woodland. Red
eye-wattle, bill and legs;
white vent and tail tips.
(Swarthelmlaksman) 22 cm

(AFRICAN) PIED STARLING
Grassveld and Karoo. Pale eyes;
orange-yellow gape; white belly
and vent. (Witgatspreeu) 25-27 cm

RED-WINGED STARLING
Widespread. Female has grey
head and mantle. Both sexes
show brick-red wings in flight.
(Rooivlerkspreeu) 27-28 cm

EUROPEAN STARLING
Southern Cape. Breeding
plumage appears black;
otherwise greenish, iridescent.
(Europese spreeu) 20-22 cm

SCARLET-CHESTED SUNBIRD
Woodland. Red breast visible when bird is perched. Iridescent green on forehead. (Rooikeelsuikerbekkie) 15 cm

RED-COLLARED WIDOW
Bushveld. Breeding male. Red collar often difficult to see unless bird is perched. (Rooikeelflap) 15-40 cm

RED-SHOULDERED WIDOW
Wetlands. Breeding male. Red shoulder retained all year. (Kortstertflap) 19 cm

THICK-BILLED WEAVER
Lowlands. White spots on forehead when breeding. (Dikbekwewer) 18 cm

RED-BILLED BUFFALO WEAVER
Thornveld. Male darker than female. Both told by red bill. (Buffelwewer) 24 cm

BLACK SUNBIRD
Woodland and forest. Male all black except for iridescent throat and forehead. (Swartsuikerbekkie) 15 cm

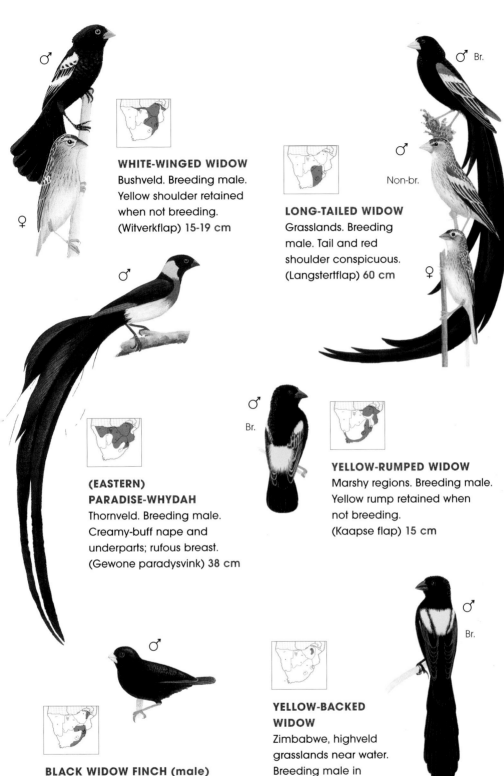

WHITE-WINGED WIDOW
Bushveld. Breeding male.
Yellow shoulder retained
when not breeding.
(Witverkflap) 15-19 cm

LONG-TAILED WIDOW
Grasslands. Breeding
male. Tail and red
shoulder conspicuous.
(Langstertflap) 60 cm

Non-br.

**(EASTERN)
PARADISE-WHYDAH**
Thornveld. Breeding male.
Creamy-buff nape and
underparts; rufous breast.
(Gewone paradysvink) 38 cm

Br.

YELLOW-RUMPED WIDOW
Marshy regions. Breeding male.
Yellow rump retained when
not breeding.
(Kaapse flap) 15 cm

BLACK WIDOW FINCH (male)
Bushveld. When breeding, whitish
bill and reddish leg colours dis-
tinguish the species from similar
widow finches in the region.
(Blouvinkies) 11 cm

**YELLOW-BACKED
WIDOW**
Zimbabwe, highveld
grasslands near water.
Breeding male in
summer only.
(Geelrugflap) 22 cm

Br.

birds with
black-and-white plumage

Blacksmith Plover

When describing black-and-white animals where the black-and-white areas are roughly equal, the term 'pied' is used; thus pied pony, Pied Crow and Pied Babbler. However, this does not apply when either black or white is dominant, as is often the case with birds. For example, the Black Eagle, with so little white on its back, could not be called a pied eagle, and this is the case with many black-and-white birds. Many seabirds have white underparts and blackish upperparts. This colour scheme, also known as counter-shading, acts as a sort of camouflage. From beneath the water the surface appears bright, which means that a white bird is not easily detected by the fish it is trying to catch. From above, the sea appears dark, and a dark bird swimming is difficult to see.

White feathers are less resistant to wear than black feathers, and this is probably the reason why, in most birds, the primary wing feathers (the 'working' feathers during flight) are usually black.

In the context of this book it should be understood that the word 'black' also covers birds that are dark brown, but appear black at a distance.

MELANISM

Birds may occasionally be encountered with abnormally black or dark brown plumage, a condition known as 'melanism'. This phenomenon can manifest itself as partially or entirely blackish plumage and may occur in a range of species. The loss of normal feather colouring is usually brought about by an excess of a black or brown feather pigment called 'melanin' which darkens the bird's usual feather colouring and may completely mask the individual's normal plumage patterns. In cases of complete melanism, the bird is probably at a disadvantage in courtship since the usual plumage patterns, essential in intra-species recognition, are lacking.

The birds you will find in this chapter

Abdim's Stork **65**
Acacia Pied Barbet **72**
African Grey Hornbill **71**
African Hawk Eagle **68**
African Penguin **62**
(African) Pied Starling **78**
African Pied Wagtail **72**
African Skimmer **62**
Arctic Tern **63**
Arnot's Chat **74**
Ashy Tit **73**
Augur Buzzard **68**
Black Harrier **69**
Black Sparrowhawk **68**
Black Stork **64**
Black-breasted Snake Eagle **68**
Black-crowned Night Heron **63**
Black-eared Canary **79**
Black-eared Finchlark **72**
Black-headed Canary **79**
Blacksmith Plover **66**
Black-winged Stilt **66**
Bronze Mannikin **79**
Brubru **76**
Buff-streaked Chat **75**
Cape Gannet **62**
Cape Gull **62**
Cape Sparrow **78**
Capped Wheatear **74**
Carp's Tit **73**
Caspian Tern **62**
Chestnut-backed Finchlark **72**
Chin-spot Batis **75**
(Common) Ostrich **67**
Common Tern **63**
Crowned Hornbill **71**
Dusky Sunbird **78**
Fiscal Flycatcher **75**
Fiscal Shrike **76**
Giant Kingfisher **70**
Great Spotted Cuckoo **69**
Horus Swift **70**
Jacobin Cuckoo **69**
Knob-billed Duck **66**
Lappet-faced Vulture **67**

Little Swift **70**
Long-tailed Shrike **76**
Long-toed Plover **66**
Marabou Stork **64**
Martial Eagle **68**
Mountain Chat **74**
Mozambique Batis **75**
Northern Grey Tit **73**
Osprey **69**
Palm-nut Vulture **67**
(Pied) Avocet **66**
Pied Crow **72**
Pied Kingfisher **70**
Pink-throated Twinspot **73**
Pin-tailed Whydah **79**
Pririt Batis **75**
Puffback **76**
Red-backed Mannikin **79**
Red-billed Hornbill **71**
Rufous-bellied Tit **73**
Sacred Ibis **65**
Saddle-billed Stork **64**
Sandwich Tern **62**
Southern Black Korhaan **67**
Southern Black Tit **73**
Southern Boubou **77**
(Southern) Pied Babbler **74**
Southern Yellow-billed Hornbill **71**
Spur-winged Goose **66**
Striped Cuckoo **69**
Striped Kingfisher **71**
Swamp Boubou **77**
Tropical Boubou **77**
Trumpeter Hornbill **71**
Whiskered Tern **63**
White Helmet Shrike **78**
White Stork **64**
White-breasted Cormorant **63**
White-eared Barbet **72**
White-headed Vulture **67**
White-rumped Swift **70**
White-tailed Shrike **77**
White-winged Tern **63**
Woolly-necked Stork **65**
Yellow-billed Stork **65**

Little Swift

AFRICAN PENGUIN
Cape coasts. Black breast-band
on white underparts diagnostic.
(Brilpikkewyn) **63 cm**

CAPE GULL
Coastal. Large gull. Yellow bill;
black upperwings; white body.
(Kelpmeeu) **60 cm**

CAPE GANNET
Coastal waters. Black legs, tail
and wing feathers on white
body; buffy-yellow on head.
(Witmalgas) **84-94 cm**

CASPIAN TERN
Inland waters, coastal lagoons
and estuaries. Black cap; large
red bill; white body.
(Reusesterretjie) **52 cm**

SANDWICH TERN
Coastal shores. White body apart
from black cap, pale grey back
and wings; long slender black bill
with yellow tip.
(Grootsterretjie) **40 cm**

AFRICAN SKIMMER
Okavango and Zambezi Valley.
Large red bill; short red legs; body
white, upperwings dark. Skims
water, bill immersed.
(Waterploeër) **38 cm**

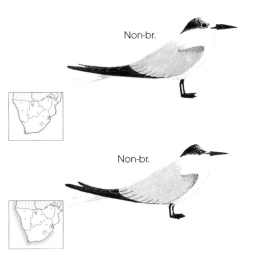

COMMON and ARCTIC TERNS
Coastal. Both similar in non-breeding plumage. Grey above, white below. Arctic Tern has shorter bill and legs.
(Gewone sterretjie) 35 cm
(Arktiese sterretjie) 35 cm

WHITE-BREASTED CORMORANT
All waters. Adult has white throat and breast; immature is entirely white below.
(Witborsduiker) 90 cm

WHISKERED TERN
Inland waters. Non-breeding bird has pale grey upper tail and black line behind eye to black nape.
(Witbaardsterretjie) 23 cm

WHITE-WINGED TERN
Inland waters. Non-breeding bird has white upper tail; black spot behind eye; blackish nape.
(Witvlerksterretjie) 23 cm

BLACK-CROWNED NIGHT HERON
Inland waters. Roosts in reeds or trees. Black above; white below; grey wings; yellow legs.
(Gewone nagreier) 56 cm

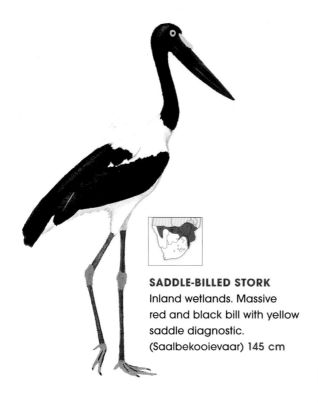

SADDLE-BILLED STORK
Inland wetlands. Massive red and black bill with yellow saddle diagnostic. (Saalbekooievaar) 145 cm

WHITE STORK
Grassveld, bushveld. Black and white with red bill and legs. Seen in large flocks or small groups in summer. (Witooievaar) 117 cm

MARABOU STORK
Bushveld and wetlands. Massive bill, bare head and neck. (Maraboe) 152 cm

BLACK STORK
Wetlands. All black excepting white belly; red bill and legs. (Grootswartooievaar) 122 cm

ABDIM'S STORK
Grassveld and bushveld. White belly, rump and whitish legs; bill horn-coloured in summer. (Kleinswartooievaar) 76 cm

WOOLLY-NECKED STORK
Wetlands. Brown plumage looks black. Head and neck white; bill and legs dark red. (Wolnekooievaar) 86 cm

SACRED IBIS
Wetlands. White bird with black head, neck and down-curved beak. (Skoorsteenveër) 89 cm

YELLOW-BILLED STORK
Inland waters. Told by yellow bill plus red face and legs. (Nimmersat) 97 cm

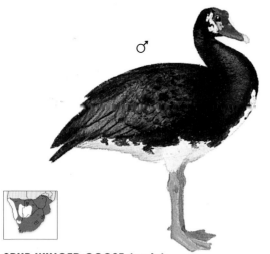

BLACKSMITH PLOVER
Wetlands, common.
Black and white with
grey wings; black bill
and legs.
(Bontkiewiet) 30 cm

SPUR-WINGED GOOSE (male)
Inland waters. Pink bill and legs.
Variable amount of white on
face and belly.
(Wildemakou) 102 cm

KNOB-BILLED DUCK (male)
Inland waters. Black-speckled head
and neck on white underparts; dark
blue-green upperparts look black.
(Knobbeleend) 64-79 cm

(PIED) AVOCET
Wetlands. Entirely pied waterbird.
Told by black, upturned bill; legs white.
(Bontelsie) 43 cm

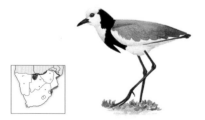

LONG-TOED PLOVER
Wetlands. Red bill and legs;
black-and-white head and
breast; white wings in flight.
(Witvlerkkiewiet) 30 cm

BLACK-WINGED STILT
Wetlands. Pied waterbird.
Told by long, straight bill
and very long red legs.
(Rooipootelsie) 38 cm

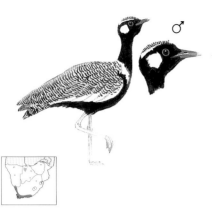

SOUTHERN BLACK KORHAAN (male)
Grasslands. White ear-patch on black head; pink bill; tawny upperparts.
(Swartkorhaan) 53 cm

PALM-NUT VULTURE
East coastal regions. White with black wings and tail; horn-coloured bill and legs.
(Witaasvoël) 60 cm

LAPPET-FACED VULTURE
Game regions. Dark brown plumage looks black. Huge size, red head and neck; yellowish bill; underparts white.
(Swartaasvoël) 115 cm

(COMMON) OSTRICH (male)
Bushveld and arid lands. Unmistakable. Tail buff, grey or white.
(Volstruis) 2 m

WHITE-HEADED VULTURE
Game regions. Dark brown plumage looks black. Red bill; pink and blue face; pink legs.
(Witkopaasvoël) 85 cm

BLACK-BREASTED SNAKE EAGLE
Bushveld and grasslands. Dark brown plumage looks black. Bare legs. In flight shows pale underwings.
(Swartborsslangarend) 63-68 cm

MARTIAL EAGLE
Game regions. Dark brown above, looks black. Legs well feathered. In flight shows dark underwings.
(Breëkoparend) 78-83 cm

AFRICAN HAWK EAGLE
Game regions. Dark brown above, looks black. White below, well spotted.
(Grootjagarend) 60-65 cm

AUGUR BUZZARD
Wooded hills. Dark brown above; white below; chestnut tail.
(Witborsjakkalsvoël) 44-53 cm

BLACK SPARROWHAWK
Tall trees. White form blackish above, white below. Long yellow legs.
(Swartsperwer) 46-58 cm

68 black-and-white plumage

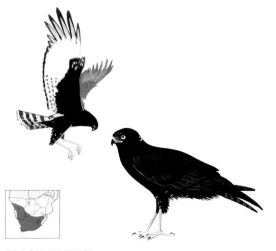

BLACK HARRIER
Moist grasslands. Black with yellow
legs. Underwings show much white.
(Witkruisvleivalk) 48-53 cm

JACOBIN CUCKOO
Woodland. Pied form:
black above, white below,
with crested head.
(Bontnuwejaarsvoël) 33-34 cm

GREAT SPOTTED CUCKOO
Woodland. Black above,
spotted white; white below;
grey crested head.
(Gevlekte koekoek) 38-40 cm

STRIPED CUCKOO
Woodland. Completely pied with
streaked breast and crested head.
(Gestreepte nuwejaarsvoël)
38-40 cm

OSPREY
Inland waters and coastal
lagoons. Dark above with
facial mask; white below.
White legs; long wings.
(Visvalk) 55-63 cm

PIED KINGFISHER
All waters. Pied with stout
black bill. Hovers over water
before plunging.
(Bontvisvanger) 28-29 cm

LITTLE SWIFT
Aerial. Small, blackish, square tail;
white throat; large white rump.
(Kleinwindswael) 14 cm

WHITE-RUMPED SWIFT
Aerial. Blackish, forked tail; white throat;
white crescent shape on back.
(Witkruiswindswael) 15 cm

HORUS SWIFT
Aerial. Black with forked tail;
white throat; large white rump.
(Horuswindswael) 17 cm

GIANT KINGFISHER
Large pied kingfisher with large
black bill. Rufous breast or belly.
(Reusevisvanger) 43-46 cm

STRIPED KINGFISHER
Woodland. Small blackish and white bird. Lower mandible and feet red; blue on back, tail and wings.
(Gestreepte visvanger) 18-19 cm

CROWNED HORNBILL
Riverine forests. Blackish above, white below; large red bill with yellow base.
(Gekroonde neushoringvoël) 50-57 cm

RED-BILLED HORNBILL
Savanna. Bright red bill and pied plumage unmistakable.
(Rooibekneushoringvoël) 42-50 cm

SOUTHERN YELLOW-BILLED HORNBILL
Savanna. Pied. Large yellow bill unmistakable.
(Geelbekneushoringvoël) 48-60 cm

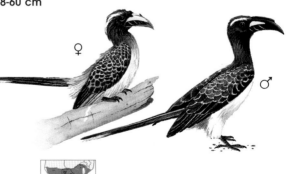

TRUMPETER HORNBILL
Riverine forest. Large pied hornbill with huge bill and casque.
(Gewone boskraai) 58-65 cm

AFRICAN GREY HORNBILL
Thornveld. Dark grey upperparts and bill; mottled brown wings. Distinctive eyebrow stripe and cream patch on bill.
(Grysneushoringvoël) 43-48 cm

WHITE-EARED BARBET
Lowland tree canopies. Dark
brown but appears black and
white; black bill, legs.
(Witoorhoutkapper) 17 cm

PIED CROW
Widespread. Black crow
with white breast and collar.
(Witborskraai) 46-52 cm

♂

ACACIA PIED BARBET
Woodland. Above black with
yellow markings; red forehead;
black throat on white underparts.
(Bonthoutkapper) 17-18 cm

BLACK-EARED FINCHLARK (male)
Scrublands. White bill on entirely black
head and body; upperparts rufous.
(Swartoorlewerik) 12-13 cm

AFRICAN PIED WAGTAIL
Wetlands. Small pied
bird with bobbing tail.
(Bontkwikkie) 20 cm

CHESTNUT-BACKED FINCHLARK
Short grassland. Black head and body
with white ear-patch and bill in male.
(Rooiruglewerik) 12-13 cm

ASHY TIT
Thornveld. All black and white, except for grey mantle and body (Acaciagrysmees) 14 cm

SOUTHERN BLACK TIT
Woodland. Small black bird with much white in wings. (Gewone swartmees) 16 cm

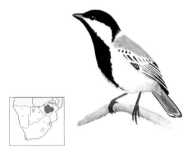

NORTHERN GREY TIT
Miombo woodland. Mantle only grey; rest of bird black and white. (Miombogrysmees) 14 cm

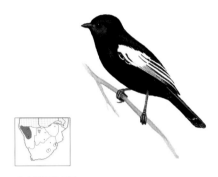

CARP'S TIT
Namibian woodland. Small black bird with much white in wings. (Ovamboswartmees) 14 cm

RUFOUS-BELLIED TIT
Miombo woodland. A pied tit with grey mantle and rufous belly. (Swartkopmees) 15 cm

PINK-THROATED TWINSPOT
Dense scrub. Pink face, breast and rump with cinnamon wings and back; belly and vent black with white spots. (Rooskeelkopensie) 12 cm

(SOUTHERN) PIED BABBLER
Woodland. White bird with black wings and tail; orange eyes. (Witkatlagter) 26 cm

ARNOT'S CHAT
Mopane woodland. White throat in female; white cap in male. Both have white shoulders. (Bontpiek) 18 cm

MOUNTAIN CHAT (male)
Rocky koppies, dry gullies. Whitish cap; white vent and shoulders; rest black. (Bergwagter) 17-20 cm

CAPPED WHEATEAR
Open veld. Pied terrestrial bird with rufous upperparts and flanks. (Hoëveldskaapwagter) 18 cm

FISCAL FLYCATCHER
Woodland. Male black and
white, female brown and white.
(Fiskaalvlieëvanger) 20 cm

MOZAMBIQUE BATIS (male)
Miombo woodland. Small pied
bird with grey cap and yellow eyes.
(Mosambiekbosbontrokkie) 10 cm

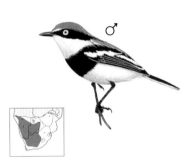

PRIRIT BATIS (male)
Thornveld. Small pied bird with
grey cap and yellow eyes.
(Priritbosbontrokkie) 12 cm

CHIN-SPOT BATIS (male)
Woodland. Small pied bird
with grey cap and yellow eyes.
(Witliesbosbontrokkie) 12-13 cm

BUFF-STREAKED CHAT (male)
Rocky grassland. Male has
striking black and pale buff
plumage; lively, demonstrative
behaviour.
(Bergklipwagter) 15-17 cm

BRUBRU
Woodland. Rufous flanks on
white underparts. Female has
brown cap and back.
(Bontroklaksman) 15 cm

LONG-TAILED SHRIKE
Woodland. Black, long tail
and bold white wing-bar.
(Langstertlaksman) 40-50 cm

PUFFBACK
Woodland. Pied with red eyes.
Male puffs out white back.
(Sneeubal) 18 cm

FISCAL SHRIKE
Suburbia. Completely pied;
stout, hooked beak.
(Fiskaallaksman) 23 cm

WHITE-TAILED SHRIKE
Woodland. Black and white
with grey mantle and flanks;
yellow eyes.
(Kortstertlaksman) 15 cm

TROPICAL BOUBOU
Woodland. Black above with
white wing-bar; below washed
cinnamon.
(Tropiese waterfiskaal) 21 cm

SWAMP BOUBOU
Riverine woodland. Black above
with white wing-bar; white below.
(Moeraswaterfiskaal) 22-23 cm

SOUTHERN BOUBOU
Woodland. Black above with white
wing-bar; white throat grades to
cinnamon belly and vent.
(Suidelike waterfiskaal) 23 cm

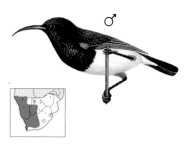

WHITE HELMET SHRIKE
Bushveld. Pied with grey crown;
orange-yellow eye-wattles and legs.
(Withelmlaksman) 22 cm

DUSKY SUNBIRD (male)
Dry woodland and scrub. Above
and breast black with coppery
iridescence; belly white.
(Namakwasuikerbekkie) 10-12 cm

CAPE SPARROW (male)
Suburbia and farmlands.
Black and white about head
and breast; mantle chestnut.
(Gewone mossie) 15 cm

(AFRICAN) PIED STARLING
Karoo and grasslands. Blackish
with white underbelly, vent; whitish
eyes; orange gape.
(Witgatspreeu) 25-27 cm

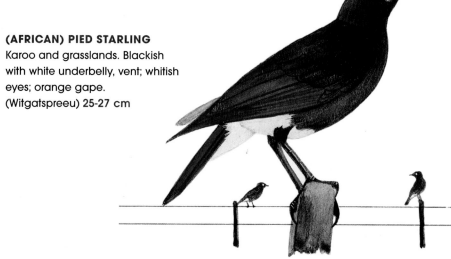

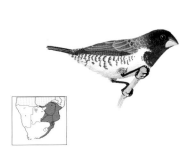

BRONZE MANNIKIN
Grass and scrub. Only head and breast black; underparts white; dull brown above.
(Gewone fret) 9cm

PIN-TAILED WHYDAH (breeding male)
Bush and suburbia. Small pied bird with red beak and very long tail.
(Koningrooibekkie) 34 cm

RED-BACKED MANNIKIN
Bush and seeding grasses. Black head and breast; white bill and underparts; rufous upperparts.
(Rooirugfret) 10 cm

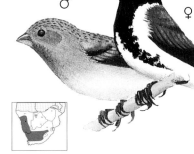

BLACK-EARED CANARY (OR SEEDEATER)
Woodland. Distinctive black mask; upperparts dark grey with streaking on head; lighter streaking on breast; gregarious.
(Swartoorkanarie) 13-14 cm

BLACK-HEADED CANARY (male)
Dry scrublands. Black of head extends to breast and belly; upperparts rufous.
(Swartkopkanarie) 15 cm

birds with
grey
plumage

Grey Waxbill

While there are very few completely grey birds in southern Africa, there are numerous species that have partially grey plumage. Most of the birds that fall under this heading qualify by having grey upperparts, such as we see in many gulls, terns and birds of prey. Grey upperparts probably have much the same disruptive value as brown upperparts, as both colours share similar tonal values. In many other birds, grey plumage is seen only on the head, back, wings, tail and so on, and this is less easily understood. The grey heads of bush shrikes, rock thrushes and others are certainly attractive to human observers, but their true value to the bird may be to serve some purpose in mate recognition.

The colour grey, as referred to in this section, is true grey, either pale or dark. Birds that are often referred to as 'grey' are frequently grey-brown or dull brown and will be included only in the section on brown birds.

Blue Crane

BLUE CRANES

The Blue Crane, an endemic species, was once common and widespread in the moister regions of South Africa. However, in recent years their numbers have so declined that its international status is now defined as 'vulnerable'. Earnest attempts are being made by crane study groups to breed these cranes in captivity for eventual release into the wild, but the process is slow, is based on small numbers of birds and many difficulties have become apparent in the experiment. Known reasons for the Blue Crane's decline are collisions with power lines and deliberate poisoning by crop farmers, but human disturbance at their breeding grounds may also be a contributing factor.

The birds you will find in this chapter

African Goshawk 88
(African) Paradise
  Flycatcher 95
African Rail 85
African Scops Owl 91
Arctic Tern 82
Ashy Tit 93
Barn Owl 91
Black-crowned Night
  Heron 83
Black-headed Heron 84
Black-shouldered
  Kite 87
Blacksmith Plover 85
Black-winged Plover 85
Blue Crane 86
Blue Korhaan 86
Blue-grey Flycatcher 95
Bokmakierie 96
Cape Rock Thrush 93
Cape Sparrow 97
Cape Turtle Dove 90
Cape Wagtail 92
Caspian Tern 82
Common Tern 82
Dark Chanting
  Goshawk 88
Dwarf Bittern 83
Eastern Red-footed
  Kestrel 90
Fairy Flycatcher 95
Fan-tailed Flycatcher 95
Gabar Goshawk 88
Giant Eagle Owl 91
Goliath Heron 84
Green-backed
  Heron 83
Grey-backed Bleating
  Warbler 95
Grey-backed
  Cisticola 92
(Grey) Crowned
  Crane 86
Grey Cuckooshrike 92
Grey Heron 84

Grey Lourie 91
Grey Penduline Tit 95
Grey Sunbird 96
Grey Waxbill 97
Grey-headed Bush
  Shrike 96
Grey-headed Gull 82
Grey-headed
  Kingfisher 92
Gymnogene 89
Hartlaub's Gull 82
Helmeted Guineafowl
  86
House Crow 93
Karoo Chat 94
Lanner Falcon 89
Laughing Dove 90
Layard's Titbabbler 94
Lesser Black-winged
  Plover 85
Lesser Grey Shrike 96
Lesser Kestrel 90
Little Banded
  Goshawk 88
Little Sparrowhawk 87
Lizard Buzzard 87
Long-tailed Wagtail 92
Marabou Stork 84
Miombo Rock
  Thrush 93
Montagu's Harrier 89
Mountain Chat 94
Neddicky 94
Ovambo Sparrowhawk
  88
Pallid Harrier 89
Pink-backed Pelican 83
Protea Canary 97
Pygmy Falcon 89
Red-backed Shrike 96
Red-chested Cuckoo 91
Rock Kestrel 90
Sandwich Tern 82
Scaly-throated
  Honeyguide 97

Secretarybird 87
Sentinel Rock Thrush 93
Short-toed Rock
  Thrush 93
Slaty Egret 83
Slender-billed
  Honeybird 97
South African
  Shelduck 84
Southern Banded
  Snake Eagle 87
Southern Grey-
  headed Sparrow 97
(Southern) Pale
  Chanting Goshawk 88
Streaky-headed
  Canary 97
Titbabbler 94
Wattled Crane 86
Western Banded
  Snake Eagle 87
Western Red-footed
  Kestrel 89
Whiskered Tern 82
White-backed
  Mousebird 92
White-crowned
  Plover 85
White-faced Scops
  Owl 91

Fan-tailed Flycatcher

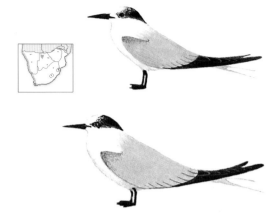

HARTLAUB'S GULL
Coastal. Grey upperwings and back only; body white; bill and legs red.
(Hartlaubse meeu) 38 cm

COMMON and ARCTIC TERNS
Coastal. Non-breeding with grey back and upperwings. Common non-breeding tern has longer bill and legs.
(Gewone sterretjie) 35cm
(Arktiese sterretjie) 35 cm

GREY-HEADED GULL
Inland and coastal. Grey head, back and upper-wings; bill and legs red.
(Gryskopmeeu) 42 cm

SANDWICH TERN
Coastal shores. White body apart from black cap, pale grey back and wings; long slender black bill with yellow tip.
(Grootsterretjie) 40 cm

CASPIAN TERN
Inland waters, coastal lagoons and estuaries. Grey upper-wings and back; white body; black cap; large red bill.
(Reusesterretjie) 52 cm

WHISKERED TERN
Inland waters. Completely grey when breeding; black cap; red bill and legs.
(Witbaardsterretjie) 23 cm

PINK-BACKED PELICAN
Inland waters. Non-breeding
bird has grey wings. Paler
when breeding.
(Kleinpelikaan) 135 cm

GREEN-BACKED HERON
Inland waters. Mantle and underbody grey; black cap; dark wings
and tail; legs orange.
(Groenrugreier) 41 cm

DWARF BITTERN
Wetlands. Upperparts
dark grey; under-
parts streaked grey.
(Dwergrietreier) 25 cm

SLATY EGRET
Floodpans. Slate-grey with rufous
throat; yellow legs and feet.
(Rooikeelreier) 60 cm

BLACK-CROWNED NIGHT HERON
Wetlands. Grey upperwings and tail;
crown and back black; body white;
legs yellow.
(Gewone nagreier) 56 cm

GREY HERON
Wetlands. Grey
wings and back.
White body; yellow
bill and legs.
(Bloureier) 100 cm

MARABOU STORK
Bushveld and wetlands.
Dark grey wings; white
underparts and legs.
Massive bill, bare head
and neck.
(Maraboe) 152 cm

SOUTH AFRICAN SHELDUCK
Brackish waters. Both sexes have
grey heads. Female has white face.
Bodies rich rufous.
(Kopereend) 64 cm

Juv.

BLACK-HEADED HERON
Grasslands. Grey with black
cap, hindneck and flight
feathers. Bill and legs grey.
(Swartkopreier) 97 cm

GOLIATH HERON
Inland waters. Upperwings,
back, tail, lower neck and
bill grey; rest rufous.
(Reusereier) 140 cm

84 grey plumage

AFRICAN RAIL
Reedbeds. Lateral head and underparts grey; upperparts rufous; bill, legs red.
(Grootriethaan) 36 cm

BLACKSMITH PLOVER
Wetlands. Grey wings on otherwise black-and-white bird.
(Bontkiewiet) 30 cm

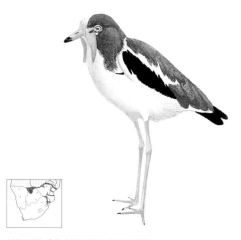

BLACK-WINGED PLOVER
Grassveld. Grey head (white forehead), neck and upper breast; above brown, below white.
(Grootswartvlerkkiewiet) 29 cm

WHITE-CROWNED PLOVER
Rivers. Lateral head and neck grey; crown and underparts white; wings black and white; bill, wattles, legs yellow.
(Witkopkiewiet) 30 cm

LESSER BLACK-WINGED PLOVER
Grassveld and woodland. Grey head; (small) white forehead, neck and upper breast; above brown, below white.
(Kleinswartvlerkkiewiet) 23 cm

grey plumage **85**

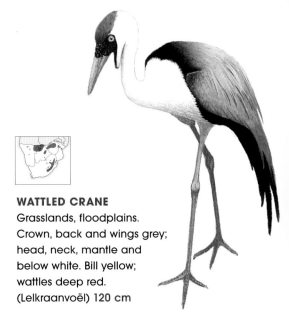

BLUE KORHAAN
Grassveld. Neck and
body blue-grey; upperparts
tawny-brown.
(Bloukorhaan) 50-58 cm

WATTLED CRANE
Grasslands, floodplains.
Crown, back and wings grey;
head, neck, mantle and
below white. Bill yellow;
wattles deep red.
(Lelkraanvoël) 120 cm

HELMETED GUINEAFOWL
Grasslands and bush. Blue
neck; red helmet; casque
and bill horn-coloured.
(Gewone tarentaal) 53-58 cm

BLUE CRANE
Grasslands, vleis. All blue-grey
except white crown, black
wing-feathers. Bill yellowish.
(Bloukraanvoël) 105 cm

(GREY) CROWNED CRANE
Grasslands, marshes. Neck and
body grey; yellow crest on black
crown; white facial patch.
(Mahem) 105 cm

SECRETARYBIRD
Grasslands. Red or orange
face; flight feathers, upper legs
and tailtip black; legs pink.
(Sekretarisvoël) 125-150 cm

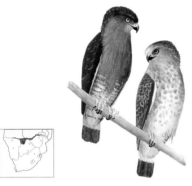

WESTERN BANDED SNAKE EAGLE
Riverine forests. Head to lower
breast ash-grey; soft parts yellow.
(Enkelbandslangarend) 55 cm

SOUTHERN BANDED SNAKE EAGLE
Riverine forests. Head to upper breast
ash-grey; soft parts yellow.
(Dubbelbandslangarend) 60 cm

LIZARD BUZZARD
Woodland. Upperparts, upper
chest grey; underparts banded.
Black throat-stripe; red cere and
legs; bold white band on black tail.
(Akkedisvalk) 35-37 cm

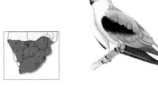

BLACK-SHOULDERED KITE
Woodland, general. Above grey
with black carpal patches; below
white; black wingtips.
(Blouvalk) 30 cm

LITTLE SPARROWHAWK
Woodland. Above grey; tail black
with two white spots; below
banded rufous; soft parts yellow.
(Kleinsperwer) 23-25 cm

AFRICAN GOSHAWK (male)
Forests. All grey above;
banded rufous below; cere
grey; eyes and legs yellow.
(Afrikaanse sperwer) 36 cm

LITTLE BANDED GOSHAWK
Woodland. Plain grey above;
banded rufous below; eyes deep
red; cere and legs yellow.
(Gebande sperwer) 30-34 cm

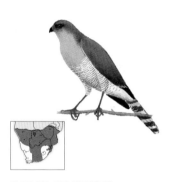

**(SOUTHERN) PALE
CHANTING GOSHAWK**
Karoo, semi-desert. Pale
grey above; secondaries
and rump white; primaries
and tail black; chest grey;
belly finely barred. Cere
and legs coral-red.
(Bleeksingvalk) 53-63 cm

GABAR GOSHAWK
Woodland. Above and breast grey;
bold white rump; eyes deep red,
cere and legs red.
(Witkruissperwer) 30-34 cm

OVAMBO SPARROWHAWK
Woodland. Above grey, below
banded grey to throat; eyes dark;
cere red, legs orange.
(Ovambosperwer) 33-40 cm

DARK CHANTING GOSHAWK
Woodland. Dark grey above; rump
white barred grey; primaries and tail
black; dark grey breast and finely barred
underparts; coral-pink cere and legs.
(Donkersingvalk) 50-56 cm

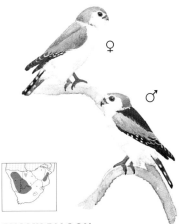

GYMNOGENE
Woodland. Wings grey, edged
black above and below; tail all
black with white band; breast
grey; underparts banded.
Cere and legs yellow.
(Kaalwangvalk) 60-66 cm

PYGMY FALCON
Thorn savanna. Grey above
(female with rufous mantle);
white below; red soft parts.
(Dwergvalk) 19,5 cm

LANNER FALCON
Grey above; russet crown;
buffy-white below; orbital rings,
cere and legs yellow.
(Edelvalk) 40-45 cm

MONTAGU'S HARRIER (male)
Grasslands. Above grey; wings
with central black bars; broad
black primaries. Chest grey;
belly and underwings white,
streaked rufous.
(Blouvleivalk) 40-47 cm

WESTERN RED-FOOTED KESTREL (male)
Grasslands. Dark grey above and below;
rufous vent. Soft parts red.
(Westelike rooipootvalk) 28-30 cm

LESSER KESTREL (male)
Grassland, Karoo. Grey head, back
and tail; grey on upper wings; rest
rufous. Soft parts yellow.
(Kleinrooivalk) 28-30 cm

ROCK KESTREL (male)
Hills. Rufous body; grey head
and tail; tail with black tip;
soft parts yellow.
(Kransrooivalk) 30-33 cm

EASTERN RED-FOOTED KESTREL
Grasslands. Both sexes grey above;
male pale grey below (rufous vent);
female white, well spotted. Soft parts
red or orange.
(Oostelike rooipootvalk) 28-30 cm

CAPE TURTLE DOVE
General. Greyest of the collared
doves; narrow collar and bill
black; legs dark red.
(Gewone tortelduif) 28 cm

LAUGHING DOVE
Diverse habitats. Pinkish head;
cinnamon breast with black flecks;
cinnamon blotched back; blue
grey wings; dark pink legs.
(Rooiborsduifie) 25 cm

90 grey plumage

WHITE-FACED SCOPS OWL
Woodland. All grey; white
facial disc with black surround;
eyes orange.
(Witwanguil) 25-28 cm

GREY LOURIE
Woodland. All grey
with crested head;
soft parts black.
(Kwêvoël) 47-50 cm

RED-CHESTED CUCKOO
Woodland, suburbia. Grey
upperparts; brick-red breast;
banded below. Orbital
ring, lower mandible
and legs yellow.
(Piet-my-vrou) 28 cm

GIANT EAGLE OWL
Woodland. All grey, paler below.
Facial disc with black outline;
eyes dark; eyelids pink.
(Reuse-ooruil) 60-65 cm

AFRICAN SCOPS OWL
Woodland. Grey plumage
streaked black resembles tree
bark; prominent 'ear' tufts.
Eyes yellow.
(Skopsuil) 18 cm

BARN OWL
Diverse habitats. Whitish heart-
shaped facial disc; pale, spotted
underparts; grey and tawny spotted
upperparts.
(Nonnetjie-uil) 30-33 cm

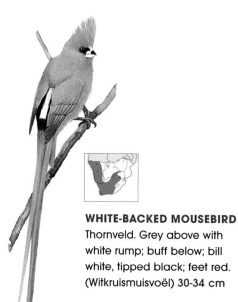

WHITE-BACKED MOUSEBIRD
Thornveld. Grey above with
white rump; buff below; bill
white, tipped black; feet red.
(Witkruismuisvoël) 30-34 cm

CAPE WAGTAIL
Wetlands and suburbia.
All greyish; chin and throat
white with black chest-band.
(Gewone kwikkie) 18 cm

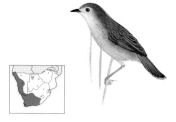

GREY-HEADED KINGFISHER
Woodland, mixed bushveld. Head,
mantle and upper breast grey; belly
chestnut-brown; wings black and
blue; tail blue; bill and legs red.
(Gryskopvisvanger) 20 cm

GREY-BACKED CISTICOLA
Fynbos, scrubland. Dark rufous
head with paler buff underparts,
grey and black streaking on back.
(Grysrugtinktinkie) 12-13 cm

LONG-TAILED WAGTAIL
Mountain streams. Very long tail.
Above grey and black; below
white; black chest-band.
(Bergkwikkie) 19-20 cm

GREY CUCKOOSHRIKE
Forest fringes. Dark grey all over;
flight feathers, tail and soft parts black.
(Bloukatakoeroe) 27 cm

HOUSE CROW
Durban region. Rear head,
breast and mantle grey;
rest black.
(Huiskraai) 43 cm

MIOMBO ROCK THRUSH (male)
Miombo woodland. Grey head and
upperparts flecked black; breast
dull orange grading to white belly.
(Angolakliplyster) 18 cm

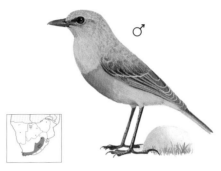

ASHY TIT
Zimbabwe thornveld. Mantle
and underparts grey; cap, throat,
central belly and tail black.
(Acaciagrysmees) 14 cm

SENTINEL ROCK THRUSH (male)
Rocky hills or grasslands. Chest, head
and mantle grey; underparts dull orange.
(Langtoonkliplyster) 21 cm

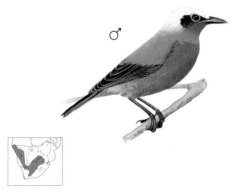

SHORT-TOED ROCK THRUSH (male)
Rocky hills. Back, mantle and throat grey;
cap white; underparts dull orange.
(Korttoonkliplyster) 18 cm

CAPE ROCK THRUSH (male)
Cliffs. Head only grey; rest of body,
including mantle, dull orange.
(Kaapse kliplyster) 21 cm

MOUNTAIN CHAT (male)
Rocky hills. Male all grey, in some areas plumage varies from dark grey or even black, with white shoulder and vent; in dry areas may have white belly; wings black.
(Bergwagter) 17-20 cm

LAYARD'S TITBABBLER
Fynbos and mountain scrub. Dark grey above; white below with spotted breast; pale eyes.
(Grystjeriktik) 15 cm

KAROO CHAT
Karoo scrub. Generally grey but for white belly; wings, upper tail blackish. Western race paler, buffy.
(Karoospekvreter) 15-18 cm

NEDDICKY (S and SE race)
Woodland and thickets. Cap rust-brown; rest of upperparts brown; underparts blue-grey.
(Neddikkie) 10-11 cm

TITBABBLER
Thorn thickets. Mostly dark grey with pale eye and chestnut vent; breast spotted.
(Bosveldtjeriktik) 15 cm

FAN-TAILED FLYCATCHER
Woodland. Mantle and back grey;
tail black with white outer feathers;
wings blackish; white underbelly.
(Waaierstertvlieëvanger) 14 cm

FAIRY FLYCATCHER
Karoo. Grey cap and upper body;
black tail; mask and black wings with
white bar; pink central breast.
(Feevlieëvanger) 12 cm

(AFRICAN) PARADISE FLYCATCHER
Woodland and suburbia. Deep blue-
grey crested head grades to grey
breast; upperparts and tail chestnut-
brown; orbital ring and bill blue.
(Paradysvlieëvanger) 23-41 cm

**GREY (OR AFRICAN)
PENDULINE TIT**
Woodland. Dark grey-green
upperparts with buff patch
extending from forehead to ear
coverts; light grey breast with
buff-coloured belly and vent.
(Gryskapokvoël) 8-9 cm

BLUE-GREY FLYCATCHER
Riverine woodland. Grey above;
pale grey below; wings blackish.
(Blougrysvlieëvanger) 14-15 cm

Non-br.

Br.

**GREY-BACKED BLEATING WARBLER
(OR CAMAROPTERA)**
Bushveld. Upperparts dark grey with
brownish-grey wings; pale greyish
throat; underparts creamy-white.
(Grysrugkwêkwêvoël) 12 cm

RED-BACKED SHRIKE (male)
Bushveld. Grey cap and nape;
chestnut back; black mask, wings
and tail; white below; hooked beak.
(Rooiruglaksman) 18 cm

BOKMAKIERIE
Suburbia. Grey crown and mantle;
rest green above, yellow below;
bold black breast-band.
(Bokmakierie) 23 cm

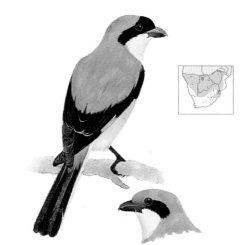

LESSER GREY SHRIKE
Bushveld. Above grey and black;
below white; stout hooked beak.
(Gryslaksman) 20-22 cm

GREY SUNBIRD
Coastal forests. Entirely grey, darker
above; slender, down-curved beak.
(Gryssuikerbekkie) 14 cm

GREY-HEADED BUSH SHRIKE
Woodland. Grey hood; heavy,
hooked bill; upperparts green;
below yellow; breast orange; eyes yellow.
(Spookvoël) 25-27 cm

CAPE SPARROW (female)
Suburbia, farmlands. Grey and white head extends to upper breast; mantle chestnut; wings black and white; underparts whitish; stout bill black.
(Gewone mossie) 15 cm

GREY WAXBILL
Woodland thickets. Grey, darker above with red eyes, rump and upper tail-base.
(Gryssysie) 11 cm

STREAKY-HEADED CANARY
Woodland. Grey-brown above; streaky crown; white eyebrow; stout blackish bill; white below.
(Streepkopkanarie) 16 cm

SOUTHERN GREY-HEADED SPARROW
Woodland. Grey head; upperparts chestnut; below whitish. Stout conical bill black or horn-coloured
(Gryskopmossie) 15-16 cm

SLENDER-BILLED
(OR GREEN-BACKED) HONEYBIRD
Woodland. Upperparts green-grey; yellow edged flight feathers; slender bill.
(Dunbekheuningvoël) 11,5 cm

PROTEA CANARY (OR SEEDEATER)
Protea woodland. Larger canary; mainly drab grey with distinct lighter bars on closed wing; heavy grey bill.
(Witvlerkkanarie) 16 cm

SCALY-THROATED HONEYGUIDE
Forest, bush. Streaky head, scaly throat with yellowish tinge; grey back with yellow bars on wings, paler underparts.
(Gevlekte heuningwyser) 19 cm

birds with
white
plumage

Hartlaub's Gull

Most white birds are waterbirds. Certainly there are many white or partially white seabirds that do not fall within the scope of this book, but there are others that occur on inland waters and at the coast. Perhaps the most familiar of these white birds is the common Cattle Egret that is seen with grazing cattle in farmlands and even in our towns. There are other white egrets, their plumages all so similar that they can cause much confusion until their specific differences are learnt. (Remember that egrets are merely a type of heron.) White plumage is strikingly bright and renders the bird highly conspicuous under normal African conditions. In northern regions, however, where the lands are often snow-bound for months, some birds actually benefit from the camouflage afforded by white plumage. This is certainly not the case with white African birds, so there must be another reason for their being white. One theory is that waterbirds are reasonably safe while standing in water since few land predators habitually hunt in water. A second theory suggests that, for a bird that forages fully exposed to the hot sun for much of the day, white feathers are the best heat reflectors.

African Spoonbill

The birds you will find in this chapter

African Spoonbill **101**
Black-shouldered Kite **101**
Cattle Egret **100**
Eastern White Pelican **100**
Great White Heron **100**
Greater Flamingo **101**
Hartlaub's Gull **100**
Little Egret **100**
Martial Eagle **101**
Wattled Starling **101**
Yellow-billed Egret **100**

Great White Heron

BIRD TERRITORIES

A territory is a region a bird or pair of birds defends against conspecifics (others of its kind) for purposes of feeding and breeding. The territory may be very small in communal breeders, perhaps half a hectare in songbirds, or may cover many square kilometres in some eagles. The male bird must select a territory of a size that is defensible and yet provide sufficient food for itself, its mate and their young.

Many small birds only defend the area of the nest site (as in many weavers) and forage for food further afield. Communal feeders, such as gulls, terns and many other ground-nesting waterbirds, space their nests closely but just out of pecking range of their immediate neighbours. Even in a crowded colony each bird is able to identify and fly directly to its own nest without interacting with those around it. In contrast, the Cape Gannet, which nests in densely-packed island colonies, requires a fairly long take-off run into wind to get airborne. In order to move through the colony to the take-off point, without being molested by the others, a departing bird must adopt a non-aggressive posture called 'sky-pointing'. The head and neck are held vertically while the bird walks between all the other nests. Should its head be lowered, even briefly, those around it will interpret the action as an aggressive one and it will be treated to a roughing-up until it readopts the sky-pointing posture.

HARTLAUB'S GULL
Coastal. Mostly white; grey upperwings; black wingtips; red bill and legs.
(Hartlaubse meeu) 38cm

LITTLE EGRET
Wetlands. All white; black bill and legs; feet yellow.
(Kleinwitreier) 64 cm

EASTERN WHITE PELICAN
Estuaries, lagoons. Adult all white; yellowish bill; pink legs. Black flight feathers.
(Witpelikaan) 180 cm

YELLOW-BILLED EGRET
Wetlands. All white; bill yellow; upper legs dull yellow; lower legs black.
(Geelbekwitreier) 68 cm

CATTLE EGRET
Pastures. All white except in summer when buff on head, neck and back. Bill, legs yellow to pink.
(Veereier) 54 cm

GREAT WHITE HERON
Wetlands. Bill yellow, black briefly when breeding; legs and feet black.
(Grootwitreier) 95 cm

BLACK-SHOULDERED KITE
Grasslands. Below white;
wingtips black. Above grey;
black shoulder-patches.
(Blouvalk) 30 cm

GREATER FLAMINGO
Salt pans and soda lakes. White
with pink and black bill; long
pink legs; red and black wings.
(Grootflamink) 140 cm

AFRICAN SPOONBILL
Wetlands. White with red
face; red and grey spatulate
bill; red legs.
(Lepelaar) 91 cm

Imm.

**MARTIAL EAGLE
(immature)**
Woodland, bushveld.
Underparts white;
upperparts brown.
Feet yellow.
(Breëkoparend) 78-83 cm

WATTLED STARLING
Open bushveld. Male whitish
when breeding; head ornamented
with black and yellow; tail black.
(Lelspreeu) 21 cm

birds with
blue
plumage

Greater Blue-eared Glossy Starling

Some of our most colourful birds owe their brilliance to blue plumage – often iridescent blue as seen, for example, in the glossy starlings, which appear metallic blue or green according to the light.

There are many birds, large and small, with dark blue plumage that appears black in all but the most favourable sunlight, which emphasises the iridescent gloss in the feathers. Among these are swallows and woodhoopoes. Many of the larger 'black' birds, such as the Spur-winged Goose, crows and certain raptors, may also appear blue-black in full sun.

Iridescence is produced by a thin layer of a substance called keratin, which occurs on the surface of the feather-barbules, or by minute granules of melanin that occur in a thin layer just below the surface of the feather-barbules. Iridescent feathers are not normally found in a bird's flight feathers.

Rollers exhibit brilliant blue wings, often described as electric blue. This is a true colour which also occurs in some bee-eaters. This non-iridescent colour is created by the scattering of light when it passes through minute air-filled cavities in the keratin of the barbules. As a result, no matter at what angle, the colour does not change.

NEST SANITATION

In the early chick-rearing period of most passerine birds, the disposal of excreta is important in the interests of nest cleanliness and the safety of the brood since predators are likely to be attracted by both smell and the sight of accumulated white droppings.

In a group of small birds, the chicks of which are confined to the nest for some weeks, the chicks' faeces are excreted in a thin but strong mucous sac, which is either swallowed by the parents or disposed of far away from the nest.

The more mobile nestlings of raptors, herons, kingfishers and others, eject their faeces from the nest in liquid form with some force.

The birds you will find in this chapter

(African) Paradise Flycatcher 113
African Pygmy Kingfisher 111
Bald Ibis 104
Black Crow 113
Blue Crane 105
Blue Korhaan 105
Blue Waxbill 115
Blue-cheeked Bee-eater 110
Broad-billed Roller 112
Brown-hooded Kingfisher 110
Burchell's Glossy Starling 114
Cape Glossy Starling 115
Cape Shoveller 104
(Common) House Martin 109
(Common) Scimitarbill 113
Crested Guineafowl 105
European Bee-eater 110
European Roller 112
European Swallow 108
Greater Blue-eared Glossy
    Starling 114
Greater Striped Swallow 107
Grey-headed Kingfisher 110
Grey-rumped Swallow 109
Half-collared Kingfisher 111
Helmeted Guineafowl 105
Hottentot Teal 104
Knob-billed Duck 104
Knysna Lourie 106
Lesser Blue-eared Glossy
    Starling 114
Lesser Striped Swallow 107
Lilac-breasted Roller 112
Long-tailed Glossy Starling 114
Maccoa Duck 104
Malachite Kingfisher 111
Meyer's Parrot 106

Mosque Swallow 107
Pearl-breasted Swallow 109
Purple Gallinule 105
Purple Roller 112
Purple-crested Lourie 106
Racket-tailed Roller 112
Red-billed Woodhoopoe 113
Red-breasted Swallow 107
Rüppell's Parrot 106
South African Cliff Swallow 108
(Southern) Carmine Bee-eater 109
Striped Kingfisher 111
Swallow-tailed Bee-eater 109
Trumpeter Hornbill 113
Violet-eared Waxbill 115
White-bellied Sunbird 115
White-throated Swallow 108
Wire-tailed Swallow 108
Woodland Kingfisher 110

Long-talied Glossy Starling

CAPE SHOVELLER
Wetlands. Pale blue upper forewings seen in flight; brightest in male.
(Kaapse slopeend) 53 cm

BALD IBIS
Montane grassland. Iridescent blue-black plumage; red cap, bill and legs.
(Kalkoenibis) 79 cm

HOTTENTOT TEAL
Wetlands. Small, brown-capped duck with blue-grey bill.
(Gevlekte eend) 35 cm

MACCOA DUCK (male)
Wetlands. Bright blue bill on black head; body chestnut.
(Bloubekeend) 46 cm

KNOB-BILLED DUCK
Wetlands. Iridescent blue above; white below; head speckled black.
(Knobbeleend) 64-79 cm

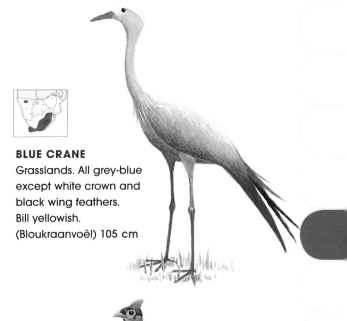

BLUE CRANE
Grasslands. All grey-blue
except white crown and
black wing feathers.
Bill yellowish.
(Bloukraanvoël) 105 cm

PURPLE GALLINULE
Wetlands. Above green; head and
below blue; frontal shield and bill
red; legs pink.
(Grootkoningriethaan) 46 cm

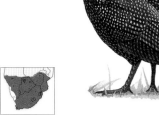

HELMETED GUINEAFOWL
Grasslands and bush. Blue neck; red
helmet; casque and bill horn-coloured.
(Gewone tarentaal) 53-58 cm

BLUE KORHAAN
Grassveld. Neck and body
grey-blue, upperwings
tawny-brown.
(Bloukorhaan) 50-58 cm

CRESTED GUINEAFOWL
Riverine thickets. Black body
with blue spots and stripes.
(Kuifkoptarentaal) 50 cm

KNYSNA LOURIE
Forest. Folded wings and upper tail iridescent blue; rest of body green; wings red in flight. (Knysnaloerie) 47 cm

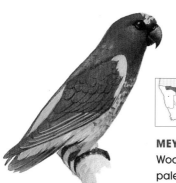

MEYER'S PARROT
Woodland. Back and rump pale blue; head, mantle and wings brown; below green. (Bosveldpapegaai) 23 cm

RÜPPELL'S PARROT
Woodland. Back, underbelly and vent deep blue, rest of body and wings dark brown. (Bloupenspapegaai) 23 cm

PURPLE-CRESTED LOURIE
Woodland. Crest blue-purple; wings and upper tail iridescent blue; body matt green with orange wash; wings red in flight. (Bloukuifloerie) 47 cm

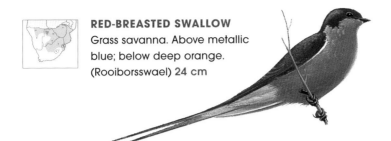

RED-BREASTED SWALLOW
Grass savanna. Above metallic
blue; below deep orange.
(Rooiborsswael) 24 cm

GREATER STRIPED SWALLOW
Grassland. Top of head orange;
rump pale orange; rest of
upperparts metallic blue;
below whitish, lightly streaked.
(Grootstreepswael) 20 cm

MOSQUE SWALLOW
Woodland. Above metallic blue; throat,
upper breast and underwings white;
rest of underbody deep orange.
(Moskeeswael) 23 cm

LESSER STRIPED SWALLOW
Bushveld. Upper half of head
and rump orange; rest of
upperparts metallic blue;
below white, heavily streaked.
(Kleinstreepswael) 16 cm

SOUTH AFRICAN CLIFF SWALLOW
Bridges, towers. Cap brownish; rump
orange; rest of upperparts dull
metallic blue; breast orange dappled
dark blue; belly white; vent orange.
(Familieswael) 15 cm

EUROPEAN SWALLOW
Aerial. Above metallic blue;
forehead and chin orange;
throat black; below white.
Forked tail.
(Europese swael) 18 cm

WHITE-THROATED SWALLOW
Wetlands. Orange forehead;
metallic-blue above; white below
with black breast-band; forked tail.
(Witkeelswael) 17 cm

WIRE-TAILED SWALLOW
Rivers. Above metallic blue;
cap orange; below white;
long tail streamers.
(Draadstertswael) 13 cm

PEARL-BREASTED SWALLOW
Open woodland; above
metallic blue; below white;
forked tail.
(Pêrelborsswael) 14 cm

SWALLOW-TAILED BEE-EATER
Woodland. Blue collar, upper
tail and belly; throat yellow;
rest green. Forked tail.
(Swaelstertbyvreter) 20-22 cm

GREY-RUMPED SWALLOW
River banks and grassy slopes.
Above metallic blue, except
greyish cap and rump.
Forked tail.
(Gryskruisswael) 14 cm

(COMMON) HOUSE MARTIN
Aerial. Above metallic blue
with white rump; below white.
Tail with shallow fork.
(Huisswael) 14 cm

(SOUTHERN) CARMINE BEE-EATER
Rivers and bushveld. Blue cap and
underbelly; rest of body carmine-red.
(Rooiborsbyvreter) 33-38 cm

EUROPEAN BEE-EATER
Aerial. Forehead and underbody blue; throat yellow; upperparts chestnut and green.
(Europese byvreter) 25-29 cm

GREY-HEADED KINGFISHER
Woodland. Back, tail and wings royal blue; wing coverts black; head and mantle grey; belly chestnut; bill red.
(Gryskopvisvanger) 20 cm

WOODLAND KINGFISHER
Woodland. Above turquoise-blue; wing coverts black; below white; bill red and black.
(Bosveldvisvanger) 23-24 cm

BROWN-HOODED KINGFISHER
Woodland. Upper body and tail blue; upper wings blue and black; head and mantle streaked brownish; below white; bill red.
(Bruinkopvisvanger) 23-24 cm

BLUE-CHEEKED BEE-EATER
Wetlands. Eyebrows, cheeks, rump and belly blue; above green; chin yellow; throat chestnut.
(Blouwangbyvreter) 27-33 cm

STRIPED KINGFISHER
Woodland. Back and tail blue;
wings blue above; coverts black;
cap streaked brown; below white;
flanks streaked; bill dark brown and red.
(Gestreepte visvanger) 18-19 cm

MALACHITE KINGFISHER
Wetlands. Above blue; below
orange-buff; white ear-patch
and throat; bill and legs red.
(Kuifkopvisvanger) 14 cm

AFRICAN PYGMY KINGFISHER
Woodland. Above entirely deep
blue; below buff; cheeks mauve;
bill and feet red.
(Dwergvisvanger) 13 cm

HALF-COLLARED KINGFISHER
Rivers. Brilliant blue above; below
throat white; underparts buffy;
bill black; legs red.
(Blouvisvanger) 20 cm

RACKET-TAILED ROLLER
Woodland. Plain blue below;
spatulate tail-shafts.
(Knopsterttroupant) 36 cm

EUROPEAN ROLLER
Woodland. Blue head and
underparts; square tail.
(Europese troupant) 30-31 cm

BROAD-BILLED ROLLER
Woodland. Blue vent and tail;
deep blue wings; yellow bill.
(Geelbektroupant) 27 cm

LILAC-BREASTED ROLLER
Woodland. Blue belly and tail;
blue wings; lilac breast.
(Gewone troupant) 36 cm

PURPLE ROLLER
Woodland. Deep blue tail
and wings; below streaked
white on maroon.
(Groottroupant) 36-40 cm

RED-BILLED WOODHOOPOE
Woodland. Deep iridescent blue; head green and blue; curved red bill; long tail.
(Gewone kakelaar) 30-36 cm

BLACK CROW
Farmlands. Entirely metallic blue-black.
(Swartkraai) 48-53 cm

(COMMON) SCIMITARBILL
Woodland. Deep iridescent purple-blue; well-curved black bill.
(Swartbekkakelaar) 24-28 cm

(AFRICAN) PARADISE FLYCATCHER
Woodland. Head blue-black; orbital ring and bill bright blue.
(Paradysvlieëvanger) 23-41 cm

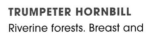

TRUMPETER HORNBILL
Riverine forests. Breast and upperparts deep metallic blue; huge bill with casque.
(Gewone boskraai) 58-65 cm

blue plumage 113

LONG-TAILED GLOSSY STARLING
Mopane woodland. Iridescent purple-blue; long, graduated tail; dark eyes. (Langstertglansspreeu) 30-34 cm

GREATER BLUE-EARED GLOSSY STARLING
Woodland. Head and breast glossy blue; wings glossy green; flanks and belly purple; eyes yellow. (Groot-blouoorglansspreeu) 21-23 cm

BURCHELL'S GLOSSY STARLING
Savanna. Iridescent blue and purple, black mask and dark eyes. (Grootglansspreeu) 30-34 cm

LESSER BLUE-EARED GLOSSY STARLING
Miombo woodland. Glossy blue-green; flanks purple; eyes yellow. (Klein-blouoorglansspreeu) 20 cm

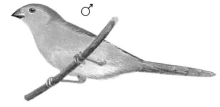

CAPE GLOSSY STARLING
Woodland and suburbia.
Glossy blue-green; head bluer;
yellow eyes.
(Kleinglansspreeu) 23-25 cm

BLUE WAXBILL
Thornveld. Underparts blue;
above brown.
(Gewone blousysie) 12-14 cm

VIOLET-EARED WAXBILL
Thornveld. Forehead and
upper tail coverts blue;
side of head violet; red bill.
(Koningblousysie) 13-15 cm

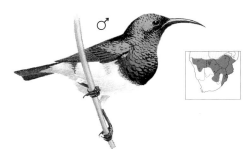

WHITE-BELLIED SUNBIRD (male)
Wooded regions. Head, breast
and mantle glossy blue; belly white;
curved black bill.
(Witpenssuikerbekkie) 11 cm

birds with
red plumage

(Southern) Red Bishop (male)

Red plumage in birds ranges from species with predominantly red plumage to those with only some conspicuous red feathers. A predominance of red makes a bird conspicuous. Usually this occurs in the male of the species and often, but not always, during the breeding season only. The male Southern Red Bishop in breeding plumage, actively displaying with feathers fluffed out, serves both to deflect attention from the incubating female and as a warning to other Southern Red Bishop males to stay away. Where the plumage is only partially red it is often found on the head or breast, or both, as seen in the Black-collared Barbet. Since this is the part of the bird presented to a rival, or to a mate, it may serve either as a warning signal or as mate recognition. Where a bird has a red cap, head or rump, its function is less obvious, but the colour may be used during courtship displays and in a variety of subtle interaction behaviours between individuals about which we understand little. The red cap or forehead of many woodpeckers, which is prominently displayed when the bird is peering from its nest-hole, probably serves to warn other woodpeckers that the territory is occupied. The brilliant red wings of the forest-dwelling Knysna Lourie serves well as a recognition feature for others in the group in dense foliage. The red colouring in the wings of many louries comes from a chemical called turacin. The name 'turaco', which is used for these birds outside southern Africa, comes from this chemical. Turacin is responsible for the red colouring in other birds, too. Birds that have red bills, red legs or facial skin are discussed in the following chapter.

The birds you will find in this chapter

Acacia Pied Barbet 120
Bearded Woodpecker 121
Bennett's Woodpecker 121
Black-cheeked Waxbill 127
Black-collared Barbet 120
Black Widow Finch 125
Blue-billed Firefinch 126
Brown Firefinch 125
Cardinal Woodpecker 121
Common Waxbill 126
Crested Barbet 120
Crimson-breasted Boubou 122
Cut-throat Finch 127
Golden-backed Pytilia 125
Golden-tailed Woodpecker 121
Gorgeous Bush Shrike 122
Greater Double-collared
  Sunbird 122
Greater Flamingo 118
Green Twinspot 126
Grey Waxbill 127
Ground Woodpecker 120
Jameson's Firefinch 126
Knysna Lourie 119
Knysna Woodpecker 121
Lesser Flamingo 118
Lesser (Southern) Double-collared
  Sunbird 122
Lilian's Lovebird 118
Long-tailed Widow 124
Marico Sunbird 123
Melba Finch 124
Narina Trogon 119
Olive Woodpecker 120
Orange-breasted Waxbill 126
Pink-throated Twinspot 126
Purple-crested Lourie 119

Red-billed Firefinch 125
Red-collared Widow 124
Red-fronted Tinkerbird 120
Red-headed Finch 127
Red-headed Quelea 123
Red-headed Weaver 123
Red-shouldered Widow 123
Red-throated Twinspot 126
Rock Pigeon 118
Rosy-faced Lovebird 118
Scarlet-chested Sunbird 123
(Southern) Carmine Bee-eater 119
(Southern) Red Bishop 124
Swee Waxbill 127
White-fronted Bee-eater 119

Crimson-breasted Boubou

ROSY-FACED LOVEBIRD
Rocky gorges. Red forecrown, face and neck on green bird; white bill. (Rooiwangparkiet) 17-18 cm

LILIAN'S LOVEBIRD
Woodland. Red forecrown, face, neck and bill on green bird. (Niassaparkiet) 17-18 cm

LESSER FLAMINGO
Salt pans. Pink bird with red wing feathers, bill and legs. (Kleinflamink) 102 cm

GREATER FLAMINGO
Wetlands. Red wings on white bird; bill and legs pink. (Grootflamink) 140 cm

ROCK PIGEON
Cliffs. Deep reddish wings spotted white; red facial skin and legs. (Kransduif) 33 cm

NARINA TROGON
Forests. Scarlet-red underparts
on iridescent green bird;
bill yellowish.
(Bosloerie) 29-34 cm

**(SOUTHERN) CARMINE
BEE-EATER**
Riverine bush. Carmine-red body
and wings; curved black bill.
(Rooiborsbyvreter) 33-38 cm

**WHITE-FRONTED
BEE-EATER**
Rivers. Red throat on tawny
underparts; curved black bill.
(Rooikeelbyvreter) 22-24 cm

KNYSNA LOURIE
Forests. Scarlet-red wings
on green bird; red bill.
(Knysnaloerie) 47 cm

PURPLE-CRESTED LOURIE
Woodland. Crimson-red wings
on blue-green bird; black bill.
(Bloukuifloerie) 47 cm

ACACIA PIED BARBET
Woodland. Forecrown only red; rest black, white and yellow.
(Bonthoutkapper) 17-18 cm

RED-FRONTED TINKERBIRD
Woodland. Red forehead (front) on black and yellow upperparts.
(Rooiblestinker) 10,5 cm

BLACK-COLLARED BARBET
Woodland. Red crown, cheeks, throat and breast; black collar.
(Rooikophoutkapper) 19-20 cm

OLIVE WOODPECKER
Forests. Red cap (male); red rump both sexes; grey head.
(Gryskopspeg) 18-20 cm

GROUND WOODPECKER
Rocks. Rump red; below streaked red on buff. Pale eyes, grey head.
(Grondspeg) 26 cm

CRESTED BARBET
Woodland. Red speckles on yellow head and breast; red rump; black-crested head.
(Kuifkophoutkapper) 23 cm

CARDINAL WOODPECKER (male)
Woodland. Red cap; brown forehead; streaked black below.
(Kardinaalspeg) 14-16 cm

GOLDEN-TAILED WOODPECKER
Woodland. Male with red cap and moustachial streak; female with red nape only; streaked black below.
(Goudstertspeg) 20-23 cm

BEARDED WOODPECKER (male)
Woodland. Red crown; black forehead; banded low.
(Baardspeg) 23-25 cm

BENNETT'S WOODPECKER
Woodland. Male with red cap and moustachial streak; female with red nape; brown face and throat; below lightly spotted.
(Bennettse speg) 22-24 cm

KNYSNA WOODPECKER
Coastal bush. Male with red cap and moustachial streak; female with black cap and red nape; both well spotted below.
(Knysnaspeg) 20 cm

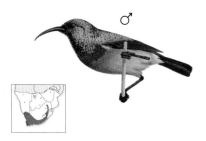

LESSER (SOUTHERN) DOUBLE-COLLARED SUNBIRD (male)
General. Narrow red lower breast-band; belly dull grey-buff; head and mantle glossy-green.
(Kleinrooibandsuikerbekkie) 12,5 cm

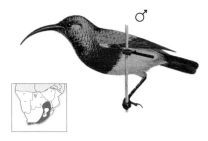

GREATER DOUBLE-COLLARED SUNBIRD (male)
Montane. Wide red lower breast-band; belly dull grey-buff; head and mantle glossy-green.
(Grootrooibandsuikerbekkie) 14 cm

CRIMSON-BREASTED BOUBOU
Thornveld. Crimson below; black above with white wing-stripe.
(Rooiborslaksman) 22-23 cm

GORGEOUS BUSH SHRIKE
Mixed bush. Red chin and throat; bold black breast-band; yellow belly.
(Konkoit) 20 cm

SCARLET-CHESTED SUNBIRD (male)
Woodland. Black with scarlet throat
and breast; green forehead.
(Rooikeelsuikerbekkie) 13-15 cm

RED-HEADED WEAVER (male)
Woodland. Red head, mantle
and breast; pink bill; belly white.
(Rooikopwewer) 15 cm

MARICO SUNBIRD (male)
Bushveld. Claret-red lower breast-
band; black belly; above head and
breast glossy-green.
(Maricosuikerbekkie) 13-14 cm

RED-HEADED QUELEA (male)
Grasslands. Red head on small,
buffy seed-eater.
(Rooikopkwelea) 11,5 cm

RED-SHOULDERED WIDOW (male)
Wetlands. Entirely black except for
red shoulder-patch; whitish bill.
(Kortstertflap) 19 cm

red plumage **123**

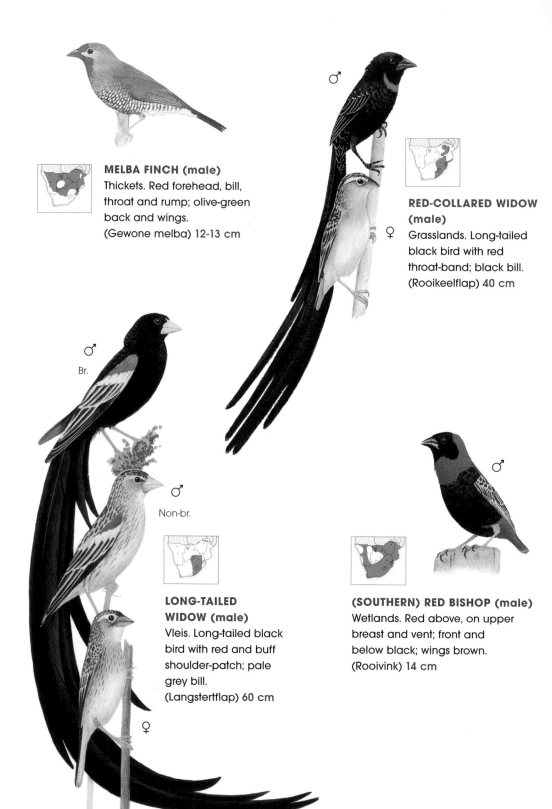

MELBA FINCH (male)
Thickets. Red forehead, bill, throat and rump; olive-green back and wings.
(Gewone melba) 12-13 cm

RED-COLLARED WIDOW (male)
Grasslands. Long-tailed black bird with red throat-band; black bill.
(Rooikeelflap) 40 cm

LONG-TAILED WIDOW (male)
Vleis. Long-tailed black bird with red and buff shoulder-patch; pale grey bill.
(Langstertflap) 60 cm

(SOUTHERN) RED BISHOP (male)
Wetlands. Red above, on upper breast and vent; front and below black; wings brown.
(Rooivink) 14 cm

124 red plumage

**GOLDEN-BACKED
PYTILIA (male)**
Thickets. Red forehead, bill,
throat, rump and upper tail;
olive-green back; orange-
edged wings.
(Geelrugmelba) 11 cm

BROWN FIREFINCH (male)
Thickets. Reddish mask, throat
and breast; rest grey-brown.
(Bruinvuurvinkie) 10 cm

RED-BILLED FIREFINCH
Bushveld. Red head, neck, breast
and upper tail coverts in male;
red lores and upper tail in female;
rest of body grey-brown.
(Rooibekvuurvinkie) 10 cm

BLACK WIDOW FINCH (male)
Bushveld. Five almost identical
species when breeding. Told
by bill and leg colours only.
(Blouvinkies) 11 cm

BLUE-BILLED FIREFINCH
Bushveld. Face, throat, breast, flanks
and rump red; above, including
crown, grey-brown; bill blue-black.
(Kaapse vuurvinkie) 11 cm

JAMESON'S FIREFINCH
Bushveld. Head, underparts and
rump pinkish-red; upperparts brown
washed pinkish-red; bill blue-black.
(Jamesonse vuurvinkie) 11 cm

RED-THROATED TWINSPOT (male)
Dense bush. Red head (not crown),
throat breast and rump. Below black
with white spots.
(Rooikeelkolpensie) 12,5 cm

**ORANGE-BREASTED WAXBILL
(male)**
Wetlands, cultivations. Red mask,
bill and vent; yellow underparts.
(Rooiassie) 9 cm

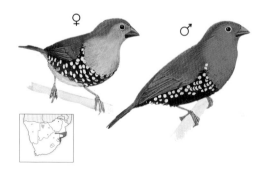

PINK-THROATED TWINSPOT
Dense scrub. Pink face, breast
and rump with cinnamon wings
and back; belly and vent black
with white spots.
(Rooskeelkopensie) 12 cm

COMMON WAXBILL
Wetlands. Red mask, bill and
central belly; brown-barred below.
(Rooibeksysie) 13 cm

126 red plumage

BLACK-CHEEKED WAXBILL
Thornveld. Rump and underparts
deep wine-red; bill and mask black.
(Swartwangsysie) 12-13 cm

GREY WAXBILL
Bushveld. Small grey bird with
red rump and upper tail coverts;
red eyes and black bill.
(Gryssysie) 11 cm

SWEE WAXBILL
Thick bush. Red back
and upper tail coverts;
red and black bill.
(Suidelike swie) 9-10 cm

RED-HEADED FINCH (male)
Thornveld. Red head; grey-brown
above; speckled below;
heavy bill.
(Rooikopvink) 13 cm

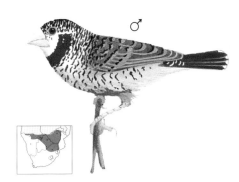

CUT-THROAT FINCH (male)
Woodland. Speckled bird with
broad red throat-band; white bill.
(Bandkeelvink) 12 cm

birds with
red bill, facial skin and legs

Pygmy Kingfisher

The title of this chapter refers to those parts of a bird that include any bare skin encircling the eyes (the orbital ring or eye-ring), bare flesh on the face or throat, its beak or bill, and its legs. Collectively these parts of a bird are called its 'soft parts' or 'bare parts' – in other words, any part of the body that is not covered by feathers. Many birds have brightly coloured bills or legs, often both, and among the larger species we frequently see bare skin around the bird's face or neck.

All too often, especially when a bird sighting is brief, we can only recall the colours of its soft parts once it has flown out of sight, and it is just this situation that this chapter caters for.

Red-headed Weaver (male)

THE CERE

At the base of the upper mandible of birds of prey, some parrots and some pigeons, there is a soft, swollen region called the cere. It is usually unfeathered, except in certain parrots. In pigeons it appears as two fleshy swellings above the nostrils, as seen in the common Feral Pigeon. The colouring of the cere may be grey, yellow (as in many birds of prey), orange or red according to the species, but its exact function is unknown.

In many birds of prey the lores, the region between the base of the bill and the eye, is bare of feathers and may be coloured red, yellow or grey. This unfeathered region probably functions as an aid to cleanliness, especially in those raptors that feed on messy food items. In the Gymnogene or Harrier-hawk the entire face and forward section of the head is bare. In many vultures the entire head and much of the neck is unfeathered for the same reason.

The birds you will find in this chapter

African Black Oystercatcher 135
African Finfoot 133
African Golden Oriole 142
African Green Pigeon 139
African Mourning Dove 138
African Pygmy Kingfisher 140
(African) Quail Finch 144
(African) Red-eyed Bulbul 142
African Skimmer 130
African Spoonbill 132
Arctic Tern 131
Bateleur 137
Black Crake 134
Black Stork 131
Black-winged Stilt 135
Brown-hooded Kingfisher 140
Bush Blackcap 142
Cape Gull 130
Caspian Tern 130
Common Tern 130
Common Waxbill 145
Crested Francolin 135
Crowned Hornbill 141
Crowned Plover 134
Dark Chanting Goshawk 137
Diederik Cuckoo 139
(Eastern) Black-headed Oriole 142
Eastern Red-footed Kestrel 138
Eurasian Golden Oriole 142
Gabar Goshawk 137
Golden-backed Pytilia 144
Grey-headed Gull 130
Grey-headed Kingfisher 140
Hartlaub's Gull 130
Helmeted Guineafowl 136
Hooded Vulture 136
Knysna Lourie 139
Lappet-faced Vulture 137
Lesser Flamingo 132
Lesser Gallinule 133
Lesser Moorhen 134
Lilian's Lovebird 139
Long-toed Plover 134
Malachite Kingfisher 140
Melba Finch 144

Monteiro's Hornbill 141
Namaqua Dove 138
Natal Francolin 136
Orange-breasted Waxbill 145
Pin-tailed Whydah 145
Purple Gallinule 133
Purple-crested Lourie 139
Red-billed Buffalo Weaver 143
Red-billed Francolin 135
Red-billed Helmet Shrike 143
Red-billed Hornbill 141
Red-billed Oxpecker 143
Red-billed Quelea 144
Red-billed Teal 133
Red-billed Wood Hoopoe 141
Red-eyed Dove 138
Red-faced Mousebird 140
Red-headed Weaver 144
Red-knobbed Coot 133
Red-necked Francolin 136
Rock Pigeon 139
Saddle-billed Stork 131
Shaft-tailed Whydah 145
Southern Bald Ibis 132
Southern Black Korhaan 135
Southern Ground Hornbill 141
Spur-winged Goose 132
Steel-blue Widow Finch 145
Swainson's Francolin 136
Three-banded Plover 134
Violet-eared Waxbill 145
Wattled Crane 135
Western Red-footed Kestrel 138
Whiskered Tern 131
White Stork 131
White-headed Vulture 137
Woodland Kingfisher 140
Yellow-billed Oxpecker 143
Yellow-billed Stork 131

African Skimmer

HARTLAUB'S GULL
Coastal. Bill and legs
deep red; plumage
white and grey.
(Hartlaubsemeeu) 38 cm

AFRICAN SKIMMER
Inland waters. Bill and
legs red; plumage dark
brown and white.
(Waterploeër) 38 cm

GREY-HEADED GULL
Inland and coastal.
Bill and legs bright red;
plumage white and grey.
(Gryskopmeeu) 42 cm

CASPIAN TERN
Inland and estuarine waters.
Large red bill; legs black;
plumage grey and white.
(Reusesterretjie) 52 cm

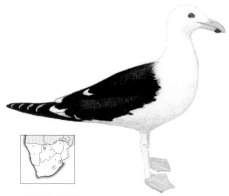

CAPE GULL
Coastal. Large yellow bill with
red spot on lower mandible;
plumage black and white.
(Swartrugmeeu) 60 cm

COMMON TERN
Coastal. Differs from Arctic Tern in
longer legs and bill; bill red with
black tip when breeding; plumage
grey and white; cap black.
(Gewone sterretjie) 35 cm

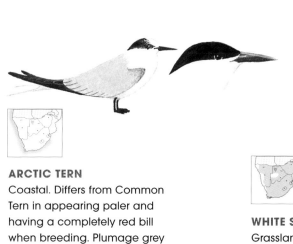

ARCTIC TERN
Coastal. Differs from Common Tern in appearing paler and having a completely red bill when breeding. Plumage grey and white; cap black. (Arktiese sterretjie) 35 cm

WHITE STORK
Grasslands, bushveld. Red bill and legs; plumage black and white. (Witooievaar) 117 cm

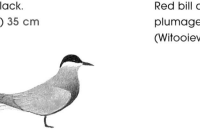

WHISKERED TERN
Inland pans. Red bill and legs when breeding; plumage grey and white; cap black. (Witbaardsterretjie) 23 cm

BLACK STORK
Inland waters. Red bill and legs; plumage black and white. (Grootswartooievaar) 122 cm

SADDLE-BILLED STORK
Wetlands. Red and black bill with yellow saddle; black-and-white plumage. (Saalbekooievaar) 145 cm

YELLOW-BILLED STORK
Wetlands. Red facial skin and legs; plumage black and white. (Nimmersat) 97 cm

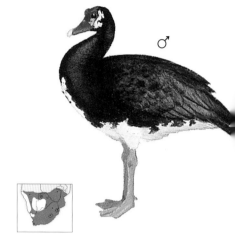

LESSER FLAMINGO
Saline waters. Bill deep red;
legs red; plumage pink.
(Kleinflamink) 102 cm

SPUR-WINGED GOOSE (male)
Wetlands. Red bill and forehead;
pink legs; plumage glossy-green.
(Wildemakou) 102 cm

AFRICAN SPOONBILL
Wetlands. Red bill and
legs; plumage white.
(Lepelaar) 91 cm

SOUTHERN BALD IBIS
Dry grasslands. Red crown and
bill; plumage iridescent blue.
(Kalkoenibis) 71 cm

RED-BILLED TEAL

Wetlands. Red bill; brown cap;
mottled-brown plumage.
(Rooibekeend) 48 cm

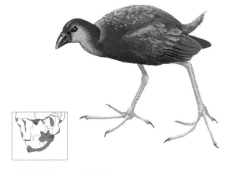

PURPLE GALLINULE

Wetlands. Red frontal shield
and bill; pink legs; plumage
glossy-green and blue.
(Grootkoningriethaan) 46 cm

RED-KNOBBED COOT

Wetlands. Red knobs on head;
red eyes; white frontal shield
and bill; black plumage.
(Bleshoender) 43 cm

AFRICAN FINFOOT

Rivers. Bill and legs red;
plumage brown and white.
(Watertrapper) 63 cm

LESSER MOORHEN
Wetlands. Red on frontal shield
and culmen; yellow bill; pink
legs; blackish plumage.
(Kleinwaterhoender) 23 cm

LONG-TOED PLOVER
Floodpans, backwaters.
Red bill with black tip;
red eye-ring and legs;
black-and-white body.
(Witvlerkkiewiet) 30 cm

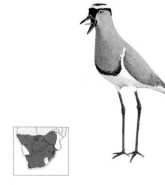

BLACK CRAKE
Wetlands. Black bird with
red legs; yellow bill.
(Swartriethaan) 20-23 cm

CROWNED PLOVER
Dry veld. Black-tipped red
bill and red legs; white ring
around black cap.
(Kroonkiewiet) 30 cm

THREE-BANDED PLOVER
Wetlands. Red bill and eye-ring;
white below with two black
chest-bands.
(Driebandstrandkiewiet) 18 cm

WATTLED CRANE
Wetlands. Large crane with a fleshy red base to its bill; grey above; white below.
(Lelkraanvoël) 120 cm

AFRICAN BLACK OYSTERCATCHER
Rocky coasts. Black bird with red bill, eye-ring and legs.
(Swarttobie) 51 cm

BLACK-WINGED STILT
Wetlands. Long red legs; white body; black bill and wings.
(Rooipootelsie) 38 cm

CRESTED FRANCOLIN
Bushveld. A bantam-like francolin with red legs.
(Bospatrys) 32 cm

SOUTHERN BLACK KORHAAN
Red bill on mostly black bird; pale yellow legs; buffy above.
(Swartkorhaan) 53 cm

RED-BILLED FRANCOLIN
Dry woodland. Red bill and legs; yellow eye-ring.
(Rooibekfisant) 30-38 cm

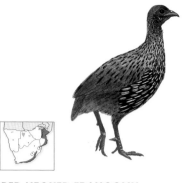

RED-NECKED FRANCOLIN
Coastal bush. Red bill, facial
and throat skin and legs;
plumage variable, may have
white about head.
(Rooikeelfisant) 32-44 cm

HELMETED GUINEAFOWL
Bushveld. Red crown on blue head;
red wattle-tips.
(Gewone tarentaal) 53-58 cm

SWAINSON'S FRANCOLIN
Bushveld. Black tip to red bill;
red facial and throat skin; legs
black; plumage dark brown.
(Bosveldfisant) 34-39 cm

HOODED VULTURE
Game regions. Reddish facial and
neck skin; slender white bill; brown
and white plumage.
(Monnikaasvoël) 70 cm

NATAL FRANCOLIN
Koppies, riverbanks. Red
and yellow bill; red legs;
speckled below.
(Natalse fisant) 30-38 cm

 WHITE-HEADED VULTURE
Game regions. Red tip to pale blue bill; pink facial and neck skin; pink legs; white and brown plumage.
(Witkopaasvoël) 85 cm

 GABAR GOSHAWK
Woodland. Small grey raptor with red cere and legs.
(Witkruissperwer) 30-34 cm

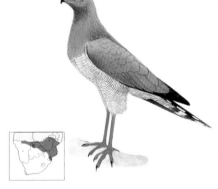

DARK CHANTING GOSHAWK
Woodland. Grey raptor with coral-red legs and pink cere.
(Donkersingvalk) 50-56 cm

LAPPET-FACED VULTURE
Game regions. Scarlet-red facial and neck skin; plumage brown and white.
(Swartaasvoël) 115 cm

BATELEUR
Game regions. Red bill and facial skin; red legs; plumage mostly black; tawny wings; short tail.
(Berghaan) 55-70 cm

red bill, facial skin and legs **137**

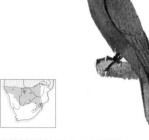

EASTERN RED-FOOTED KESTREL (male)
Grasslands. Small, pale grey raptor with red cere, eye-ring and legs.
(Oostelike rooipootvalk) 28-30 cm

WESTERN RED-FOOTED KESTREL (male)
Grasslands. Small, dark grey raptor with red cere, eye-ring and legs.
(Westelike rooipootvalk) 28-30 cm

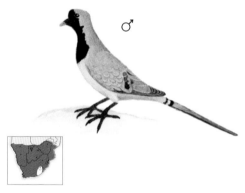

RED-EYED DOVE
Wooded regions. Red eye-ring around red eyes; wide black collar; grey crown; grey-pink underparts.
(Grootringduif) 33-36 cm

NAMAQUA DOVE (male)
Dry veld. Red bill with yellow tip; red legs; black forehead, throat and breast; long tail.
(Namakwaduifie) 27 cm

AFRICAN MOURNING DOVE
Riverine woodland. Red eye-ring around yellow eyes; red legs; grey head; black collar; pink breast.
(Rooioogtortelduif) 30 cm

138 red bill, facial skin and legs

ROCK PIGEON
Cliffs. Red mask; yellow eye; red legs; upperparts dull red, spotted white.
(Kransduif) 33 cm

KNYSNA LOURIE
Forests. Red bill and eye-ring on green bird with crested head.
(Knysnaloerie) 47 cm

AFRICAN GREEN PIGEON
Riverine woodland. Red bill with white tip; red legs; white eye; green upperparts.
(Papegaaiduif) 30 cm

PURPLE-CRESTED LOURIE
Red eye-ring on green head with purple crest.
(Bloukuifloerie) 47 cm

LILIAN'S LOVEBIRD
Zambezi Valley. Red bill on rose-red head; whitish eye-ring; rest green.
(Niassaparkiet) 17-18 cm

DIEDERIK CUCKOO
Wooded habitats. Red eye-rings on glossy-green cuckoo; juvenile has pinkish-red bill and no eye-ring.
(Diederikkie) 18,5 cm

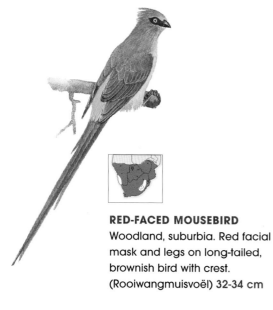

RED-FACED MOUSEBIRD
Woodland, suburbia. Red facial
mask and legs on long-tailed,
brownish bird with crest.
(Rooiwangmuisvoël) 32-34 cm

BROWN-HOODED KINGFISHER
Woodland. Red bill on brown-streaked
head and body; red legs; black and
blue wings and tail.
(Bruinkopvisvanger) 23-24 cm

WOODLAND KINGFISHER
Woodland. Blue and white;
bill red above, black below;
juvenile has all-red bill.
(Bosveldvisvanger) 23-24 cm

AFRICAN PYGMY KINGFISHER
Woodland. Red bill and legs on
small kingfisher; blue above; sandy
below; mauve sides to head.
(Dwergvisvanger) 13 cm

GREY-HEADED KINGFISHER
Woodland. Red, dagger-like
bill on grey head; red legs.
(Gryskopvisvanger) 20 cm

MALACHITE KINGFISHER
Streams. Red bill and legs on
small kingfisher; glossy-blue
above; orange-buff below.
(Kuifkopvisvanger) 14 cm

RED-BILLED WOOD HOOPOE
Curved red bill; red legs on long-tailed, glossy blue-green bird.
(Gewone kakelaar) 30-36 cm

MONTEIRO'S HORNBILL
Red bill with white base; dark head and breast; dark upperparts; white below.
(Monteirose neushoringvoël) 54-58 cm

RED-BILLED HORNBILL
Woodland. Prominent red bill on black-and-white hornbill; upperparts speckled white.
(Rooibekneushoringvoël) 42-50 cm

CROWNED HORNBILL
Lowland forests. Prominent red bill with yellow base; dark brown above; white below.
(Gekroonde neushoringvoël) 50-57 cm

SOUTHERN GROUND HORNBILL
Woodland. Large black, terrestrial bird with red facial and throat skin.
(Bromvoël) 90 cm

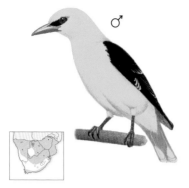

EURASIAN GOLDEN ORIOLE
Woodland. Coral-red bill on
yellow bird with black wings.
(Europese wielewaal) 24 cm

BUSH BLACKCAP
Hillside scrub. Red bill on greyish
bird with black cap; orange legs.
(Rooibektiptol) 17 cm

AFRICAN GOLDEN ORIOLE (male)
Woodland. Coral-red bill on
yellow bird with black mask.
(Afrikaanse wielewaal) 24 cm

(AFRICAN) RED-EYED BULBUL
Semi-arid bush. Yellow-vented bulbul
with red eye-ring on black head.
(Rooioogtiptol) 19-21 cm

**(EASTERN) BLACK-HEADED
ORIOLE**
Woodland. Coral-red bill on
yellow bird with black head.
(Swartkopwielewaal) 25 cm

RED-BILLED HELMET SHRIKE
Riverine forests. Black bird with red bill, eye-wattles and legs; white vent.
(Swarthelmlaksman) 22 cm

YELLOW-BILLED OXPECKER
Game regions. Red-tipped yellow bill on brown bird.
(Geelbekrenostervoël) 22 cm

RED-BILLED BUFFALO WEAVER
Woodland. Stout red bill on blackish weaver.
(Buffelwewer) 24 cm

RED-BILLED OXPECKER
Game regions. Red bill; red eye with yellow eye-wattle on brown bird.
(Rooibekrenostervoël) 20-22 cm

RED-BILLED QUELEA
Croplands. Red or pinkish bill on small, weaver-type bird; male has blackish face.
(Rooibekkwelea) 13 cm

GOLDEN-BACKED PYTILIA
Thornveld thickets. Red bill on grey head; golden-orange wings.
(Geelrugmelba) 11 cm

(AFRICAN) QUAIL FINCH
Grassveld. Very small finch; male has red bill; female has red and black bill; banded breast.
(Gewone kwartelvinkie) 9,5 cm

RED-HEADED WEAVER (male)
Woodland. Coral-red bill on weaver with red head, mantle and breast.
(Rooikopwewer) 15 cm

MELBA FINCH
Thornveld thickets. Red bill on grey head; male with red forehead and throat; male and female banded below.
(Gewone melba) 12-13 cm

ORANGE-BREASTED WAXBILL
Wetlands. Red bill; grey above;
yellow below with banded flanks.
(Rooiassie) 8,5-9 cm

PIN-TAILED WHYDAH
(male)
Suburbia and general.
Black-and-white, long-tailed
bird with red bill.
(Koningrooibekkie) 34 cm

COMMON WAXBILL
Reedbeds. Red-billed waxbill
with red mask and underbelly.
(Rooibeksysie) 13 cm

SHAFT-TAILED WHYDAH
Thornveld. Red bill and legs;
black above; buffy below;
very long tail-shafts.
(Pylstertrooibekkie) 34 cm

VIOLET-EARED WAXBILL
Dry thornveld. Red-billed waxbill
with longish tail; violet cheeks.
(Koningblousysie) 13-15 cm

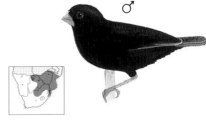

STEEL-BLUE WIDOW FINCH (male)
Mixed bush. Small, black bird
with red bill and legs.
(Staalblouvinkie) 11 cm

birds with
orange
plumage

Natal Robin

There are 32 southern African birds with partly orange plumage or soft parts, especially beaks and legs. Orange as a plumage colour is particularly attractive since it is often set against a yellow background, as seen, for example, in the beautiful Orange-breasted Bush Shrike. Like certain other bright colours, orange probably has an important signalling function in species recognition, and perhaps courtship or pair-bonding rituals, as suggested by the fact that the orange colour most often occurs on the bird's breast, forehead or bill, where it is most easily seen by others.

Orange-breasted Sunbird (male)

PELLETS

Many birds regurgitate undigested food items in the shape of oval or round pellets. The action involves a series of convulsive movements of the extended head and neck with the bill open. In owls, which swallow prey whole, the pellet consists mainly of fur and small mammal bones. In kingfishers, herons and other fish-eaters, the pellets contain fish bones, scales and similar hard materials. Even shrikes, rollers and others that prey on large insects and small reptiles will regurgitate such indigestable items as beetle carapaces, claws and small bones. The disection and examination of bird pellets therefore provides an insight to the bird's preferred diet.

The birds you will find in this chapter

African Pygmy Goose **148**
Black-fronted Bush Shrike **153**
Cape Eagle Owl **148**
Cape Robin **151**
Chorister Robin **152**
(Common) Ringed Plover **148**
Golden-breasted Bunting **153**
Greater Striped Swallow **149**
Grey-headed Bush Shrike **153**
Grey Penduline Tit **152**
Half-collared Kingfisher **149**
Heuglin's Robin **152**
Karoo (Sombre) Thrush **150**
Kurrichane Thrush **150**
Lesser Crested Tern **148**
Lesser Striped Swallow **149**
Malachite Kingfisher **149**
Natal Robin **152**
Olive Thrush **150**
Orange-breasted Bush Shrike **152**
Orange-breasted Rock-jumper **151**
Orange-breasted Sunbird **153**
Orange-breasted Waxbill **153**
Orange-throated Longclaw **150**
Ruddy Turnstone **148**
Sentinel Rock Thrush **151**
Short-toed Rock Thrush **151**
White-faced Scops Owl **148**
White-throated Robin **151**
Wire-tailed Swallow **149**
Yellow-fronted Tinkerbird **150**

Short-toed Rock Thrush

Black-fronted Bush Shrike

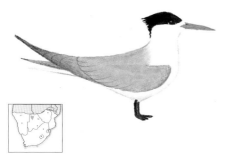

LESSER CRESTED TERN
Coastal. Orange bill only. Black or partially black cap; grey above; white below with black legs. (Kuifkopsterretjie) 40 cm

RUDDY TURNSTONE (breeding)
Shorelines. Orange legs; black bill; head and below white; black facial marks and breast-band; rufous wings. (Steenloper) 22 cm

AFRICAN PYGMY GOOSE
Quiet waters. Orange bill and orange-buff underparts in both sexes; upperparts dark green. (Dwerggans) 33 cm

WHITE-FACED SCOPS OWL
Woodland. Deep orange eyes in white facial disc with black border; plumage grey. (Witwanguil) 25-28 cm

(COMMON) RINGED PLOVER
Shorelines. Black-tipped orange bill and orange legs; bold black breast-band on white underparts. (Ringnekstrandkiewiet) 18 cm

CAPE EAGLE OWL
Rocky valleys. Orange eyes in immature; orange-yellow in adult. Large 'eared' owl; dark above; blotched dark below. (Kaapse ooruil) 48-55 cm

LESSER STRIPED SWALLOW
Lowveld. Cap, ear coverts and rump rich orange; below white, well streaked black.
(Kleinstreepswael) 16 cm

GREATER STRIPED SWALLOW
Highveld. Orange cap and pale orange rump; whitish below, lightly streaked black.
(Grootstreepswael) 20 cm

MALACHITE KINGFISHER
Ponds. Orange-buff below; blue above; bill and legs red.
(Kuifkopvisvanger) 14 cm

WIRE-TAILED SWALLOW
Lowveld rivers. Orange cap; black mask; white below with fine tail-streamers.
(Draadstertswael) 13 cm

HALF-COLLARED KINGFISHER
Quiet rivers. Orange wash on belly and vent; throat white; above blue; bill black; legs red.
(Blouvisvanger) 20 cm

orange plumage **149**

KAROO (OR SOMBRE) THRUSH
Highveld and scrubland. Dark grey-
brown except for orange underbelly, orange-yellow legs and bill.
(Brynluister) 24 cm

KURRICHANE THRUSH
Woodland. Orange bill, eye-ring,
legs and flanks; white belly;
black moustachial streaks.
(Rooibeklyster) 22 cm

YELLOW-FRONTED TINKERBIRD
Woodland. Yellow forehead normally
looks orange; above black, speckled
white and yellow; below pale yellow.
(Geelblestinker) 12 cm

**ORANGE-THROATED
LONGCLAW**
Grasslands. Orange throat
with black border; underparts
yellow; above grey-brown.
(Oranjekeelkalkoentjie) 20 cm

OLIVE THRUSH
Forests and suburbia.
Orange bill and belly;
orange-yellow legs;
speckled throat.
(Olyflyster) 24 cm

150 orange plumage

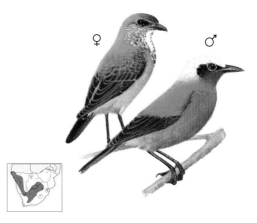

SENTINEL ROCK THRUSH
Rocky hills. Orange rump and
outer tail feathers; light orange wash
to underparts; breast speckled. Male
has dull grey head, breast and mantle;
orange lower breast to vent.
(Langtoonkliplyster) 21 cm

SHORT-TOED ROCK THRUSH
Rocky hills. Orange below with white throat;
above grey-brown with orange rump.
Male has grey throat and mantle, white cap;
breast to vent rich orange.
(Korttoonkliplyster) 18 cm

WHITE-THROATED ROBIN
Thickets. Grey, black and white
above; below white chin to
lower breast; flanks and belly
washed orange.
(Witkeeljanfrederik) 16-18 cm

CAPE ROBIN
Forest fringes and gardens.
Orange breast, rump, upper tail
coverts and tail fringes; white
eyebrows; underbody grey-buff.
(Gewone janfrederik) 18 cm

ORANGE-BREASTED ROCK-JUMPER (male)
Rocky grasslands. Rump and upper tail coverts
orange; below orange lower breast; paler towards belly.
(Oranjeborsberglyster) 21 cm

HEUGLIN'S ROBIN
Thickets. Underparts entirely rich orange
extending to rump and tail fringes;
white eyebrows on black hood.
(Heuglinse janfrederik) 19-20 cm

CHORISTER ROBIN
Forests. Underparts entirely
orange; hood black; wings
and upper tail dark grey.
(Lawaaimakerjanfrederik) 20 cm

**GREY (OR AFRICAN)
PENDULINE TIT**
Woodland. Dark grey-green
upperparts with buff patch
extending from forehead to ear
coverts; light grey breast with
buff-coloured belly and vent.
(Gryskapokvoël) 8-9 cm

NATAL ROBIN
Forests. Entirely orange
except for brownish crown
and silver-grey wings.
(Nataljanfrederik) 18-20 cm

ORANGE-BREASTED BUSH SHRIKE
Bushveld. Grey cap and mantle;
olive-green wings and upper tail;
below yellow with orange breast-patch.
(Oranjeborsboslaksman) 18-19 cm

152 orange plumage

ORANGE-BREASTED SUNBIRD (male)
Fynbos. Head and throat glossy-green; breast-band purple; breast orange grading to yellow at vent; tail longish. (Oranjeborssuikerbekkie) 15 cm

BLACK-FRONTED BUSH SHRIKE
Forests. Chin to underbelly rich orange; vent yellow; above olive-green; cap grey. (Swartoogboslaksman) 19 cm

ORANGE-BREASTED WAXBILL
Reedbeds. Small waxbill with red bill and mask; below yellow with orange wash on breast; orange vent; banded flanks. (Rooiassie) 8,5-9 cm

GREY-HEADED BUSH SHRIKE
Riverine forests. Yellow chin to vent, except for orange breast; head grey; rest olive-green; eyes orange-yellow; heavy bill black. (Spookvoël) 25-27 cm

GOLDEN-BREASTED BUNTING
Bushveld. Head black with white stripes; chin to lower breast yellow, with orange wash on breast; vent white. (Rooirugstreepkoppie) 16 cm

birds with
yellow colouring

African Golden Oriole

Of all the bright colours seen in birds, yellow is probably the most common. In the majority of birds with yellow plumage it is their underparts that carry this colour, many being yellow from chin to tail. Other birds have white underparts, or some light colour such as cream, buff or beige, and this arrangement of pale underparts serves a purpose known as counter-shading. A bird receives most sunlight on its darker upperparts, while its pale underparts are in shade. The contrast between the dark upper surface and pale under-surface is thereby reduced so that the bird does not stand out from its background. For example, a bird that is olive-green above and yellow below will tend to appear the same colour all over since its shaded yellow underparts will take on a greenish appearance.

In this chapter only true yellow, a colour likely to make a lasting impression on an observer, is included. Waterbirds that are identifiable by their yellow bills or legs are included, but not the many birds of prey that have yellow ceres and legs, since these cannot be regarded as specific identification features.

Collared Sunbird

THE WARBLERS

This is a somewhat ambiguous term used to describe a host of small songbirds belonging to various groups found in both temperate and tropical regions. In southern Africa, the term is used in particular for the many small European birds that migrate over very long distances to spend their non-breeding months (our summer) in the sub-tropics, namely the Palearctic warblers. In general terms, the warblers also include the apalises, penduline tits, eremomelas, crombecs, grass warblers (cisticolas), prinias and titbabblers. The Palearctic warblers, frequently referred to as just LBJs, are among the more difficult little brown birds to identify unless you are familiar with their habitats and songs.

The birds you will find in this chapter

Acacia Pied Barbet 161
African Emerald Cuckoo 159
African Golden Oriole 163
(African) Red-eyed Bulbul 164
(African) Wattled Plover 158
(African) Yellow White-eye 168
Bar-throated Apalis 165
Black Crake 158
Black Cuckooshrike 163
Black Egret 157
Black-eyed Bulbul 164
Black-throated Canary 173
Bokmakierie 167
Broad-billed Roller 160
Bully Canary 172
Cabanis's Bunting 173
Cape Bulbul 164
Cape Canary 172
Cape Gannet 156
Cape Gull 156
Cape Penduline Tit 165
Cape Siskin 173
Cape Weaver 169
Cape White-eye 168
Collared Sunbird 168
Crested Barbet 161
Cuckoo Finch 172
Drakensberg Siskin 173
(Eastern) Black-headed Oriole 163
Eastern White Pelican 156
Eurasian Golden Oriole 163
European Bee-eater 160
Forest Weaver 168
Golden Bishop 170
Golden-breasted Bunting 173
Golden-rumped Tinkerbird 161

Gorgeous Bush Shrike 167
Great White Heron 157
Greater Honeyguide 162
Green Coucal 159
Grey-headed Bush Shrike 167
Icterine Warbler 165
(Large) Golden Weaver 169
Lemon-breasted Canary 173
Lesser Masked Weaver 170
Little Bee-eater 160
Little Egret 157
Meyer's Parrot 159
Orange-breasted Bush Shrike 167
Orange-breasted Waxbill 171
Orange-throated Longclaw 162
Pink-backed Pelican 156
Red-fronted Tinkerbird 161
Red-headed Weaver 170
Ruddy Turnstone 158
Rüppell's Parrot 159
Saddle-billed Stork 157
Saffron Prinia 166
Scaly-throated Honeyguide 166
Slender-billed Honeybird 166
(Southern) Brown-throated Weaver 169
(Southern) Masked Weaver 170
Southern Yellow-billed Hornbill 160
Spectacled Weaver 169
Spotted-backed Weaver 170
Starred Robin 164
Swallow-tailed Bee-eater 160

Swee Waxbill 171
Swift Tern 156
White-crowned Plover 158
White-throated Canary 173
White-winged Widow 171
Willow Warbler 167
Yellow Canary 172
Yellow Wagtail 162
Yellow Warbler 165
Yellow Weaver 169
Yellow-backed Widow 171
Yellow-bellied Bulbul 164
Yellow-bellied Eremomela 166
Yellow-bellied Sunbird 168
Yellow-billed Duck 158
Yellow-billed Egret 157
Yellow-billed Kite 159
Yellow-billed Stork 157
Yellow-breasted Apalis 165
Yellow-eyed Canary 172
Yellow-fronted Tinkerbird 161
Yellow-rumped Widow 171
Yellow-spotted Nicator 163
Yellow-throated Longclaw 162
Yellow-throated (Woodland) Warbler 166

CAPE GANNET
Coastal. This mostly white
seabird has a distinctive
yellow wash over its head
and hind-neck.
(Witmalgas) 84-94 cm

PINK-BACKED PELICAN
Inland and coastal.
Yellow bill-pouch and feet.
(Kleinpelikaan) 135 cm

CAPE GULL
Coastal. Black-and-white
gull with yellow bill and
a red spot on the lower
mandible.
(Swartrugmeeu) 60 cm

EASTERN WHITE PELICAN
Inland and coastal. When
breeding it has a yellow
bill-pouch and yellow patch
on its upper breast; legs
are pinkish.
(Witpelikaan) 180 cm

SWIFT TERN
Coastal. A fairly large tern
with a yellow bill.
(Geelbeksterretjie) 50 cm

BLACK EGRET
Wetlands. A blackish
egret with yellow feet.
(Swartreier) 66 cm

GREAT WHITE HERON
Wetlands. A large heron.
When not breeding it has
a yellow bill and black legs.
(Grootwitreier) 95 cm

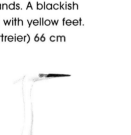

LITTLE EGRET
Wetlands. A white
egret with yellow feet
and black legs.
(Kleinwitreier) 64 cm

SADDLE-BILLED STORK
Wetlands. Huge pied stork
with large red and black bill,
and a yellow 'saddle' on the
upper mandible.
(Saalbekooievaar) 145 cm

YELLOW-BILLED STORK
Wetlands. Yellow, slightly
curved bill on white stork
with red face and legs.
(Nimmersat) 97 cm

YELLOW-BILLED EGRET
Wetlands. A medium-size, robust
white egret with a yellow bill.
(Geelbekwitreier) 68 cm

YELLOW-BILLED DUCK
Wetlands. The only duck with
a distinctive yellow bill with
a black saddle.
(Geelbekeend) 53-58 cm

(AFRICAN) WATTLED PLOVER
Wetlands. Yellow bill with black
tip; yellow wattles and legs;
entire breast greyish.
(Lelkiewiet) 35 cm

BLACK CRAKE
Wetlands. Small black
waterbird with yellow bill;
red legs.
(Swartriethaan) 20-23 cm

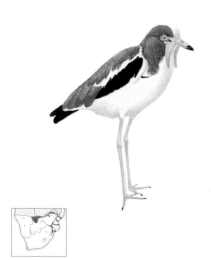

RUDDY TURNSTONE
Coastal. In non-breeding
plumage has yellow legs.
(Steenloper) 22 cm

WHITE-CROWNED PLOVER
Wetlands. Yellow bill with black tip;
long yellow wattles and
yellow legs; underparts white.
(Witkopkiewiet) 30 cm

 AFRICAN EMERALD CUCKOO
Forests. The only green
cuckoo with a yellow belly.
(Mooimeisie) 20 cm

 YELLOW-BILLED KITE
Aerial. Brown kite with forked tail;
yellow bill, cere and legs.
(Geelbekwou) 55 cm

 GREEN COUCAL
Coastal forests. A dull green
coucal with a yellow bill.
(Groenvleiloerie) 23 cm

 MEYER'S PARROT
Woodland. Small, brown-headed
parrot with yellow forehead
and shoulders; green belly;
pale blue back.
(Bosveldpapegaai) 23 cm

 RÜPPELL'S PARROT
Woodland. Small, dark brown parrot
with yellow shoulders and underwing
coverts; deep-blue belly; female with
deep-blue belly and back.
(Bloupenspapegaai) 23 cm

yellow colouring **159**

SWALLOW-TAILED BEE-EATER
Kalahari woodland. Blue and
green bee-eater with forked tail
and yellow throat.
(Swaelstertbyvreter) 20-22 cm

BROAD-BILLED ROLLER
Palm woodland. The
only yellow-billed roller.
(Geelbektroupant) 27 cm

**SOUTHERN YELLOW-
BILLED HORNBILL**
Woodland. Pied hornbill with
a prominent yellow bill.
(Geelbekneushoringvoël) 48-60 cm

EUROPEAN BEE-EATER
Wooded regions. Yellow throat;
blue forehead and underparts.
(Europese byvreter) 25-29 cm

LITTLE BEE-EATER
Woodland. Small bee-eater with
yellow throat, black upper breast
patch and orange-buff underparts.
(Kleinbyvreter) 17 cm

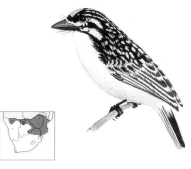

GOLDEN-RUMPED TINKERBIRD
Forests. Black above with yellow
wing edges and rump; whitish
below with yellow belly.
(Swartblestinker) 10 cm

YELLOW-FRONTED TINKERBIRD
Woodland. Black-and-white above
with yellow wing-feather edges;
orange forehead; pale yellow below.
(Geelblestinker) 12 cm

ACACIA PIED BARBET
Woodland. Red forehead; yellow
eyebrows and edges to wing and
tail feathers.
(Bonthoutkapper) 17-18 cm

RED-FRONTED TINKERBIRD
Lowland forests. Black-and-white
above with yellow wing-feather edges;
red forehead; pale yellow below.
(Rooiblestinker) 10,5 cm

CRESTED BARBET
Woodland. Bill pale yellow; head
and underparts yellow with red
spotting; above black with white
feather edges.
(Kuifkophoutkapper) 23 cm

Imm.

♀

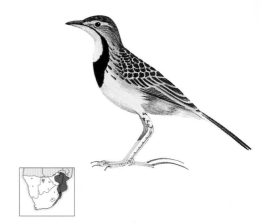

GREATER HONEYGUIDE (immature)
Woodland. The young bird is brown above and yellow below, grading to paler at vent.
(Grootheuningwyser) 19-20 cm

YELLOW-THROATED LONGCLAW
Open woodland. Above eyebrows and feather edges yellow; below yellow with black gorget.
(Geelkeelkalkoentjie) 20 cm

ORANGE-THROATED LONGCLAW
Grasslands. Eyebrows and below yellow; throat orange bordered black.
(Oranjekeelkalkoentjie) 20 cm

YELLOW WAGTAIL
Wetlands. Below yellow; above green-grey; various head patterns.
(Geelkwikkie) 18 cm

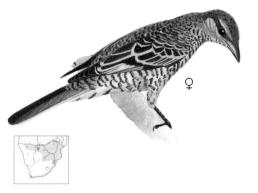

BLACK CUCKOOSHRIKE (female)
Woodland. Dull olive-brown above
with yellow wing-feathers and tail
edges; below banded black on white.
(Swartkatakoeroe) 22 cm

(EASTERN) BLACK-HEADED ORIOLE
Woodland. Black head and throat;
pink bill; rest yellow except black
primaries; green upper tail.
(Swartkopwielewaal) 25 cm

EURASIAN GOLDEN ORIOLE
Woodland. Entirely yellow except for
black wings, tail feathers and lores;
bill pink.
(Europese wielewaal) 24 cm

AFRICAN GOLDEN ORIOLE
Woodland. Entirely yellow except
for black mask, primaries and central
tail feathers; female greener; bill pink.
(Afrikaanse wielewaal) 24 cm

YELLOW-SPOTTED NICATOR
Dense bush. Greenish above; wing
feathers and tail tipped yellow;
underbelly, thighs and vent yellow.
(Geelvleknikator) 23 cm

YELLOW-BELLIED BULBUL
Riverine forests. Below
(including underwings) yellow;
head grey; rest olive-brown.
(Geelborswillie) 20-23 cm

CAPE BULBUL
Coastal bush. Dark brown
head and breast; white
eye-rings; yellow vent.
(Kaapse tiptol) 21 cm

BLACK-EYED BULBUL
Woodland and gardens. Black
eyes and tufted head; yellow vent.
(Swartoogtiptol) 20-22 cm

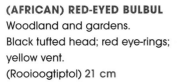

(AFRICAN) RED-EYED BULBUL
Woodland and gardens.
Black tufted head; red eye-rings;
yellow vent.
(Rooioogtiptol) 21 cm

STARRED ROBIN
Forests. Underparts yellow;
head grey; rest deep olive-green.
(Witkoljanfrederik) 15-16 cm

164 yellow colouring

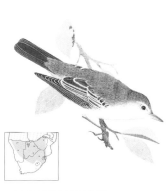

ICTERINE WARBLER
Acacia thornveld. Brown above with yellow flight-feather edges; below yellow.
(Spotvoël) 14-15 cm

YELLOW-BREASTED APALIS
Bushveld. Yellow-green above; some grey on head; yellow breast; white throat and belly; small central breast-bar often absent.
(Geelborskleinjantjie) 10-12,5 cm

YELLOW (OR DARK CAPPED YELLOW) WARBLER
Reeds and forest fringes. Yellow below; above olive-brown; wing feathers and tail edged yellow.
(Geelsanger) 14-15 cm

CAPE PENDULINE TIT
Woodland. Very small size; forehead blackish; throat white; rest of underparts yellow.
(Kaapse kapokvoël) 9-10 cm

BAR-THROATED APALIS
Woodland. The northern race is yellow below the black breast-band; throat white; above greyish; eyes whitish.
(Bandkeelkleinjantjie) 12-13 cm

YELLOW-BELLIED EREMOMELA
Bushveld. Yellow belly on small, greyish bird; paler on breast; darker above; tail short.
(Geelpensbossanger) 9-10 cm

SAFFRON PRINIA
Forest fringes. Eyebrows and below saffron-yellow; above brown; tail long.
(Gevlekte langstertjie) 14 cm

SCALY-THROATED HONEYGUIDE
Forest, bush. Streaky head, scaly throat with yellowish tinge; grey back with yellow bars on wings, paler underparts.
(Gevlekte heuningwyser) 19 cm

**SLENDER-BILLED
(OR GREEN-BACKED) HONEYBIRD**
Woodland. Upperparts green-grey; yellow edged flight feathers; slender bill.
(Dunbekheuningvoël) 11,5 cm

**YELLOW-THROATED (WOODLAND)
WARBLER**
Forests. Olive-green above. Chestnut cap; eyebrows and breast yellow; belly white.
(Geelkeelsanger) 11 cm

WILLOW WARBLER
Diverse bushy habitats; summer
visitor. Upperparts olive-green
with darker tail and flight feathers;
pale yellow underparts. Distinctive
yellowish eyebrow and notch in tail.
(Hofsanger) 12 cm

BOKMAKIERIE
Bush and suburbia. Above grey cap
and mantle; rest olive-green; yellow
below with black gorget.
(Bokmakierie) 23 cm

GORGEOUS BUSH SHRIKE
Dense bush. Red throat; black gorget;
yellow belly with orange wash; above
olive-green; yellow eyebrows.
(Konkoit) 20 cm

ORANGE-BREASTED
BUSH SHRIKE
Woodland. Yellow eyebrows
and underparts; orange breast;
above grey and olive-green.
(Oranjeborsboslaksman) 18-19 cm

GREY-HEADED BUSH SHRIKE
Bushveld. Heavy bill; yellowish eyes;
grey hood; rest olive-green; throat
and underbelly yellow; breast orange.
(Spookvoël) 25-27 cm

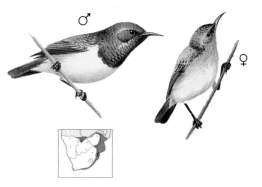

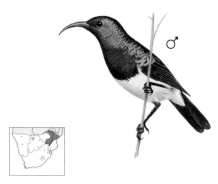

COLLARED SUNBIRD
Riverine woodland. Male has glossy-green upperparts, head and breast; lower breast to vent yellow; female entirely yellow below, duller. (Kortbeksuikerbekkie) 10 cm

YELLOW-BELLIED SUNBIRD (male)
Riverine forests and bush. Head and above glossy-green; breast violet; belly yellow. (Geelpenssuikerbekkie) 11 cm

(AFRICAN) YELLOW WHITE-EYE
Woodland. Above yellow-green; below entirely clear yellow. (Geelglasogie) 10,5 cm

 FOREST WEAVER
Forests. Yellow below; dark brown above; whitish bill and legs. (Bosmusikant) 16 cm

CAPE WHITE-EYE
Woodland and gardens. Various races but all with underlying yellow plumage; greener above. (Kaapse glasogie) 12 cm

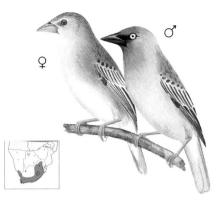

CAPE WEAVER
General. Male yellow all over; darker above; orange wash over head and throat; pale eyes. Female paler; yellow wash over head and breast; eyes dark; belly white.
(Kaapse wewer) 16-18 cm

(SOUTHERN) BROWN-THROATED WEAVER
Wetlands. All-yellow; male has brown throat-patch; black bill. Female greener above; white belly; bill horn-coloured.
(Bruinkeelwewer) 15 cm

YELLOW WEAVER
Wetlands. Both sexes all-yellow; bill dark.
(Geelwewer) 16 cm

(LARGE) GOLDEN WEAVER
Wetlands. Large yellow weaver; greener above; eyes pale yellow; bill black; male with orange throat in NW regions.
(Goudwewer) 18 cm

SPECTACLED WEAVER
Wetlands. All-yellow; wings darker; head with orange wash; bill and eye-stripe black; male with black bib; eyes pale.
(Brilwewer) 15-16 cm

yellow colouring **169**

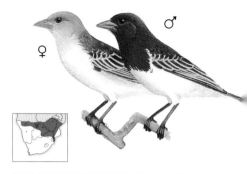

(SOUTHERN) MASKED WEAVER
Wetlands and gardens. Breeding male yellow with black mask from forehead to throat; black bill; red eyes. Female greener above, whitish below with yellow wash on breast.
(Swartkeelgeelvink) 15 cm

RED-HEADED WEAVER (female)
Woodland. White below with yellowish head; orange-pink bill; yellow feather edges to dark wings.
(Rooikopwewer) 15 cm

LESSER MASKED WEAVER
Wetlands. Both sexes yellow; greener above; eyes pale yellow. Male has black mask from central crown to throat.
(Kleingeelvink) 14 cm

SPOTTED-BACKED WEAVER
Wetlands. Male yellow with dark wings; yellow-speckled mantle; black mask from eyebrows to throat, or entirely black head; bill black; eyes red. Female lacks speckled mantle and mask; throat and breast yellow; belly whitish; eyes red; bill pinkish.
(Bontrugwewer) 17 cm

GOLDEN BISHOP (male)
Wetlands. Breeding male has yellow crown, nape and back; below black; bill black; legs pink.
(Goudgeelvink) 12 cm

WHITE-WINGED WIDOW (male)
Thornveld and cultivations. Breeding male all-black with yellow and white shoulder-patch; bill pale grey.
(Witvlerkflap) 19 cm

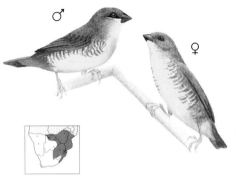

YELLOW-RUMPED WIDOW (male)
Vleis. Breeding male all-black with yellow rump and shoulder-patch.
(Kaapse flap) 15 cm

ORANGE-BREASTED WAXBILL
Reedbeds. Yellow below with barred flanks; male with red mask, breast-patch and vent; above grey-brown.
(Rooiassie) 8,5-9 cm

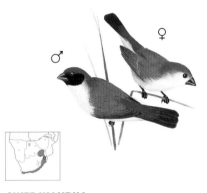

SWEE WAXBILL
Wooded streams. Yellow belly and vent in both sexes; breast whitish; dark green above; red rump and tail coverts; male has black mask.
(Suidelike swie) 9-10 cm

YELLOW-BACKED WIDOW (male)
Marshes. Breeding male all-black with yellow mantle and shoulder-patches.
(Geelrugflap) 22 cm

CUCKOO FINCH
Vleis. Small yellow bird;
dark wings with yellow-edged
feathers; black bill and legs.
(Koekoekvink) 12-13 cm

CAPE CANARY
General. Grey nape
and mantle; rest yellow;
greenish wings with
feathers edged yellow.
(Kaapse kanarie) 13-14 cm

YELLOW-EYED CANARY
Wooded regions. Below yellow; eyebrows
and cheeks yellow; crown to nape grey; rest
greenish with yellow-edged wing feathers.
(Geeloogkanarie) 12 cm

♂

YELLOW CANARY (male)
Dry bush. Eyebrows, cheeks
and underparts yellow;
upperparts olive-green,
paler in W, darkest in SE.
(Geelkanarie) 13-14 cm

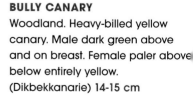

BULLY CANARY
Woodland. Heavy-billed yellow
canary. Male dark green above
and on breast. Female paler above
below entirely yellow.
(Dikbekkanarie) 14-15 cm

WHITE-THROATED CANARY

Karoo. Heavy-billed, greyish canary with yellow rump. (Witkeelkanarie) 14-15 cm

LEMON-BREASTED CANARY (male)

Bush and grasslands. Yellow breast and rump; belly white; dull greenish above. (Geelborskanarie) 10 cm

BLACK-THROATED CANARY

Grassy woodland. Small, greyish canary with blackish throat and yellow rump. (Bergkanarie) 11-12 cm

♂

♀

♂

CABANIS'S BUNTING

Miombo woodland. Yellow below; black head with white streaks; back brown with white-edged shoulder feathers. (Geelstreepkoppie) 15 cm

CAPE and DRAKENSBERG SISKINS

Montane scrub. Small, dark canary-like birds with greenish-yellow underparts. (Kaapse pietjiekanarie) (Bergpietjiekanarie) 13 cm

GOLDEN-BREASTED BUNTING

Woodland. Yellow below with orange breast; belly and vent white; head black with white streaks; mantle brown with white shoulder-patch. (Rooirugstreepkoppie) 16 cm

birds with
green plumage

Purple-banded Sunbird

Green plumage in many birds, from bright greens to dull olive, serve as cryptic coloration within the predominantly green habitat in which they live. Even bright green lovebirds, for example, are very difficult to detect when settled in a leafy tree canopy or feeding in fresh green grass, unless they move. Dull olive-green upperparts, as seen in many small birds, certainly help to render the wearers inconspicuous when seen from above, and this is particularly important for those that forage in the understorey or on the ground. Few waterbirds have green plumage, an exception being the green upperparts of the Pygmy Goose, which lives among floating water lily leaves. Some dabbling ducks have an iridescent green patch on the upperwings called a speculum. The speculum probably functions as an intraspecific visual stimulant or 'advertisement' used by the male bird to establish its status within a flock. This is done frequently when the male bird stands erect and flaps its wings, thereby displaying the colourful speculae.

SUNBIRDS

Sunbirds are the small, brightly iridescent birds with slender, decurved beaks that feed mostly on flower nectar. The bill is adapted to probe into tubular flowers such as those of aloes and ericas. There are many misconceptions about sunbirds, resulting in the local usage of such misleading names as 'honey-sucker' and 'sugarbird', the latter name properly referring to the unrelated genus *Promerops*, the Cape Sugarbird and Gurney's Sugarbird. It is also often assumed that sunbirds are a type of African hummingbird, whereas nothing could be further from the truth. Hummingbirds are found only in the Americas; Africa is the home of sunbirds. Their appearance, food and feeding habits are similar but the two families are quite unrelated. Hummingbirds feed while hovering, with wing-beats of well over 4 000 per minute in some species, and can even fly backwards, whereas sunbirds are able to hover only very briefly and must settle to feed.

The birds you will find in this chapter

African Green Pigeon 177
African Pygmy Goose 176
Blue-cheeked Bee-eater 180
Bokmakierie 183
Brown-headed Parrot 178
Bully Canary 185
Cape Parrot 178
Cape Shoveller 176
Cape Teal 176
Cape White-eye 184
Collared Sunbird 183
Diederik Cuckoo 179
Eastern Olive Sunbird 184
Emerald Cuckoo 179
Emerald-spotted Wood-dove 177
Feral Pigeon 177
Forest Canary 185
Glossy Ibis 177
Gorgeous Bush Shrike 182
Greater Double-collared
  Sunbird 183
Green-backed Bleating
  Warbler 182
Grey-headed Bush Shrike 183
Klaas's Cuckoo 179
Knysna Lourie 179
Lesser Double-collared Sunbird 183
Lilian's Lovebird 178
Little Bee-eater 180
Malachite Sunbird 183
Marico Sunbird 184
Melba Finch 185
Meyer's Parrot 178
Narina Trogon 179
Olive Bush Shrike 182
Orange-breasted Sunbird 184
Purple Gallinule 177
Purple-banded Sunbird 184
Rose-ringed Parakeet 178

Rosy-faced Lovebird 178
Rudd's Apalis 182
Sombre Bulbul 181
Spur-winged Goose 176
Stripe-cheeked Bulbul 181
Swallow-tailed Bee-eater 180
Swee Waxbill 185
White-fronted Bee-eater 180
Woodpeckers 181
Yellow Canary 185
Yellow-bellied Sunbird 184
Yellow-billed Duck 176
Yellow-breasted Apalis 182

Knysna Loerie

CAPE SHOVELLER
Wetlands. In flight, upperwings show green secondaries separated from blue forewings by a white line. (Kaapse slopeend) 53 cm

AFRICAN PYGMY GOOSE
Lily pans. Upperparts dark green; underparts orange-beige; short yellow bill. (Dwerggans) 33 cm

CAPE TEAL
Wetlands. In flight, upperwings show white secondaries with green central panel. Pale duck with pink bill. (Teeleend) 46 cm

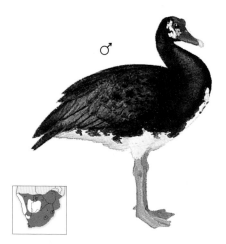

SPUR-WINGED GOOSE (male)
Wetlands. Upperparts blackish with green iridescence; below white; bill and legs pink. (Wildemakou) 102 cm

YELLOW-BILLED DUCK
Wetlands. In flight, upperwings show green secondaries bordered with white. Speckled duck with yellow bill. (Geelbekeend) 53-58 cm

176 green plumage

GLOSSY IBIS
Wetlands. A brown-bronze water-bird with iridescent green wings, long legs and a long curved bill. (Glansibis) 71 cm

PURPLE GALLINULE
Wetlands. Head and below blue; back, tail and wings green; bill and frontal shield red; legs pink. (Grootkoningriethaan) 46 cm

EMERALD-SPOTTED WOOD-DOVE
Woodland. Emerald-green spots on the wings; double black bars on the back; rufous flight feathers. (Groenvlekduifie) 20 cm

FERAL PIGEON
Urban. Many individuals of this variable pigeon have glossy-green neck feathers. (Tuinduif) 33 cm

AFRICAN GREEN PIGEON
Riverine woodland. Predominantly green; eyes whitish; bill red and white; legs red; thighs yellow. (Papegaaiduif) 30 cm

ROSE-RINGED PARAKEET
Urban. Apple-green parrot with long tail, red bill and pale eyes.
(Ringnekpapegaai) 40 cm

CAPE PARROT
Forests. Green body and wings; yellow-brown (or grey) head and neck; orange-red forehead and shoulders.
(Grootpapegaai) 35 cm

BROWN-HEADED PARROT
Woodland. Pale green body; dark green wings; brown head.
(Bruinkoppapegaai) 23 cm

ROSY-FACED LOVEBIRD
Rocky gorges. Rose-red head with pale bill; green body and wings; blue back.
(Rooiwangparkiet) 17-18 cm

MEYER'S PARROT
Woodland. Brown head, neck and wings; blue back and green underparts; yellow shoulders.
(Bosveldpapegaai) 23 cm

LILIAN'S LOVEBIRD
Zambezi Valley. Rose-red head with red bill; rest entirely green.
(Niassaparkiet) 17-18 cm

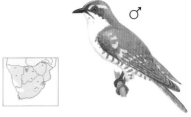

DIEDERIK CUCKOO
Woodland. Male bright green above; white below; bill black; eyes red. Female similar, but with coppery mantle.
(Diederikkie) 18,5 cm

NARINA TROGON
Forests. Glossy-green head, breast and upperparts; scarlet-red below. Female lacks green breast; bill greenish-yellow.
(Bosloerie) 29-34 cm

EMERALD CUCKOO
Forests. Male bright green above, beak to tail, plus breast; belly yellow; eyes dark; beak green. Female brown above; white below with heavy green banding overall.
(Mooimeisie) 20 cm

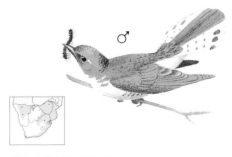

KNYSNA LOURIE
Forests. Green crested head, nape and underparts; glossy-blue folded wings and tail; red flight feathers.
(Knysnaloerie) 47 cm

KLAAS'S CUCKOO
Woodland. Male entirely bright green above, bill to tail; white below; eyes dark. Female duller; green above; white below; heavily banded brown; eyes yellow.
(Meitjie) 17 cm

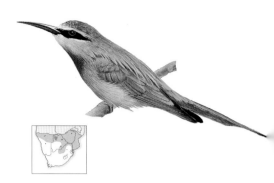

SWALLOW-TAILED BEE-EATER
Western savanna.
Green above and upper
breast; throat yellow with
blue band; belly and forked
tail blue. Immature apple-
green above and below.
(Swaelstertbyvreter) 20-22 cm

BLUE-CHEEKED BEE-EATER
Wetlands. Entirely green above;
pale blue eyebrows, cheeks and
belly; chin yellow; throat rufous.
(Blouwangbyvreter) 27-33 cm

LITTLE BEE-EATER
Woodland. Green
above; rufous below;
yellow throat; black
upper breast-patch.
(Kleinbyvreter) 17 cm

WHITE-FRONTED BEE-EATER
Riverine woodland. Back, wings
and upper tail green; forehead and
chin white; throat red; nape and
breast cinnamon; belly to vent blue.
(Rooikeelbyvreter) 22-24 cm

SOMBRE BULBUL
Forest fringes. In the south, a
dull-green bird with whitish eyes;
Zambezi and beyond brighter
green above, yellow-green below.
(Gewone willie) **19-24 cm**

Cardinal
Woodpeckers

WOODPECKERS
Woodland. Several woodpeckers
have dull-green wings, usually with
small white or yellow spots. Best
identified by their breast and
head markings, and their calls.
(Spegte)

STRIPE-CHEEKED BULBUL
Forest fringes. Overall dull green
(yellow-green below); grey cap;
white eyelids and cheek-stripes.
(Streepwangwillie) **19-21 cm**

green plumage **181**

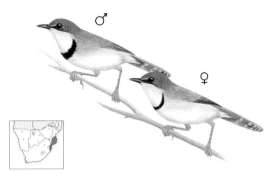

GREEN-BACKED BLEATING WARBLER
Dull olive-green above; white below;
tail usually raised.
(Groenrugkwêkwêvoël) 12 cm

RUDD'S APALIS
Coastal bush. Grey cap;
olive-green back and tail;
white below with black chest-band.
(Ruddse kleinjantjie) 10,5-12 cm

OLIVE BUSH SHRIKE
Forests. Olive-green above with or
without grey cap (male with black
mask); cinnamon or yellow breast.
(Olyfboslaksman) 17 cm

YELLOW-BREASTED APALIS
Bushveld. Grey hood; yellow-green
upperparts; white chin and belly;
yellow breast with small black
breast-bar sometimes present.
(Geelborskleinjantjie) 10-12,5 cm

GORGEOUS BUSH SHRIKE
Dense bush. Olive-green above;
red throat and breast with broad
black gorget; yellow-orange
belly and vent.
(Konkoit) 20 cm

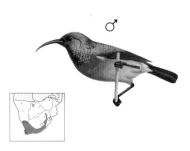

BOKMAKIERIE
Diverse habitats. Grey cap, nape and mantle; green upperparts; yellow underparts with broad black gorget. (Bokmakierie) 23 cm

♂

LESSER (SOUTHERN) DOUBLE-COLLARED SUNBIRD (male)
Woodlands. Glossy-green head and mantle; blue and narrow red breast-bands, greyish belly. (Kleinrooibandsuikerbekkie) 12,5 cm

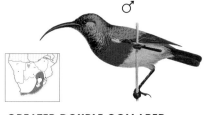

♂

GREY-HEADED BUSH SHRIKE
Riverine bush. Grey hood; yellow eyes; heavy bill; green upperparts; yellow below with broad orange breast. (Spookvoël) 5-27 cm

GREATER DOUBLE-COLLARED SUNBIRD (male)
Montane. Glossy-green head and mantle; blue and wide red breast-bands; greyish belly. (Grootrooibandsuikerbekkie) 14 cm

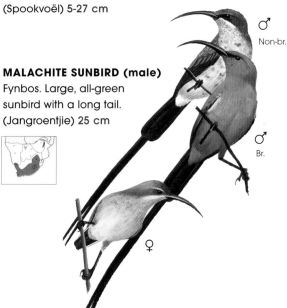

♂ Non-br.

MALACHITE SUNBIRD (male)
Fynbos. Large, all-green sunbird with a long tail. (Jangroentjie) 25 cm

♂ Br.

♀

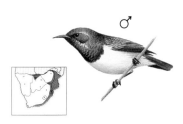

♂

COLLARED SUNBIRD
Riverine forests. Glossy-green upperparts, head and upper breast; rest of underparts yellow. Female has entirely yellow underparts. (Kortbeksuikerbekkie) 11 cm

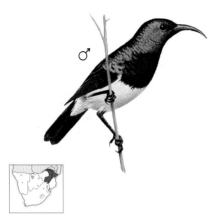

ORANGE-BREASTED SUNBIRD (male)
Fynbos. Glossy-green head and
mantle; upper breast purple; rest
of underparts orange grading to
yellow vent; tail extended.
(Oranjeborssuikerbekkie) 15 cm

YELLOW-BELLIED SUNBIRD (male)
Broad-leaved woodland. Glossy
blue-green head and mantle;
purple breast; yellow belly.
(Geelpenssuikerbekkie) 11 cm

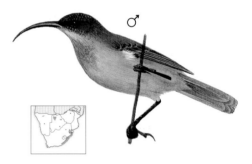

EASTERN OLIVE SUNBIRD (male)
Lowland forests. A large sunbird.
Dull olive-green, darker above,
paler below.
(Olyfsuikerbekkie) 13-15 cm

MARICO SUNBIRD (male)
Thornveld. Upperparts, head
and breast glossy-green;
lower breast with purple and
red bands; belly black.
(Maricosuikerbekkie) 13-14 cm

CAPE WHITE-EYE
Woodland. Various races: grey
to yellow below; yellow-green above;
white eye-rings.
(Kaapse glasogie) 12 cm

MELBA FINCH

Thorn thickets. Yellow-green mantle
and wings; red bill (red forehead
and throat in male); red rump and
upper tail; banded underparts.
(Gewone melba) 12-13 cm

FOREST CANARY

Forest fringes. Olive-green head
and upperparts with darker
streaks; underparts yellow
well streaked with green.
(Gestreepte kanarie) 13 cm

YELLOW CANARY (male)

Dry bush and Karoo scrub.
Above light to dark olive-green;
eyebrow and underparts yellow.
(Geelkanarie) 13-14 cm

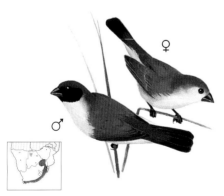

SWEE WAXBILL

Forest fringes. Dark olive-green back
and wings; red lower bill, rump and
upper tail coverts; grey cap (male
with black mask); below grey-white.
(Suidelike swie) 9-10 cm

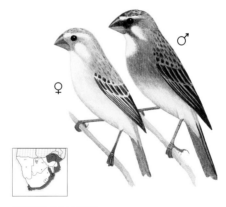

BULLY CANARY

Wooded habitats. Above dark
or light olive-green; dark race
with olive-green breast; eyebrows
and below yellow. Bill thick.
(Dikbekkanarie) 14-15 cm

birds with
purple,
lilac
or violet
plumage

*Violet-backed
Sunbird (male)*

♂

To the human eye these colours are certainly pleasing. Their purpose may appear to be purely decorative, but seen through the eyes of a bird they may have a very different function. Research has determined quite recently that many, if not all, birds can see the ultraviolet spectrum, something that is not normally visible to the human eye. The bird's ultraviolet vision may render colours such as purple more brilliant than the human eye can perceive.

Purple Roller

The birds you will find in this chapter

Black Sunbird 191
Broad-billed Roller 188
Burchell's Glossy Starling 190
(Common) Scimitarbill 189
European Starling 189
Greater Blue-eared Glossy
    Starling 190
Lesser Blue-eared Glossy
    Starling 190
Lilac-breasted Roller 188
Long-tailed Glossy Starling 189
Plum-coloured Starling 189
Purple Gallinule 188
Purple Roller 188
Purple-crested Lourie 188
Violet-eared Waxbill 191
Yellow-bellied Sunbird 190
(Western) Violet-backed
    Sunbird 191

Plum-coloured Starling

BROOD PATCHES

Birds have developed various ways to maintain the temperature of their eggs during incubation. The Emperor Penguin of the Antarctic rests the single egg on its feet and allows the ample folds of its belly-skin to cover them. The Mallee Fowl of Australia deposits its eggs in a self-made compost mound and regulates the internal temperature of the mound by adding or removing compost. However, in the majority of birds, egg-temperature is maintained by transmitting heat from the sitting bird's body. Since one of the primary functions of a bird's plumage is the maintenance of body-heat through insulation, it follows that insufficient heat would normally reach the eggs. This apparent *impasse* is solved by the development of brood patches during the breeding season. These are areas of bare skin that come directly into contact with the eggs, permitting the direct transfer of body heat when the bird is sitting. In some birds it can be a single patch of bare skin, in others several small patches equal to the number of eggs laid. In ducks, the female bird plucks its down feathers and uses them as a nest-lining.

PURPLE GALLINULE
Wetlands. The underparts of this bird are a deep purple-blue, appearing more purple than blue as the bird moves. (Grootkoningriethaan) **46 cm**

PURPLE ROLLER
Woodland. This many-coloured roller has purple shoulder-patches and undertail coverts. (Groottroupant) **36-40 cm**

BROAD-BILLED ROLLER
Palm savanna. This small, yellow-billed roller has purple underparts and cinnamon upperparts. (Geelbektroupant) **27 cm**

PURPLE-CRESTED LOURIE
Riverine woodland. Has a purple crest on a shiny green head; red eye-ring and flight feathers. (Bloukuifloerie) **47 cm**

LILAC-BREASTED ROLLER
Bushveld. Named for its lilac breast, it also has blue underparts and flight feathers. (Gewone troupant) **36 cm**

PLUM-COLOURED STARLING (male)
Woodland. Its iridescent upperparts
appear purple or coppery; white below.
(Witborsspreeu) 18-19 cm

(COMMON) SCIMITARBILL
Woodland. Seen at close range,
the head, mantle and wings
are deep purple.
(Swartbekkakelaar) 24-28 cm

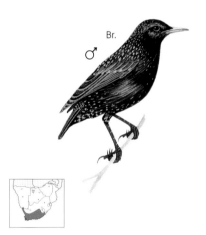

EUROPEAN STARLING (breeding)
Suburbia. Its green-black plumage
shows a purple sheen about the
upper breast and mantle.
(Europese spreeu) 20-22 cm

LONG-TAILED GLOSSY STARLING
Mopane woodland. Shows much
purple in its mantle and upper tail.
(Langstertglansspreeu) 30-34 cm

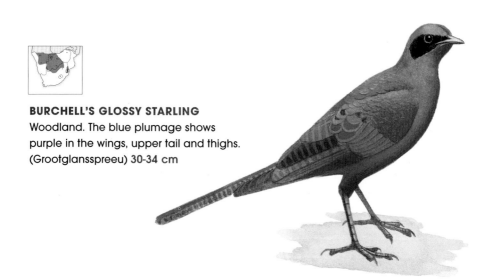

BURCHELL'S GLOSSY STARLING
Woodland. The blue plumage shows
purple in the wings, upper tail and thighs.
(Grootglansspreeu) 30-34 cm

LESSER BLUE-EARED GLOSSY STARLING
Woodland. Shows magenta thighs in good light.
(Klein-blouoorglansspreeu) 20 cm

**GREATER BLUE-EARED GLOSSY
STARLING**
Woodland. This blue-green bird shows
purple-blue flanks in good light.
(Groot-blouoorglansspreeu) 21-23 cm

YELLOW-BELLIED SUNBIRD (male)
Broad-leaved woodland. Green head and
upperparts; purple breast; yellow belly.
(Geelpenssuikerbekkie) 11 cm

BLACK SUNBIRD (male)
Woodland. Has an iridescent
purple throat and shoulder-
patches.
(Swartsuikerbekkie) 15 cm

VIOLET-EARED WAXBILL
Dry thornveld. Both sexes have
violet ear coverts and red bills.
(Koningblousysie) 13-15 cm

(WESTERN) VIOLET-BACKED SUNBIRD (male)
Broad-leaved woodland. Chin and upperparts
entirely violet; below white.
(Blousuikerbekkie) 12,5-14 cm

birds with
rufous
plumage
including chestnut

Violet-eared Waxbill

The term rufous refers to the reddish-brown colour that is common in many birds, especially birds of prey. The colouring of the Rock Kestrel is a good example. Another brownish colour found in some bird plumages, and often mistaken for rufous, is what, for lack of a better description, is accurately called chestnut, the colour of a fruit that does not even grow in southern Africa! For the sake of those who may never have set eyes on a chestnut (even worse, not savoured the flavour of a roasted chestnut) we include this colour in the rufous range, although it is a little more yellow than true rufous.

Goliath Heron

ACCIPITERS AT REST

When perched, sparrowhawks and goshawks are notoriously difficult to approach on foot, but are often more tolerant of a motor vehicle. Since the general colouring of their upperparts is grey or dark brown according to age and sex, rather concentrate on the colours of their soft parts and the patterns of barring or streaking on their underparts. Eye colours can be yellow, deep red or dark brown; the ceres yellow, red or grey according to species and age. Yellow is by far the most common leg colour, while orange is common to some immatures and to the Ovambo Sparrowhawk. Red legs and ceres are found only in adult Gabar Goshawks. Most adult birds have close barring, rufous or grey, on their underparts, with the exception of the Gabar Goshawk which also has a grey upper breast. Immature Little Banded and Gabar goshawks have the upper breast streaked and the belly barred, while both immature Little Sparrowhawks and African Goshawks have heavily-spotted underparts. The Rufous-breasted Sparrowhawk and some immature Ovambo Sparrowhawks stand apart in having non-barred, entirely rufous breast and belly.

The birds you will find in this chapter

(African) Crowned Eagle **198**
African Cuckoo Hawk **200**
African Darter **194**
African Fish Eagle **198**
African Hoopoe **204**
African Jacana **197**
(African) Paradise Flycatcher **210**
African Stonechat **207**
Barlow's Lark **205**
Black-crowned Tchagra **211**
Black-headed Canary **213**
Brubru **210**
Buff-spotted Flufftail **196**
Burchell's Coucal **203**
Burchell's Courser **198**
Burchell's Sandgrouse **202**
Cape Batis **209**
Cape Bunting **213**
Cape Rock Thrush **207**
Cape Rock-jumper **207**
Cape Sparrow **212**
Caspian Plover **197**
Chestnut-backed Finchlark **206**
Chestnut-banded Plover **197**
Chin-spot Batis **209**
Cinnamon Dove **202**
Cinnamon-breasted Warbler **208**
Collared Palm Thrush **208**
Coppery-tailed Coucal **203**
Crested Francolin **198**
Dabchick **195**
Eastern Red-footed Kestrel **202**

Egyptian Goose **195**
Eurasian Hobby **201**
Giant Kingfisher **204**
Goliath Heron **194**
Great Sparrow **212**
Greater Kestrel **201**
Grey-backed Cisticola **196**
Grey-headed Kingfisher **204**
House Sparrow **211**
Jackal Buzzard **199**
Kalahari Robin **208**
Karoo Korhaan **204**
Karoo Lark **205**
Lanner Falcon **200**
Lesser Kestrel **201**
Little Banded Goshawk **199**
Little Sparrowhawk **199**
Maccoa Duck **195**
Miombo Rock Thrush **206**
Mocking Chat **207**
Ovambo Sparrowhawk **199**
Painted Snipe **196**
Pink-billed Lark **206**
Purple Roller **204**
Pygmy Falcon **200**
Red Lark **205**
Red-backed Mannikin **212**
Red-backed Shrike **210**
Red-chested Flufftail **196**
Red-necked Falcon **200**
Red-throated Wryneck **205**
Rock Bunting **213**
Rock Kestrel **201**
Rock Pigeon **202**
Rockrunner **209**
Ruddy Turnstone **197**

Rufous-bellied Heron **194**
Rufous-breasted Sparrowhawk **199**
Rufous-eared Warbler **209**
Rufous-naped Lark **205**
Senegal Coucal **203**
Sentinel Rock Thrush **207**
Short-toed Rock Thrush **206**
South African Shelduck **195**
Southern Grey-headed Sparrow **211**
Southern Tchagra **210**
Spike-heeled Lark **206**
Temminck's Courser **198**
Three-streaked Tchagra **211**
Titbabbler **208**
Violet-eared Waxbill **212**
Western Red-footed Kestrel **202**
White-backed Night Heron **194**
White-browed Coucal **203**
White-browed Scrub Robin **208**
White-faced Duck **195**

Cape Rock-jumper

Juv.

WHITE-BACKED NIGHT HERON
Inland rivers. Rufous neck and mantle; black cap; yellow facial skin and legs (Witrugnagreier) **53 cm**

AFRICAN DARTER (male)
Inland waters. Front of neck rufous; crown and body very dark brown; front of neck sandy in female.
(Slanghalsvoël) **79 cm**

RUFOUS-BELLIED HERON
Wetlands. Very dark small heron; rich rufous below and on wings. Bill and legs normally yellow.
(Rooipensreier) **58 cm**

GOLIATH HERON
Wetlands. Huge heron with rufous head, neck and underparts; upperparts grey.
(Reusereier) **140 cm**

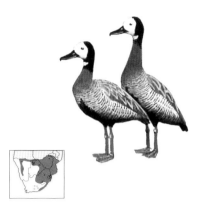

MACCOA DUCK (male)
Inland waters. Chestnut body; black head with bright blue bill; stiff tail.
(Bloubekeend) 46 cm

WHITE-FACED DUCK
Wetlands. White face on black head; rufous neck and upper breast.
(Nonnetjie-eend) 48 cm

SOUTH AFRICAN SHELDUCK
Brackish waters. Grey head (female has white face) on rufous body; black bill and legs.
(Kopereend) 64 cm

DABCHICK (breeding)
Inland waters. Chestnut sides to head and neck; distinctive creamy patch at base of bill.
(Kleindobbertjie) 20 cm

EGYPTIAN GOOSE
Wetlands. Rufous neck and upper body; pale below; pink legs.
(Kolgans) 71 cm

GREY-BACKED CISTICOLA
Fynbos, scrubland. Dark rufous
head with paler buff underparts,
grey and black streaking on back.
(Grysrugtinktinkie) 12-13 cm

RED-CHESTED FLUFFTAIL (male)
Marshlands. Small, secretive. Head,
nape and upper breast chestnut.
(Rooiborsvleikuiken) 15-17 cm

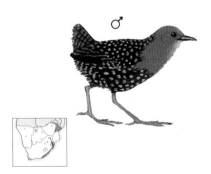

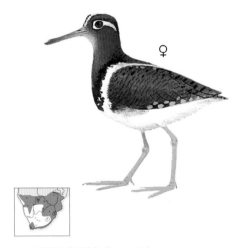

BUFF-SPOTTED FLUFFTAIL (male)
Forests. Small, secretive. Head,
nape and upper breast chestnut;
buff spots on dark back.
(Gevlekte vleikuiken) 17 cm

PAINTED SNIPE (female)
Pond fringes. Rufous from above the
eyes to nape and breast; olive-green
back; white on central crown, eye-
stripe and shoulders; legs yellow.
(Goudsnip) 28-32 cm

CASPIAN PLOVER (male)
Semi-arid plains. Medium plover.
Brown above; white below with
broad rufous breast-band.
(Asiatiese strandkiewiet) 21-23 cm

Br. Non-br.

RUDDY TURNSTONE (breeding)
Shorelines. Chestnut above with black
and white about head, neck and breast;
white below.
(Steenloper) 22 cm

CHESTNUT-BANDED PLOVER (male)
Salt pans. Small plover. Buff-grey above;
white below with chestnut breast-band.
(Rooibandstrandkiewiet) 15 cm

AFRICAN JACANA
Lily pans. Rufous-bodied waterbird
with long legs and toes; head and
neck black above, white below.
(Grootlangtoon) 40 cm

BURCHELL'S COURSER
Short grasslands. Mainly chestnut colouring; grey nape; white belly and legs.
(Bloukopdrawwertjie) 23 cm

CRESTED FRANCOLIN
Bushveld. Rufous brown above with black-and-white facial marks; well-spotted breast; red legs.
(Bospatrys) 32 cm

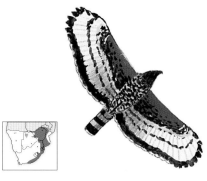

TEMMINCK'S COURSER
Short grasslands. Rufous cap and lower breast; white underbelly and legs.
(Trekdrawwertjie) 23 cm

(AFRICAN) CROWNED EAGLE
Forests. Rufous underwing coverts in flight.
(Kroonarend) 80-90 cm

AFRICAN FISH EAGLE
Wetlands. White head, breast and mantle on rufous body; darker above.
(Visarend) 63-73 cm

Imm.

JACKAL BUZZARD
Mountains. Dark buzzard with rufous breast and tail; distinctive black-and-white underwings.
(Rooiborsjakkalsvoël) **44-53 cm**

LITTLE BANDED GOSHAWK
Woodland. Banded rufous below chin to belly; above grey. Immature has rufous streaks and bands below.
(Gebande sperwer) **30-34 cm**

♂ ♀

Imm.

RUFOUS-BREASTED SPARROWHAWK
Open woodland. Underbody and underwing coverts rufous; dark above; eyes and legs yellow.
(Rooiborssperwer) **33-40 cm**

LITTLE SPARROWHAWK
Riverine forests. Entire underbody and underwings banded rufous; above grey; white spots on upper tail.
(Kleinsperwer) **23-25 cm**

OVAMBO SPARROWHAWK (immature)
Woodland. Rufous morph of the immature has the entire head and body that colour; cere yellow; legs orange.
(Ovambosperwer) **33-40 cm**

AFRICAN CUCKOO HAWK
Woodland. This hawk, with its crested
grey head and barred tail, is broadly
barred rufous on breast, belly and
underwing coverts.
(Koekoekvalk) **40 cm**

RED-NECKED FALCON
Kalahari thornveld.
Well-barred falcon with
rufous cap and nape.
(Rooinekvalk) **36 cm**

♀

PYGMY FALCON (female)
Dry acacia veld. Rufous mantle;
red eye-ring, cere and legs.
(Dwergvalk) **19,5 cm**

LANNER FALCON
Cliffs. Told by rufous crown;
upperparts grey;
underparts creamy-white.
(Edelvalk) **40-45 cm**

EURASIAN HOBBY
Light woodland. Dark above; heavily streaked below with rufous thighs. (Europese boomvalk) 30-35 cm

ROCK KESTREL
Hills and grasslands. Grey head; rufous upperwings and under-parts; upper tail grey; well-barred in female, single bar in male. (Kransrooivalk) 30-33 cm

GREATER KESTREL
Grasslands. Entirely rufous upperparts and body; white underwings and undertail. (Grootrooivalk) 36 cm

LESSER KESTREL
Grasslands. Both sexes have rufous upperwings; male has grey head, secondary coverts, back and upper tail. (Kleinrooivalk) 28-30 cm

EASTERN RED-FOOTED KESTREL (male)
Grasslands. Slate-grey above; pale
grey below with rufous vent; white
underwings; red cere and legs.
(Oostelike rooipootvalk) 28-30 cm

**WESTERN RED-FOOTED
KESTREL (male)**
Grasslands. Entirely dark
grey with rufous vent;
dark underwings, red
cere and legs.
(Westelike rooipootvalk)
28-30 cm

**WESTERN RED-FOOTED
KESTREL (female)**
Grasslands. Head and
underparts (including
underwing coverts)
rufous; upperwings grey.
Cere and legs red.
(Westelike rooipootvalk)
29-30 cm

CINNAMON DOVE
Forests. Forehead and
chin white; rest rufous;
wings greenish.
(Kaneelduifie) 25-30 cm

BURCHELL'S SANDGROUSE
Kalahari. Face grey in male; yellow in
female. Below rufous; spotted white.
(Gevlekte sandpatrys) 25 cm

ROCK PIGEON
Cliffs. Streaked neck;
wings and upper body rufous;
wings with white spots.
(Kransduif) 33 cm

BURCHELL'S COUCAL
Thickets. Rufous wings; black cap
and tail; faint barring on upper tail
coverts; underparts white.
(Gewone vleiloerie) **44 cm**

SENEGAL COUCAL
Dense thickets. Rufous wings; black
cap and tail; white underparts.
(Senegalvleiloerie) **41 cm**

WHITE-BROWED COUCAL
Thickets. Black crown grades
onto rufous mantle and wings;
white eyebrow; white streaking
from head to mantle.
(Witbrouvleiloerie) **44 cm**

COPPERY-TAILED COUCAL
Reedbeds. Rufous wings, darker on
nape; cap and tail coppery-black.
(Grootvleiloerie) **44-50 cm**

PURPLE ROLLER
Woodland. Large roller with
rufous underparts streaked white.
(Groottroupant) 36-40 cm

KAROO KORHAAN
Arid areas. Cinnamon brown with
greyish neck, black throat patch
and plain head.
(Vaalkorhaan) 56-60 cm

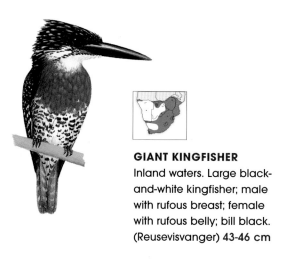

GIANT KINGFISHER
Inland waters. Large black-
and-white kingfisher; male
with rufous breast; female
with rufous belly; bill black.
(Reusevisvanger) 43-46 cm

AFRICAN HOOPOE
Woodland. Rufous crest,
head and body; black-
and-white wings.
(Hoephoep) 27 cm

GREY-HEADED KINGFISHER
Woodland. Red bill; grey head,
breast and mantle; chestnut belly.
(Gryskopvisvanger) 20 cm

KAROO LARK
Karoo. Some races have rich rufous upperparts and facial colouring.
(Karoolewerik) 17 cm

RED-THROATED WRYNECK
Woodland. Above speckled brown and black; below rufous throat and upper breast on creamy-white.
(Draaihals) 18 cm

RED LARK
Bushmanland. May have brick-red to rich rufous upperparts.
(Rooilewerik) 19 cm

RUFOUS-NAPED LARK
Open bushveld. Eastern race with rufous crest and wings; body washed rufous; pale western race with rufous on wings only.
(Rooineklewerik) 18-19 cm

BARLOW'S LARK
Namib dunes. Some races have chestnut upperparts and facial colouring.
(Barlowse lewerik) 19 cm

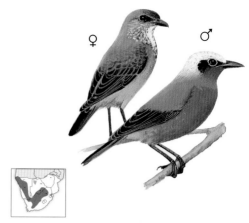

SPIKE-HEELED LARK
Grasslands and scrub.
SE race has rufous colouring
overall; short tail.
(Vlaktelewerik) 15-16 cm

SHORT-TOED ROCK THRUSH (male)
Rocky hills. Grey above with white crown;
rufous below from upper breast to vent.
(Korttoonkliplyster) 18 cm

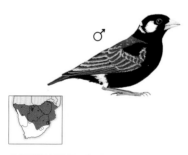

PINK-BILLED LARK
Short grasslands. SE race has rich
rufous plumage; pink bill and legs.
(Pienkbeklewerik) 12 cm

**CHESTNUT-BACKED FINCHLARK
(male)**
Grassy plains. Male has chestnut
nape and wings; black head
and body; white ear-patch.
(Rooiruglewerik) 12-13 cm

MIOMBO ROCK THRUSH (male)
Woodland. Pale grey above to throat;
upper breast rufous; belly whitish.
(Angolakliplyster) 18 cm

SENTINEL ROCK THRUSH (male)
Rocky uplands. Grey head, mantle
and breast; lower breast to vent rufous.
(Langtoonkliplyster) 21 cm

MOCKING CHAT (female)
Rocks with bushes. Entirely grey-black
above; dark rufous below.
(Dassievoël) 20-23 cm

CAPE ROCK THRUSH
Rocky slopes and cliffs. Both sexes have
rufous underparts, rump and tail; male
with rufous mantle, grey head and neck;
female speckled brown above.
(Kaapse kliplyster) 21 cm

AFRICAN STONECHAT (male)
Vleis. Mainly black upperparts; white
rump and half-collar; underparts rufous.
(Gewone bontrokkie) 14 cm

CAPE ROCK-JUMPER
Rocky hillsides. Male has black-
and-white upperparts and throat;
rufous breast and rump. Female
rufous below with streaked breast;
speckled above.
(Kaapseberglyster) 25 cm

TITBABBLER
Woodland. Greyish bird
with well-streaked breast,
pale eyes and rufous vent.
(Bosveldtjeriktik) 15 cm

WHITE-BROWED SCRUB ROBIN
Scrub. Rufous rump and upper
tail coverts; well-streaked breast;
white wing-markings.
(Gestreepte wipstert) 15 cm

CINNAMON-BREASTED WARBLER
Dry, rocky bushveld. Dark brown
above; lower breast and vent rufous.
(Kaneelborssanger) 13-14 cm

KALAHARI ROBIN
Thornveld. Predominantly
rufous above, including
rump and tail coverts;
whitish below.
(Kalahariwipstert) 16-17 cm

COLLARED PALM THRUSH
Palm savanna. Rufous upperparts and vent; black collar
to creamy throat; grey flanks.
(Palmmôrelyster) 19 cm

208 rufous plumage

ROCKRUNNER
Rocky and bushy hillsides.
Heavily streaked head and
mantle; white throat and breast;
rufous back, belly and vent.
(Rotsvoël) 17 cm

CAPE BATIS
Forest fringes. Female has
rufous throat, breast-band and
flanks on white underparts; yellow
eyes; red eye-rings.
(Kaapse bosbontrokkie) 12-13 cm

CHIN-SPOT BATIS (female)
Woodland. Small rufous
chin-spot and broad rufous
breast-band; yellow eyes.
(Witliesbosbontrokkie) 12-13 cm

RUFOUS-EARED WARBLER
Dry scrub veld. Rufous mask and
ear coverts; black breast-band
on white underparts; erect tail.
(Rooioorlangstertjie) 16 cm

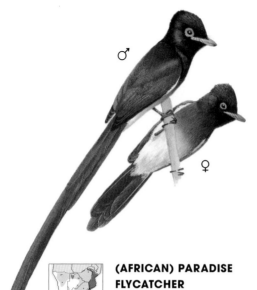

(AFRICAN) PARADISE FLYCATCHER
Woodland. Blue-black head and breast; blue eye-rings and bill; rufous upperparts and tail. (Paradysvlieëvanger) 23-41 cm

BRUBRU
Woodland. Small pied bird with rufous flanks on white underparts. (Bontroklaksman) 15 cm

SOUTHERN TCHAGRA
Coastal bush and thickets. Brown crown and mantle. Rufous wings; heavy bill. (Grysborstjagra) 21 cm

RED-BACKED SHRIKE (male)
Bushveld. Grey head, nape and rump; black mask; rufous mantle and back; white underparts. (Rooiruglaksman) 18 cm

THREE-STREAKED TCHAGRA
Thornveld thickets. Grey-brown
crown and mantle; black border
to crown; chestnut wings.
(Rooivlerktjagra) 19 cm

BLACK-CROWNED TCHAGRA
Mixed woodland. Black crown;
beige mantle; rufous wings.
(Swartkroontjagra) 21-23 cm

**SOUTHERN
GREY-HEADED SPARROW**
Chestnut upperparts with grey
head; small white wing-bar;
bill black or horn-coloured.
(Gryskopmossie) 15-16 cm

HOUSE SPARROW (male)
Human settlements. Crown grey;
nape dark brown grading into chestnut
back and wings; small white wing-bar;
lores to bib black.
(Huismossie) 14 cm

CAPE SPARROW
Farmlands and suburbia. Crown, face and upper breast black in male, grey in female; mantle grey; back, rump and wings chestnut with small white wing-bar.
(Gewone mossie) 15 cm

VIOLET-EARED WAXBILL (male)
Dry thornveld. Rufous crown, wings and body; red bill and eye-rings; blue rump; black tail.
(Koningblousysie) 15 cm

GREAT SPARROW
Dry thornveld. Grey crown; chestnut nape, back and wings with small white wing-bar; male only with conspicuous black bib.
(Grootmossie) 15-16 cm

RED-BACKED MANNIKIN
Dune forests, bushveld. Black head and breast; rufous upperparts; white bill and underparts.
(Rooirugfret) 9,5-10 cm

BLACK-HEADED CANARY
Arid scrub. Both sexes have chestnut back and wings; head, throat and central breast black or black-and-white in male, greyish in female.
(Swartkopkanarie) 12-15 cm

CAPE BUNTING
Various dry habitats. Black-and-white streaked head; rufous wings, crown, mantle; below washed grey-brown.
(Rooivlerkstreepkoppie) 16 cm

ROCK BUNTING
Rocky koppies. Black-and-white streaked head (blackest in male); rest cinnamon-brown.
(Klipstreepkoppie) 13-14 cm

birds with
dark brown plumage

Wahlberg's Eagle

Brown is probably the most common plumage colour found in birds. Not only are the numerous 'little brown jobs' mostly brownish all over, but most birds of prey and many plovers, francolins and other terrestrial birds are dressed partially or entirely in brown. For those with a mainly terrestrial way of life, brown feathers or brown upperparts serve well to render the bird inconspicuous, while much the same applies to the LBJs which live in the shadowy interiors of dense thickets.

I find that many people tend to describe small brown birds as 'greyish', which is not very helpful when you are attempting to identify in retrospect the 'one that got away'. I am not sure whether this 'grey' description stems from a tendency to generalise broadly or a genuine inability to differentiate between colours. (I understand that some 40% of men have some degree of colour-blindness which, in many cases, results in their being unable to separate tones in the red-brown spectrum.) Whatever the reason, in this chapter I have selected only medium brown to dark brown birds, but I do accept that they may appear dark grey or blackish to some birders.

THE GENUS *ACCIPITER*

Accipiter (pronounced ak-sip-iter) is merely the Latin name for a hawk and is specifically the generic name for the sparrowhawk group of raptors – mostly small, short-winged, longish-tailed hawks. Most hunt other small birds in woodland and forest from a hidden perch, surprising their quarry in a brief, rapid and agile chase. Sparrowhawks have long, slender legs and feet with an elongated central toe. The larger species are often called goshawks, which, although lacking the long central toe, are basically similar.

Related to the accipiters is the genus *Melierax*, the grey chanting goshawks to which the small Gabar Goshawk rightly belongs. The two species of chanting goshawks in southern Africa are moderately large hawks with reddish ceres and long red legs (yellow in immatures). They either still-hunt for terrestrial prey from a perch or forage on the ground like small Secretarybirds.

The birds you will find in this chapter

African Barred Owl 228
African Black Duck 217
(African) Crowned
Eagle 224
African Cuckoo Hawk 226
(African) Dusky Flycatcher
238
African Finfoot 216
African Fish Eagle 224
African Goshawk 225
African Grass Owl 228
African Grey Hornbill 231
African Hawk Eagle 223
African Marsh Harrier 225
African Palm Swift 230
(African) Pied Starling 240
African Rail 218
(African) Red-eyed
Bulbul 233
African Scops Owl 229
African Sedge Warbler 232
(African) White-backed
Vulture 221
African Wood Owl 228
Arrow-marked Babbler 234
Augur Buzzard 225
Banded Martin 230
Barred Warbler 236
Bat Hawk 226
Black-breasted Snake
Eagle 222
Black-chested Prinia 238
Black-eyed Bulbul 233
Black-necked Grebe 217
Black-winged Plover 219
Black-winged Pratincole
219
Blue-mantled (Crested)
Flycatcher 239
Booted Eagle 222
Brown Snake Eagle 222
Brown-headed Parrot 227
Brown-throated Martin 230
Burnt-necked Eremomela
236
Bush Blackcap 233
Cape Bulbul 233
Cape Eagle Owl 229
Cape Francolin 220
Cape (Griffon) Vulture 221
Cape Siskin 241

Chat Flycatcher 239
Cinnamon-breasted
Warbler 237
(Common) Ostrich 220
Common Sandpiper 218
Crowned Hornbill 231
Dabchick 217
Drakensberg Siskin 241
(European) Honey
Buzzard 225
European Sand Martin 230
Familiar Chat 235
Forest Buzzard 224
Forest Weaver 241
Garden Warbler 236
Glossy Ibis 216
Great Crested Grebe 218
Greater Honeyguide 232
Groundscraper Thrush 235
Hamerkop 216
Hartlaub's Babbler 234
Hooded Vulture 221
Indian Myna 240
Jackal Buzzard 225
Karoo Prinia 238
Karoo Robin 236
Karoo (Sombre) Thrush 234
Kurrichane Thrush 234
Lappet-faced Vulture 221
Lesser Black-winged
Plover 219
Lesser Honeyguide 232
Lesser Spotted Eagle 222
Long-crested Eagle 223
Maccoa Duck 217
Marico Flycatcher 239
Marsh Owl 228
Martial Eagle 224
Meyer's Parrot 227
Monteiro's Hornbill 231
Mountain Chat 235
Namaqua Warbler 238
Natal Francolin 220
Neddicky 237
Olive Thrush 234
Osprey 226
Pallid Flycatcher 239
Pearl-spotted Owl 228
Rameron Pigeon 227
Rattling Cisticola 234
Red-billed Buffalo

Weaver 240
Red-billed Oxpecker 240
Red-faced Cisticola 237
Red-necked Francolin 220
Red-winged Pratincole 219
Reed Cormorant 216
Rock Martin 230
Rock Pratincole 219
Rüppell's Parrot 227
Saffron Prinia 238
Sharp-billed Honeybird
232
Sickle-winged Chat 235
(Southern) Ant-eating
Chat 235
Southern Pochard 217
Southern White-rumped
Babbler 234
Spotted Eagle Owl 229
Spotted Flycatcher 239
Spotted Thrush 235
Spur-winged Goose 217
Steppe Buzzard 224
Steppe Eagle 223
Stierling's Barred
Warbler 237
Swainson's Francolin 220
Tambourine Dove 227
Tawny-flanked Prinia 236
Terrestrial Bulbul 233
Thick-billed Weaver 241
Three-banded Plover 218
Victorin's Warbler 232
Wahlberg's Eagle 223
White-breasted Cormorant
216
White-browed Sparrow-
weaver 241
White-eared Barbet 231
White-headed Vulture 221
Wood Sandpiper 218
Woolly-necked Stork 216
Yellow-bellied Eremomela
236
Yellow-billed Kite 222
Yellow-billed Oxpecker
240

Imm.

REED CORMORANT (immature)
Wetlands. Entirely dark brown except
for drab pale brown underbody;
bill dull yellow.
(Rietduiker) 60 cm

HAMERKOP
Wetlands. Entirely
dark brown waterbird;
bill and legs black.
(Hamerkop) 56 cm

**WHITE-BREASTED
CORMORANT**
Wetlands. Upperwings
and tail dark brown;
wing feathers
edged black.
(Witborsduiker) 90 cm

Non-br.   Br.

GLOSSY IBIS
Wetlands. Bronze-brown
with iridescent green on
wings; long curved bill.
(Glansibis) 71 cm

WOOLLY-NECKED STORK
Wooded wetlands. Dark brown
above and on breast; head,
neck and underbelly white.
(Wolnekooievaar) 86 cm

AFRICAN FINFOOT (female)
Quiet rivers. Above dark brown
(grey in male); bill and legs
bright red.
(Watertrapper) 63 cm

Imm.

SPUR-WINGED GOOSE (immature)
Wetlands. Large; completely dark brown, with red bill.
(Wildemakou) 102 cm

AFRICAN BLACK DUCK
Rivers. Dark brown with white-spotted upperparts; bill grey; legs orange.
(Swarteend) 51-54 cm

SOUTHERN POCHARD
Wetlands. Female has dark upperparts only; male entirely dark brown with bronzy sheen.
(Bruineend) 51 cm

DABCHICK
Wetlands. Small waterbird; dark brown above, pale below; when breeding plumage has chestnut face and neck, and creamy spot at base of bill.
(Kleindobbertjie) 20 cm

BLACK-NECKED GREBE
Saline waters. Above dark blackish-brown; eyes red; has golden ear coverts and flanks when breeding; whitish below when not breeding.
(Swartnekdobbertjie) 28 cm

Non-br.

Br.

MACCOA DUCK (female)
Dams with reeds. Small; dark brown with white neck and horizontal cheek-stripe; bill grey.
(Bloubekeend) 46 cm

GREAT CRESTED GREBE
Wetlands. Dark brown upperparts; 'horned' crest and golden flanks when breeding; head, neck and underparts white at other times. (Kuifkopdobbertjie) 50 cm

COMMON SANDPIPER
Inland water shorelines. Upperparts and breast-band dark brown; below white extending around the folded wing; white upper tail barred brown. (Gewone ruiter) 20 cm

AFRICAN RAIL
Reedbeds. Dark brown above; grey below to lower breast; black-and-white barred belly and flanks; bill red. (Grootriethaan) 36 cm

WOOD SANDPIPER
Inland water shorelines. Upperparts dark brown with white speckling; white eyebrows; buffy breast; white belly; yellow-green legs. (Bosruiter) 20 cm

THREE-BANDED PLOVER
Inland water shorelines. Small plover told by white underparts with two black breast-bands; above dark brown; bill and eye-rings red. (Driebandstrandkiewiet) 18 cm

BLACK-WINGED PLOVER
Grasslands. Folded upper wings dark olive-brown; head to breast grey; large white forehead; white belly; eyes yellow; eye-ring red. Black-and-white underwings in flight.
(Grootswartvlerkkiewiet) 29 cm

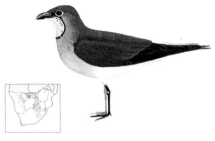

BLACK-WINGED PRATINCOLE
Wetlands and farmlands. Dark brown above; buff throat edged black; buff breast; white belly and rump; underwings show all black.
(Swartvlerksprinkaanvoël) 25 cm

LESSER BLACK-WINGED PLOVER
Moist grasslands. Folded upper wings dark olive-brown; head to breast grey; small white forehead; eyes yellow. Black-and-white underwings in flight.
(Kleinswartvlerkkiewiet) 23 cm

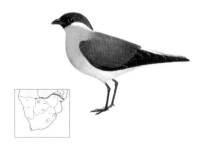

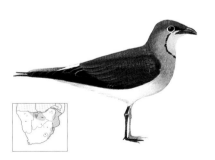

ROCK PRATINCOLE
River rapids. Dark brown above, separated from grey breast by white collar; white belly and rump; red legs.
(Withalssprinkaanvoël) 18 cm

RED-WINGED PRATINCOLE
Wetlands. Dark brown above; buff throat edged black; buff breast; white belly and rump; underwings show red-brown.
(Rooivlerksprinkaanvoël) 25 cm

CAPE FRANCOLIN
Fynbos. Large, dark francolin; dark brown above with feathers edged pale buff; black below; feathers streaked white; legs reddish.
(Kaapse fisant) 40-45 cm

NATAL FRANCOLIN
Riverine bush. Dark brown above with black streaking; speckled black and white below; bill red and yellow; legs red.
(Natalse fisant) 30-38 cm

RED-NECKED FRANCOLIN
Dense bush. Eastern races are dark brown above, streaked black; below black streaked white; all bare parts red.
(Rooikeelfisant) 32-44 cm

SWAINSON'S FRANCOLIN
Bushveld. Entirely dark brown; red facial skin and neck; dark grey legs.
(Bosveldfisant) 34-39 cm

(COMMON) OSTRICH (female)
Grasslands and woodland. The female has a dark brown body with some whitish wing feathers; head, neck and legs whitish.
(Volstruis) 2 m

220 dark brown plumage

CAPE (GRIFFON) VULTURE (immature)
Highveld and bushveld. Young birds are medium brown with pale streaks below; head, neck and breast-patches red with white downy covering. (Kransaasvoël) 105-115 cm

(AFRICAN) WHITE-BACKED VULTURE (immature)
Game regions. Young birds are dark brown streaked white below; blackish head and neck with a white downy covering; no white back. (Witrugaasvoël) 90-98 cm

WHITE-HEADED VULTURE
Game regions. Dark brown back, wings and upper breast; crown, nape and below white (female has white inner secondaries); bare parts pink; bill blue and red. (Witkopaasvoël) 85 cm

HOODED VULTURE
Game regions. Dark brown at all ages; adults have white legs, thighs, pectoral feathers and downy hood; neck and facial skin pink; bill slender. (Monnikaasvoël) 70 cm

LAPPET-FACED VULTURE
Game regions. Above and wings dark brown; below white; breast streaked dark brown; head and neck red; bill horn-coloured. (Swartaasvoël) 115 cm

BOOTED EAGLE
Dry, montane regions. Small eagle.
Above dark brown; below dark
brown, buff or white; cere and
feet pale yellow.
(Dwergarend) 48-52 cm

YELLOW-BILLED KITE
Wide ranging. Entirely dark brown
with forked tail and yellow soft parts.
(Geelbekwou) 55 cm

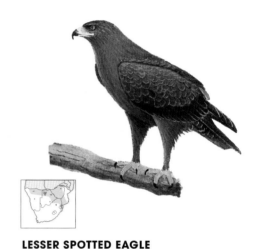

BLACK-BREASTED SNAKE EAGLE
Bushveld. Above entirely dark brown
to head and breast; below white;
underwings with some black barring;
eyes yellow.
(Swartborsslangarend) 63-68 cm

LESSER SPOTTED EAGLE
Game regions. Dark brown eagle
with closely feathered legs; immature
with white spots on folded wings.
Cere and feet yellow.
(Gevlekte arend) 65 cm

BROWN SNAKE EAGLE
Woodland. Large, dark brown eagle
with yellow eyes and whitish legs.
Distinctive upright stance.
(Bruinslangarend) 71-76 cm

222 dark brown plumage

WAHLBERG'S EAGLE
Woodland. Entirely blackish-brown, dark brown or white with brown wings; cere and feet yellow. In flight looks square-tailed, square-winged. (Bruinarend) 55-60 cm

LONG-CRESTED EAGLE
Hilly, forested regions. Almost entirely blackish-brown with distinctive long crest; feathered legs may be dappled white; striking black-and-white underwing pattern.
(Langkuifarend) 53-58 cm

AFRICAN HAWK EAGLE
Woodland. Dark brown above; white below with dark breast-streaks; eyes, cere and feet yellow. Underwing shows white 'windows'; tail with black terminal band.
(Grootjagarend) 60-65 cm

STEPPE EAGLE
Game regions. Adult large, dark brown; gape and feet orange-yellow.
(Steppe-arend) 75 cm

(AFRICAN) CROWNED EAGLE
Forests. Large eagle; dark brown above; heavily mottled dark below; underwings with orange-brown coverts, dark trailing edge and barred tail.
(Kroonarend) 80-90 cm

STEPPE BUZZARD
Open country. Plumage variable, dark brown to red-brown; darkest above; streaked and banded below.
(Bruinjakkalsvoël) 45 cm

AFRICAN FISH EAGLE
Wetlands. Wings dark brown; belly chestnut-brown; head, breast and mantle white; cere and legs yellow.
(Visarend) 63-73 cm

MARTIAL EAGLE
Woodland. All dark brown except for white belly and legs with brown spots; cere grey; feet yellow.
(Breëkoparend) 78-83 cm

FOREST BUZZARD
Exotic plantations. Small buzzard; dark brown above; white below with brown blotching; central breast region usually white; flanks only blotched in immatures.
(Bosjakkalsvoël) 45 cm

224 dark brown plumage

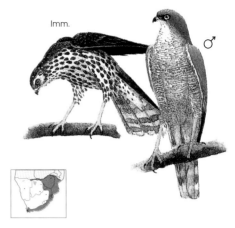

Imm. ♂

(EUROPEAN) HONEY BUZZARD
Woodland. Dark brown above with greyish head; below variable: dark brown, spotted brown on white or buff (immature); underwings well barred.
(Wespedief) 54-60 cm

AFRICAN GOSHAWK
Forests. Male grey above, female dark brown above; both barred brown below; immature browner above. Long bare legs yellow.
(Afrikaanse sperwer) 40 cm

JACKAL BUZZARD
Hilly regions. Dark brown all over, except for chestnut-brown breast and tail; underwings dark brown and white.
(Rooiborsjakkalsvoël) 44-53 cm

AUGUR BUZZARD
Wooded hills. Dark brown above; white below; chestnut-brown tail, white underwing edged dark.
(Witborsjakkalsvoël) 44-53 cm

AFRICAN MARSH HARRIER
Marshlands. Dark brown, long-winged hawk; paler brown below; underwings well barred; flies low.
(Afrikaanse vleivalk) 44-49 cm

dark brown plumage **225**

BAT HAWK
Riverine forests. Entirely dark brown hawk with pale eyes and white legs; immature with white breast and belly. (Vlermuisvalk) 45 cm

OSPREY
Lakes and lagoons. Upperparts dark brown; head with dark mask, whitish crown; underparts white; legs pale grey. (Visvalk) 55-63 cm

AFRICAN CUCKOO HAWK
Riverine forests. Dark brown above with crested greyish head; throat pale grey; breast and belly broadly barred chestnut. (Koekoekvalk) 40 cm

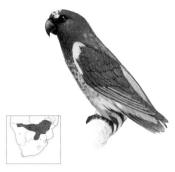

TAMBOURINE DOVE
Forest fringes. Above dark brown; eyebrow, forehead and underparts white. (Witborsduifie) 23 cm

MEYER'S PARROT
Woodland. Upperparts brown except for pale blue back; belly green; forehead and shoulders yellow. (Bosveldpapegaai) 23 cm

RAMERON PIGEON
Forests and plantations. Dark, purple-brown with grey head and purple-grey neck; eye-rings, bill and legs bright yellow. (Geelbekbosduif) 40 cm

RÜPPELL'S PARROT
Dry woodland. Very dark brown with deep-blue back and belly; yellow shoulders. (Bloupenspapegaai) 23 cm

BROWN-HEADED PARROT
Woodland. Brown head and neck; body and wings green. (Bruinkoppapegaai) 40 cm

MARSH OWL
Vleis and marshes. Dark brown above
(with small 'ear' tufts); pale buff below;
wings show chestnut in flight.
(Vlei-uil) 36 cm

PEARL-SPOTTED OWL
Woodland. Dark brown above
well spotted white; streaked
brown and white below with
large white pearl-like spots.
(Witkoluil) 15-18 cm

AFRICAN WOOD OWL
Forests. Dark brown above including
surround of facial disc; finely barred brown
on whitish underparts; no 'ear' tufts.
(Bosuil) 30-36 cm

AFRICAN GRASS OWL
Moist grasslands. Dark brown above
with small white spots; creamy below
with small brown spots; no 'ear' tufts.
(Grasuil) 34-37 cm

SPOTTED EAGLE OWL
Widespread. Dark brown above with prominent 'ear' tufts; dark border to facial disc; below finely barred and blotched with dark brown, white and buff; eyes yellow.
(Gevlekte ooruil) 43-50 cm

AFRICAN SCOPS OWL
Mixed bushveld. Woodbark camouflage; very mottled grey-brown colour, with flecks of white and black; small ear tufts.
(Skopsuil) 15-18 cm

CAPE EAGLE OWL
Rocky valleys. Dark brown above with prominent 'ear' tufts; orange eyes; below buffy with brown and white blotching.
(Kaapse ooruil) 48-55 cm

AFRICAN BARRED OWL
Woodland. Dark brown above including head, with fine white barring plus band of large white wing-spots; below white with brown bars and spots.
(Gebande uil) 20 cm

EUROPEAN SAND MARTIN

Estuaries. Small martin; above dark brown; below white with narrow brown chest-band; tail with shallow fork. (Europese oewerswael) 12 cm

BROWN-THROATED MARTIN

Inland rivers. Small martin; belly white; rest dark brown (a few birds all brown). (Afrikaanse oewerswael) 13 cm

BANDED MARTIN

Inland waters. Large martin; above dark brown; below white with wide brown chest-band; small white eyebrow, square tail. (Gebande oewerswael) 17 cm

ROCK MARTIN

Cliffs. Dark brown, broad-winged; paler below; tail square with white 'windows'. (Kransswael) 15 cm

AFRICAN PALM SWIFT

Vicinity of palm trees. Small, slender-winged brown swift with deeply forked tail. (Palmwindswael) 17 cm

AFRICAN GREY HORNBILL

Mixed bushveld. Dark brown above to upper breast; wing feathers edged creamy; eyebrows white; bill black; upper mandible and casque creamy (reduced in female); below white from lower breast to vent. (Grysneushoringvoël) 43-48 cm

WHITE-EARED BARBET

Coastal forest fringes. Dark brown with white ear-stripes and underbelly. (Witoorhoutkapper) 18 cm

CROWNED HORNBILL

Lowland forest fringes. Dark brown above; mostly white below; large red bill with yellow base; yellow eyes. (Gekroonde neushoringvoël) 50-57 cm

MONTEIRO'S HORNBILL

Rocky regions. Above dark brown to breast; wings with white spots; secondaries and outer tail feathers white; lower breast to vent white; bill red. (Monteirose neushoringvoël) 54-58 cm

Imm.

♀

♂

GREATER HONEYGUIDE
Woodland. Adult dark brown above with faint yellow shoulder; male has pink bill and dark throat-patch; female has black bill; below whitish in both sexes; white outer tail feathers; immature yellow below. (Grootheuningwyser) 19-20 cm

LESSER HONEYGUIDE
Woodland. Dark greenish-brown above; wing feathers edged paler; outer tail feathers white; breast dusky; belly white; white patch above the base of the stumpy bill. (Kleinheuningwyser) 15 cm

VICTORIN'S WARBLER
Dense scrub. Brown upperparts; cinnamon-buff below; distinct orange-yellow eyes. (Rooiborsruigtesanger) 16 cm

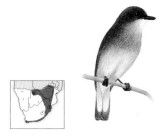

SHARP-BILLED HONEYBIRD
Wooded regions. Small; dark brown above with white outer tail feathers; below white with dusky breast; bill black. (Skerpbekheuningvoël) 13 cm

AFRICAN SEDGE WARBLER (OR LITTLE RUSH-WARBLER)
Dense vegetation over water. Dark brown above with rounded tail; noticeable eye-stripe; faint markings on upper breast. (Kaapse Vleisanger) 17 cm

TERRESTRIAL BULBUL
Forests and thickets. Dark brown
above; white throat contrasts with
dusky breast and flanks.
(Boskrapper) 21-22 cm

**(AFRICAN) RED-EYED
BULBUL**
Bush and gardens. Tufted head;
bill and legs black; eye-rings
red; upperparts dark brown;
below dusky white; vent yellow.
(Rooioogtiptol) 21 cm

BUSH BLACKCAP
Upland scrub on forest fringes.
Told by black cap, red bill
and legs; wings and tail dark
brown; breast grey; belly white.
(Rooibektiptol) 17 cm

CAPE BULBUL
Coastal scrub, gardens. Tufted head
to breast and upperparts dark brown;
eye-rings white; belly dusky white;
vent yellow; bill and legs black.
(Kaapse tiptol) 21 cm

BLACK-EYED BULBUL
Woodland and gardens. Tufted
head, eyes, bill and legs black;
upperparts dark brown; below
dusky white; vent yellow.
(Swartoogtiptol) 20-22 cm

ARROW-MARKED BABBLER
Mixed bushveld and thickets. Above dark brown; breast grey-brown; belly tawny; white arrow marks all over; eyes orange with red eye-rings; bill and legs black.
(Pylvlekkatlagter) 23-25 cm

KURRICHANE THRUSH
Broad-leaved woodland. Dark grey-brown above; eyebrows and throat white with black moustachial streaks; upper breast greyish; flanks washed orange; belly white; eye-rings, bill and legs orange.
(Rooibeklyster) 22 cm

HARTLAUB'S (OR SOUTHERN WHITE-RUMPED) BABBLER
Riverine woodland. Upperparts and breast dark brown; all feathers fringed white; rump, belly and vent white; eyes yellow with red eye-rings.
(Witkruiskatlagter) 26 cm

RATTLING CISTICOLA
Bushveld. Buff and dark brown upperparts; pale underparts. Distinctive rattle at end of song; often sings from top of bush.
(Bosveldtinktinkie) 14-16 cm

KAROO (OR SOMBRE) THRUSH
Highveld and scrubland. Dark grey-brown except for orange under-belly, orange-yellow legs and bill.
(Brynluister) 24 cm

OLIVE THRUSH
Montane forests and gardens. Dark, olive-brown above; throat speckled black on white; underparts orange (highveld race with brown breast); vent white or dusky; bill and legs orange-yellow.
(Olyflyster) 24 cm

SPOTTED THRUSH
Coastal forests. Above dark brown with two white wing-bars; face and under-parts white, heavily marked and spotted black; bill black; legs pink.
(Natallyster) 23 cm

FAMILIAR CHAT
Rocky ground and farm-yards. Dark brown above, slightly paler below, rump rich chestnut-brown, tail same with black tip and central feathers.
(Gewone spekvreter) 15 cm

SICKLE-WINGED CHAT
Grasslands and Karoo scrub. Dark brown above with rufous-edged wing feathers and pale chestnut rump; off-white below with dusky breast.
(Vlaktespekvreter) 15 cm

GROUNDSCRAPER THRUSH
Woodland. Dark grey-brown above; below white with bold black facial markings and spots; bill black above and orange below; legs pale orange.
(Gevlekte lyster) 22 cm

MOUNTAIN CHAT (female)
Boulder-strewn slopes. Dark brown with white rump and outer tail feathers; bill and legs black.
(Bergwagter) 17-20 cm

(SOUTHERN) ANT-EATING CHAT
Short grasslands. Entirely dark brown or blackish-brown; only primary feathers show paler in flight.
(Swartpiek) 18 cm

BURNT-NECKED EREMOMELA
Acacia woodland. Grey-brown above; yellow-buff below; brown throat-bar not always present; pale eyes with brown eye-rings.
(Bruinkeelbossanger) 12 cm

KAROO ROBIN
Karoo. Dark brown above and only slightly paler below; white eyebrows, moustachial streaks and throat; tail-tips white; vent white spotted black.
(Slangverklikker) 17 cm

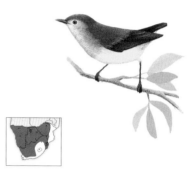

YELLOW-BELLIED EREMOMELA
Mixed bushveld or scrub. Grey-brown upperparts; pale grey breast; yellow belly; soft parts black.
(Geelpensbossanger) 9-10 cm

GARDEN WARBLER
Parks and gardens. Nondescript warbler; dark brown above; whitish below; no prominent features.
(Tuinsanger) 5 cm

BARRED WARBLER
Woodland thickets. Dark brown above, buffy below and well barred brown; has dark breast in summer.
(Gebande sanger) 13-15 cm

Br.

Non-Br.

STIERLING'S BARRED WARBLER
Woodland thickets. Dark brown
above; white below and well
barred blackish.
(Stierlingse sanger) 11,5-13 cm

NEDDICKY
Thickets. Above plain dark brown
except for rusty cap; below blue-grey
(southern and eastern regions);
buffy elsewhere.
(Neddikkie) 10-11 cm

RED-FACED CISTICOLA
Reedbeds and rank grass. Dark
brown above; white below;
face, flanks and breast washed
rufous; most noticeably in winter.
(Rooiwangtinktinkie) 12-13 cm

CINNAMON-BREASTED WARBLER
Upper tail black; rest of upperparts dark
brown, except for cinnamon forehead;
breast, flanks and rump cinnamon;
throat pale with dark barring.
(Kaneelborssanger) 13-14 cm

TAWNY-FLANKED PRINIA
Riverine vegetation and gardens.
Dark brown above with white eye-
brows and dark eye-stripe; white
below; flanks, vent and rump tawny.
(Bruinsylangstertjie) 10-15 cm

NAMAQUA WARBLER
Karoo scrub. Dark brown above; white below with buffy wash to flanks and vent; breast lightly spotted. (Namakwalangstertjie) 14 cm

BLACK-CHESTED PRINIA
Dry thorn scrub. Dark brown above; eyebrow to vent white with broad black breast-band; yellow below in winter. (Swartbandlangstertjie) 15 cm

(AFRICAN) DUSKY FLYCATCHER
Forest fringes. Dark grey-brown above and on breast; throat and underbelly whitish; breast has indistinct dark smudges; soft parts black. (Donkervlieëvanger) 12-13 cm

KAROO PRINIA
Fynbos and Karoo scrub. Dark brown above; eyebrows and underparts very pale yellow; breast and flanks streaked black. (Karoolangstertjie) 14 cm

SAFFRON PRINIA
Upland vleis and matted scrub. Dark brown above; eyebrows and underparts saffron-yellow; breast lightly spotted. (Gevlekte langstertjie) 14 cm

CHAT FLYCATCHER
Kalahari and Karoo. Grey-brown
above; wing feather edges paler;
below whitish with a brown wash to
the breast and belly; soft parts black.
(Grootvlieëvanger) 20 cm

SPOTTED FLYCATCHER
Woodland. Dark grey-brown above,
crown streaked dark; below whitish;
breast and flanks indistinctly streaked
brown; soft parts black.
(Europese vlieëvanger) 14-15 cm

PALLID FLYCATCHER
Broad-leaved woodland. Dull
grey-brown overall; paler on throat;
soft parts black; eye-rings pale.
(Muiskleurvlieëvanger) 15-17 cm

MARICO FLYCATCHER
Acacia thornveld. Dark brown
above; clear white below;
soft parts black.
(Maricovlieëvanger) 18 cm

**BLUE-MANTLED (CRESTED)
FLYCATCHER**
Forest fringes. Dark brown above with
white wing-bar; crested head black;
throat and breast black in male, finely
spotted in female; belly and vent white.
(Bloukuifvlieëvanger) 17-18 cm

RED-BILLED OXPECKER
Game and cattle regions. Upperparts and entire head dark brown; underparts and rump yellow-buff; bill and eyes red; eye-rings yellow. (Rooibekrenostervoël) 20-22 cm

(AFRICAN) PIED STARLING
Karoo, roadsides. Very dark brown with white underbelly and vent; eyes whitish; gape orange. (Witgatspreeu) 25-27 cm

INDIAN MYNA
Towns. Head, mantle and breast black; rest brown; darker above; belly white; bill, facial skin and legs yellow. (Indiese spreeu) 25 cm

YELLOW-BILLED OXPECKER
Game regions. Upperparts and entire head dark brown; underparts and rump yellow-buff; bill yellow with red tip, eyes yellow. (Geelbekrenostervoël) 22 cm

RED-BILLED BUFFALO WEAVER
Mixed woodland. Red bill in both sexes; male blackish-brown, wing feather edges white, female paler on breast. (Buffelwewer) 24 cm

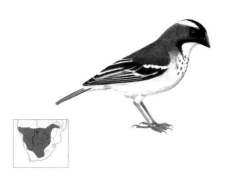

WHITE-BROWED SPARROW-WEAVER
Thornveld. Dark brown above with white eyebrows, wing-bars and feather edges; below white, with or without spotted breast; bill black; legs pink.
(Koringvoël) 18 cm

CAPE SISKIN
Cape mountain slopes.
Dark brown above with streaky crown; dull yellow below; female has streaky breast.
(Kaapse pietjiekanarie) 13 cm

THICK-BILLED WEAVER
Reedbeds and adjacent bush.
Male blackish-brown all over, with a white wing-spot and white forehead when breeding; bill black; female dark brown above, whitish below, heavily streaked dark brown; bill horn-coloured.
(Dikbekwewer) 18 cm

FOREST WEAVER
Forests. Dark brown above; yellow below; throat speckled, bill pale grey.
(Bosmusikant) 16 cm

DRAKENSBERG SISKIN
Drakensberg mountain slopes. Dark brown above; male with streaky head, greenish-yellow below; female buffy below with streaked throat and breast.
(Bergpietjiekanarie) 13 cm

birds with
light brown plumage

Kalahari Robin

Light brown plumage, as with dark brown plumage, is mostly found on the upperparts of the bird where, on sandy terrain especially, or on mudflats, it serves to render the bird less obvious from above. On the following pages it will be seen that many birds with this colouring are shorebirds or those that frequent dry regions. In certain other species, light brown, in its various tones, is the drab plumage of female birds or males in their non-breeding plumage.

Bearded Vulture

SHOREBIRDS OR WADERS

'Shorebirds' or 'waders' are two words describing the same group of birds. These are the countless small water-associated birds that migrate to southern Africa each year, arriving here in September and departing again for their northern breeding grounds in March. The term 'shorebird' accurately describes their habitat and activities; they feed in shallow water, both fresh and saline, on our coastlines and on the shores of estuaries, rivers, lagoons and most other inland waters. In the Old World the term 'wader' is commonly applied to these little greyish birds whereas in the New World 'shorebird' is used. Since the term 'wader' correctly applies also to the many large water-feeding birds, such as herons, spoonbills, stilts, avocets, oystercatchers, gallinules and some plovers, the more specific American term 'shorebird' is used in this book.

The birds you will find in this chapter

African Cuckoo Hawk 251
African Darter 244
African Hawk Eagle 250
African Scops Owl 250
(African) Wattled Plover 247
(African) White-backed Vulture 249
Barlow's Lark 252
Barn Owl 250
Bearded Robin 254
Bearded Vulture 249
Black Sunbird 255
Black-bellied Korhaan 248
Black-eared Canary 245
Bronze-winged
   Courser 248
Buff-streaked Chat 253
Cape (Griffon) Vulture 249
Caspian Plover 245
Chestnut-banded
   Plover 245
Collared Palm-thrush 245
(Common) Greenshank 246
(Common) Ringed Plover 246
Crowned Plover 247
Dune Lark 252
Flappet Lark 252
Fulvous Duck 245
Gray's Lark 253
Greater Double-
   collared Sunbird 254
Gymnogene 251
Hadeda Ibis 244
Herero Chat 253
Jackal Buzzard 250
Kalahari Robin 254
Karoo Chat 253
Kittlitz's Plover 246
Kori Bustard 248
Lark-like Bunting 255
Lesser (Southern) Double-
   collared Sunbird 254
Little Bittern 244
Little Stint 247
Long-billed Larks 252
Long-toed Plover 247

Marico Sunbird 255
Marsh Sandpiper 246
Martial Eagle 250
Namaqua Dove 251
Purple Heron 244
(Red) Knot 247
Red-billed Firefinch 255
Red-billed Francolin 249
Red-capped Lark 252
Red-faced Mousebird 251
Rufous-breasted
   Sparrowhawk 250
Rufous-naped Lark 252
Rüppell's Korhaan 248
Sabota Lark 252
Sociable Weaver 255
(Southern) White-crowned
   Shrike 254
Speckled Mousebird 251
Squacco Heron 244
Stark's Lark 253
Steppe Eagle 250
Striped Crake 245
Tawny Eagle 249
Temminck's Courser 248
Terek Sandpiper 247
Tractrac Chat 253
Water Dikkop (Thick-knee) 255
White-browed Scrub Robin 254
White-crowned Plover 248
White-fronted Plover 246

*Bronze-winged
Courser*

Imm.

AFRICAN DARTER (immature)
Wetlands. Young birds have pale,
rufous-brown necks and bodies,
becoming darker with age.
(Slanghalsvoël) **79 cm**

PURPLE HERON
Wetlands. Adult
has red-brown
neck; young birds
mostly light brown;
below white.
(Rooireier) **89 cm**

LITTLE BITTERN
Wetlands. Male has black
crown, back and flight feathers
(dark brown in female); rest of
body, both sexes, buffy-brown,
streaked white below.
(Woudapie) **26 cm**

♀ Juv. ♂

SQUACCO HERON
Wetlands. In breeding plumage
upperparts pale red-brown;
non-breeding plumage pale
tawny-brown; below white.
(Ralreier) **43 cm**

Br. Non-br.

HADEDA IBIS
Wetlands and gardens. The head
and neck are dull grey-brown;
rest greenish-black with
iridescent shoulder.
(Hadeda) **76 cm**

244 light brown plumage

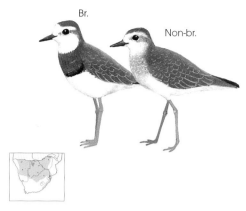

FULVOUS DUCK
Wetlands. Head and body fulvous brown with white flank feathers; wings and back dark brown.
(Fluiteend) **46 cm**

CASPIAN PLOVER
Dry plains. Above light brown; sides of head and below white with dusky breast-band (non-breeding) or broad chestnut breast-band (breeding).
(Asiatiese strandkiewiet) **21-23 cm**

STRIPED CRAKE
Wetlands. Above dark brown with white feather edges; below buffy-brown.
(Gestreepte riethaan) **24 cm**

CHESTNUT-BANDED PLOVER
Pans and gravel pits. Light brown above; white forehead, face and underparts, with narrow chestnut or buffy throat-band.
(Rooibandstrandkiewiet) **15 cm**

BLACK-EARED CANARY (OR SEEDEATER)
Woodland. Distinctive black mask; upperparts dark grey with streaking on head; lighter streaking on breast; gregarious.
(Swartoorkanarie) **13-14 cm**

COLLARED PALM-THRUSH
Palm savanna. Russet brown head, back and tail; pale eye; grey neck with distinctive black-bordered cream throat patch.
(Palmmôrelyster) **19 cm**

MARSH SANDPIPER
Wetlands. Above sandy-brown
with white feather edges and back;
below white, slender black bill;
long yellow-green legs.
(Moerasruiter) 23 cm

(COMMON) RINGED PLOVER (male)
Wetlands. Light brown above; white below
and on forehead; male has black mask
and bold black band encircling breast
and mantle; bill and legs orange-yellow.
(Ringnekstrandkiewiet) 18 cm

KITTLITZ'S PLOVER
Wetlands. Light brown above with
white and black bands around head
and throat; belly white; breast buff.
(Geelborsstrandkiewiet) 16 cm

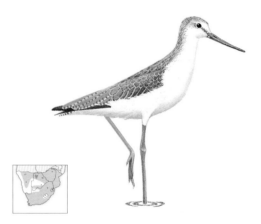

(COMMON) GREENSHANK
Wetlands. Above sandy-brown
with white feather edges and back;
below white; black bill slightly upturned;
long legs greenish.
(Groenpootruiter) 32 cm

WHITE-FRONTED PLOVER
Coastal and river shores. Sandy-brown
above; male with darker forecrown;
white below and on forehead.
(Vaalstrandkiewiet) 18 cm

LITTLE STINT
Wetlands. Small shorebird.
Non-breeding plumage sandy-brown
above; feathers edged white; below
white; short black bill and black legs.
(Kleinstrandloper) 14 cm

LONG-TOED PLOVER
Floodpans. Above light brown; wing
feathers white; frontal half of head and
neck white; rear of head, hindneck and
breast black; belly white; soft parts red.
(Witvlerkkiewiet) 30 cm

TEREK SANDPIPER
Coastal shorelines. Sandy-
brown above; white below; long
up-turned bill, and yellow legs.
(Terekruiter) 23-25 cm

CROWNED PLOVER
Dry veld. Crown black with
encircling white band; upperparts, neck and breast light
brown; belly white; eyes
yellow; bill and legs red.
(Kroonkiewiet) 30 cm

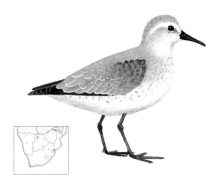

(RED) KNOT
Shorelines. Small, bulky-
bodied shorebird; sandy-
brown above; white below;
shortish black bill and legs.
(Knoet) 25 cm

(AFRICAN)
WATTLED PLOVER
Moist grassland. Forecrown
white; rear of crown dark
brown; neck streaked black;
rest of upperparts and breast
pale grey-brown; belly white;
wattles, bill and legs yellow.
(Lelkiewiet) 35 cm

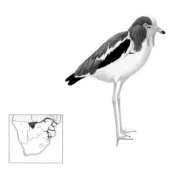

WHITE-CROWNED PLOVER
Large rivers. Head grey with white central crown band; upperparts light brown; folded wings white and black; below white; wattles, bill and legs yellow.
(Witkopkiewiet) 30 cm

RÜPPELL'S KORHAAN
Desert plains. Light brown upperparts; white below; pale grey head and neck with black-and-white markings.
(Woestynkorhaan) 56-60 cm

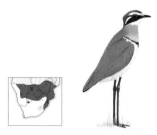

BRONZE-WINGED COURSER
Woodland. Light brown above and on upper breast; dark mask; eyebrows, throat and underparts white; eye-rings and legs red.
(Bronsvlerkdrawwertjie) 25 cm

BLACK-BELLIED KORHAAN
Grasslands. Tawny above and on neck with black markings; male has black-and-white head marking plus black belly; female white below; legs pale yellow.
(Langbeenkorhaan) 58-65 cm

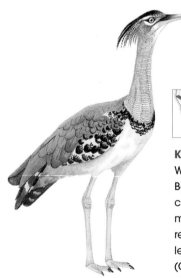

KORI BUSTARD
Woodland and grasslands. Back and wings light brown; coverts with black-and-white markings; head with crest at rear; neck grey; below white; legs pale yellow.
(Gompou) 134 cm

TEMMINCK'S COURSER
Short grasslands. Light brown upperparts and breast; rufous cap above white eyebrow; black eye-stripe; rufous lower breast; white belly and legs.
(Trekdrawwertjie) 20 cm

RED-BILLED FRANCOLIN
Dry scrub and thickets. Above light brown finely dappled black; below white with dense black barring; eye-rings yellow; bill and legs red. (Rooibekfisant) 30-38 cm

BEARDED VULTURE
Montane cliffs. Black mask and beard on white face; rest of body ginger-brown; wings and tail dark brown; eyes pale yellow and red; feet whitish. (Baardaasvoël) 110 cm

(AFRICAN) WHITE-BACKED VULTURE
Game regions. Grey-brown above and below; back white; flight feathers, neck skin and soft parts black. (Witrugaasvoël) 90-98 cm

TAWNY EAGLE
Woodland. Various colour forms: light brown, tawny and gingery-brown. Tawny form only has black dappling on upperwing covert; all have black flight feathers and tail; cere and legs yellow. (Roofarend) 65-72 cm

CAPE (GRIFFON) VULTURE
Wide ranging. Mature birds have wings and body feathers very pale brown; flight feathers and tail black; neck skin blue-grey; eyes honey-coloured. (Kransaasvoël) 105-115 cm

Imm.

Imm.

STEPPE EAGLE (immature)
Woodland. Immature birds light brown;
can be confused with similar Tawny
Eagle but for wider gape and white
trailing edge to wings.
(Steppe-arend) 75 cm

JACKAL BUZZARD (immature)
Hilly country. Young birds have
buffy-brown bodies with dark streaks
on flanks and thighs.
(Rooiborsjakkalsvoël) 44-53 cm

Imm.

Imm.

**MARTIAL EAGLE
(immature)**
Woodland. Young
birds are light brown
above; white below.
(Breëkoparend) 78-83 cm

**AFRICAN HAWK EAGLE
(immature)**
Woodland. Young birds have
entirely red-brown heads
and bodies; dark brown
wings; soft parts yellow.
(Grootjagarend) 60-65 cm

**RUFOUS-BREASTED
SPARROWHAWK**
Wooded patches in hills.
Above dark brown; below
rufous-brown; underwings and
tail well barred; soft parts yellow.
(Rooiborssperwer) 33-40 cm

BARN OWL
Diverse habitats. Whitish heart-shaped
facial disc; pale, spotted underparts;
grey and tawny spotted upperparts.
(Nonnetjie-uil) 30-33 cm

AFRICAN SCOPS OWL
Mixed bushveld. Woodbark camouflage;
very mottled grey-brown colour, with
flecks of white and black; small ear tufts.
(Skopsuil) 15-18 cm

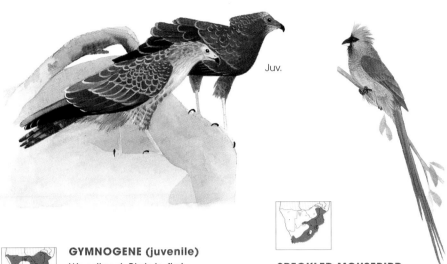

Juv.

GYMNOGENE (juvenile)
Woodland. Birds in first plumage are light brown; flight feathers and tail darker; soft parts pale yellow.
(Kaalwangvalk) 60-66 cm

SPECKLED MOUSEBIRD
Bush and suburbia. Brown wings and upper tail; light brown crested head and underparts; mask and upper mandible black; lower mandible white; legs black.
(Gevlekte muisvoël) 30-35 cm

AFRICAN CUCKOO HAWK
Riverine woodland. Grey head; dark brown upper-parts; whitish below broadly barred light brown; under-wing coverts light brown.
(Koekoekvalk) 40 cm

RED-FACED MOUSEBIRD
Thornveld and suburbia. Light brown above; wings and tail darker; rump and underparts grey-white; eyes blue; bill black; mask and legs red.
(Rooiwangmuisvoël) 32-34 cm

♀

NAMAQUA DOVE (female)
Farmlands. Light brown above with purple wing-spots; light brown breast; underparts whitish; legs maroon-red.
(Namakwaduifie) 27 cm

RUFOUS-NAPED LARK
Grassland with bush. Eastern birds light brown to rufous-brown, crest and wings redder; western birds paler, greyer.
(Rooineklewerik) 18-19 cm

FLAPPET LARK
Grassland. Brown upperparts; rufous head and wing edges; streaked back. Distinctive spurts of territorial wing-clapping in flight when breeding.
(Laeveldklappertjie) 16 cm

LONG-BILLED LARKS
Hills and Karoo scrublands in western parts of region. Whitish below with rufous wash on spotted breast; long bill conspicuous.
(Karoo langbeklewerik) 20-22 cm

SABOTA LARK
Bushveld. Well-streaked dark grey and buff upperparts, distinctive white eyebrow, and pale outer tail feathers.
(Sabotalewerik) 15 cm

RED-CAPPED LARK
Dry pans, short grass. Light brown above with rufous cap and pectoral tufts; whitish below.
(Rooikoplewerik) 15 cm

DUNE LARK
Namib dunes. Above, from head to tail, pale sand dune-brown; below white with small breast-spots.
(Duinlewerik) 17 cm

BARLOW'S LARK
Scrub-vegetated dunes. Above pale red-brown from head to tail; bold facial markings; below white with boldly spotted breast.
(Barlowse lewerik) 19 cm

252 light brown plumage

STARK'S LARK
Arid grasslands. Pale fawn above; all feathers with dark centres; below white, fawn wash on lightly spotted breast; stubby bill pinkish. (Woestynlewerik) 13 cm

KAROO CHAT
Karoo. Eastern race grey. Namibian race has pale brown upperparts, pale brown breast, white belly and vent; pale brown rump and white outer tail feathers. (Karoospekvreter) 15-18 cm

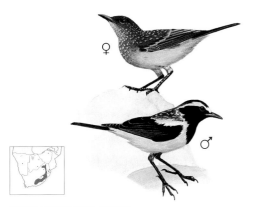

BUFF-STREAKED CHAT
Rocky grassland. Male has striking black and pale buff plumage; lively, demonstrative behaviour. (Bergklipwagter) 15-17 cm

HERERO CHAT
Arid, rocky ground. Above light brown; rump and outer tail feathers rufous; below white faintly streaked brown; white eyebrow above black facial mask. (Hererospekvreter) 17 cm

TRACTRAC CHAT
Arid plains. Southern race is light grey-brown above; Namibian race very pale brown, almost white above; both races white below; rump buff or white. (Woestynspekvreter) 14-15 cm

GRAY'S LARK
Desert gravel plains. Above pale fawn; below white with fawn wash on breast; appears all white at distance. (Namiblewerik) 14 cm

WHITE-BROWED SCRUB ROBIN
Bushveld thickets. Light brown above
to below eyes; white eyebrows; rump
and upper tail rufous; below white,
breast and flanks streaked black.
(Gestreepte wipstert) 15 cm

(SOUTHERN) WHITE-CROWNED SHRIKE
Woodland. White crown; light brown
mantle; dark wings; tail, lores and ear
coverts, throat and breast white; belly
to vent light brown.
(Kremetartlaksman) 23-25 cm

♀

**GREATER DOUBLE-COLLARED
SUNBIRD (female)**
Upland forest fringes. Similar to Lesser
Double-collared Sunbird (below), but
bill longer than head.
(Grootrooibandsuikerbekkie) 14 cm

BEARDED ROBIN
Broad-leaved and riverine woodland.
Light brown above to below eyes;
eyebrows white edged black; lores
black; throat white; moustachial
streak black; breast, flanks and
rump orange; belly white.
(Baardwipstert) 16-18 cm

♀

**LESSER (SOUTHERN)
DOUBLE-COLLARED SUNBIRD (female)**
Lowland woodland. Dull grey-brown overall; darker
above; paler below; curved bill length of head.
(Kleinrooibandsuikerbekkie) 12 cm

KALAHARI ROBIN
Kalahari thornveld. Above light brown;
rump and upper tail rufous; cap grey;
white eyebrows; black eye-stripe; below
white washed pale rufous.
(Kalahariwipstert) 16-17 cm

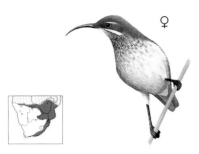

BLACK SUNBIRD (female)
Woodland and gardens. Light brown above; creamy-white below with creamy moustachial streak and dark mottled throat. (Swartsuikerbekkie) 15 cm

SOCIABLE WEAVER
Dry acacia woodland. Scaled light grey-brown above; cap light brown; lores and chin black; rest of underparts white. (Versamelvoël) 14 cm

MARICO SUNBIRD (female)
Thornveld. Light brown above; pale orange-yellow below with dusky throat; bill longer than head. (Maricosuikerbekkie) 13-14 cm

LARK-LIKE BUNTING
Dry regions. Light brown above with buffy feather edges; pale eye-brows; below pale cinnamon-brown. (Vaalstreepkoppie) 14 cm

RED-BILLED FIREFINCH
Riverine bush. Male has upper wings grey-brown; female mostly grey-brown; lighter below; lores and rump red. (Rooibekvuurvinkie) 10 cm

WATER DIKKOP (OR THICK-KNEE)
Near water. Buffy with dark streaks; dark moustachial stripe; distinctive grey wing bar edged black. (Waterdikkop) 40 cm

birds with
speckled plumage

African Scops Owl

including freckled, dappled, brindled and mottled

Many birds have speckled or dappled plumage as a result of individual feathers having pale margins that give a scalloped effect, or having dark centres, dark stripes or dark spots. These feathers may, in addition, be overlaid with stripes or bars of black or white, the overall result producing a confusing spotty pattern as seen, for example, in the African Snipe. In several cases these birds are best told by bill shape, bill length or colour, or leg length or colour. These features, coupled with their spotted plumage, are the surest guide to their identity.

Spotted Dikkop

WOODPECKERS

Woodpeckers are well known for their habit of tapping audibly on trees with their sharp, chisel-like beaks, but the reason for this behaviour is not always understood. The actual excavation of nest holes apart, normal tapping has the function of disturbing insects beneath the bark or loosening the bark in search of wood beetle burrows. Tapping on hollow logs is also used by many species as a means of territorial communication, a much heard woodland example of this being the far-carrying, rythmic tapping of the Bearded Woodpecker.

For actual feeding, woodpeckers are equipped with very long, sticky tongues in the case of ant and termite feeders or barbed tongues in those that feed on wood beetle grubs. In the latter, the tongue, with its backward projecting barbs, is inserted deep into the burrow of the beetle grub until the prey is hooked and extracted.

The birds you will find in this chapter

(African) Crowned Eagle **261**
African Scops Owl **258**
African Snipe **259**
Bearded Vulture **261**
Black Cuckooshrike **263**
Black-eared Finchlark **263**
Burchell's Sandgrouse **262**
Cape Shoveller **258**
Cape Teal **258**
Chestnut-backed Finchlark **263**
Common Quail **260**
(Common) Whimbrel **260**
Cut-throat Finch **263**
Double-banded Sandgrouse **262**
(Eurasian) Curlew **260**
European Starling **263**
Grey Plover **259**

Grey-backed Finchlark **263**
Grey-winged Francolin **260**
Hottentot Teal **258**
Namaqua Sandgrouse **262**
Natal Francolin **261**
Nightjars **262**
Orange River Francolin **260**
Red-billed Teal **258**
Red-winged Francolin **261**
Ruddy Turnstone **259**
Ruff **259**
Shelley's Francolin **261**
Spotted Creeper **262**
Spotted Dikkop **260**
White-backed Duck **258**
Yellow-billed Duck **259**
Yellow-throated Sandgrouse **262**

Spotted Creeper

AFRICAN SCOPS OWL
Mixed bushveld. Woodbark camouflage; very mottled grey-brown colour, with flecks of white and black; small ear tufts. (Skopsuil) 15-18 cm

RED-BILLED TEAL
Wetlands. Red bill; dark brown hood and upperparts; all feathers edged creamy; neck dusky; underparts white; all feathers with dark centres. (Rooibekeend) 48 cm

WHITE-BACKED DUCK
Secluded wetlands. Head and neck buff but densely spotted black (darkest on crown); a white spot at base of black bill; rest of upperparts spotted and barred dark brown; rufous and white. (Witrugeend) 43 cm

CAPE SHOVELLER
Wetlands. Large drab duck. Black, broad-tipped bill; orange-yellow legs; speckled all over dark brown on pale grey. Male has paler head. In flight, shows pale blue on upper wings. (Kaapse slopeend) 53 cm

CAPE TEAL
Brackish pans. Pale duck with pink bill. Above dark brown; feathers edged creamy; head and below white, well spotted dark brown. (Teeleend) 46 cm

HOTTENTOT TEAL
Wetlands. Small duck with slate-blue bill; dark brown hood and wing feathers; mantle feathers edged white; rest of head and underparts creamy; breast to thighs spotted black. (Gevlekte eend) 35 cm

YELLOW-BILLED DUCK
Upland wetlands. Yellow bill with black saddle. Above dark brown, all feathers edged white; head and underparts white, all feathers with dark brown centres, densely so on head and neck.
(Geelbekeend) 53-58 cm

RUFF
Wetlands. Orange legs in adult, dark in immature. Head and rear of neck dappled light brown; back and wings dark brown; all feathers boldly edged white; below white.
(Kemphaan) 24-30 cm

RUDDY TURNSTONE (non-breeding)
Coastal shores. Short black bill; yellow legs. Head light brown; upperparts mottled dark brown and blackish; neck and below white; various black markings on breast plus broken black breast-band.
(Steenloper) 22 cm

Non-br.

Non-br.

AFRICAN SNIPE
Marshes. Very long, straight black bill. Head, breast and upperparts buff; heavily streaked and spotted dark brown, lower breast to belly white; flanks barred dark brown.
(Afrikaanse snip) 32 cm

GREY PLOVER (non-breeding)
Tidal flats. Bill, legs black. Above mottled light grey-brown and white; eyebrows and forehead white; below white; breast streaked light grey-brown; in flight 'armpits' black.
(Grysstrandkiewiet) 30 cm

speckled plumage **259**

(EURASIAN) CURLEW
Tidal waters. Very large shorebird with very long, down-curved bill; head, mantle and breast buff, well streaked dark brown with buffy-white feather edges; wing feathers edged white; underbelly white.
(Grootwulp) 59 cm

(COMMON) WHIMBREL
Coastal lagoons. Large shorebird with long, black, down-curved bill. Dark brown crown with central white stripe; above dark brown mottled white; below white, streaked brown on breast and flanks.
(Kleinwulp) 43 cm

COMMON QUAIL
Grasslands. Above rufous, mottled and streaked black and white; head with white markings; throat dark; below pale rufous; flanks streaked white.
(Afrikaanse kwartel) 18 cm

GREY-WINGED FRANCOLIN
Grassy hills. Black bill; yellow legs. Upperparts tawny barred black and streaked white; head markings rufous; throat white well spotted black; below grey.
(Bergpatrys) 31-33 cm

SPOTTED DIKKOP
Stony grassland. Large yellow eyes; yellow bill with black tip; long yellow legs. Above buffy; heavily streaked and spotted dark brown; below white, chest streaked blackish.
(Dikkop) 44 cm

ORANGE RIVER FRANCOLIN
Dry grasslands. Legs dull yellow. Above dark grey-brown, mottled black with white streaks; head rufous, black and white; throat white; below rufous (paler in west) spotted and dappled red-brown.
(Kalaharipatrys) 33-35 cm

SHELLEY'S FRANCOLIN
Grassy woodland. Legs dull yellow. Above dark grey-brown, blotched black and streaked white; throat white; below white, breast blotched red-brown, belly barred black. (Laeveldpatrys) 33 cm

BEARDED VULTURE (immature)
Maluti mountains. Bill and legs whitish; eyes yellow; head, beard and upper breast dark brown; rest of plumage (except flight feathers) dappled dark and light brown and white. (Baardaasvoël) 110 cm

RED-WING FRANCOLIN
Grassy hills. Legs dull yellow. Above dark brown, blotched black and streaked white; ear coverts and lateral neck rufous; throat white; upper breast mottled black and white; underparts pale rufous streaked red-brown. (Rooivlerkpatrys) 38-40 cm

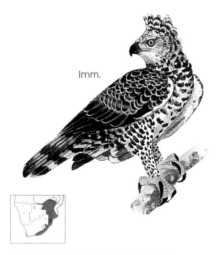

NATAL FRANCOLIN
Granite koppies. Bill yellow and red; legs red. Above dark brown streaked black; below throat to vent speckled black and white. (Natalse fisant) 30-38 cm

(AFRICAN) CROWNED EAGLE (immature)
Forests. Eyes and feet orange-yellow. Above dark brown, all feathers edged white; head and underparts white, dappled and barred dark brown and orange. (Kroonarend) 80-90 cm

DOUBLE-BANDED SANDGROUSE
Broad-leaved woodland. Usually in pairs. Female almost completely speckled. Male has distinctive white and black band on breast. White spots on back.
(Dubbelbandsandpatrys) 25 cm

YELLOW-THROATED SANDGROUSE (female)
Kalahari. Face and throat yellow; crown, hindneck, upperparts and breast pale yellow heavily dappled blackish; belly dusky; vent rufous.
(Geelkeelsandpatrys) 30 cm

BURCHELL'S SANDGROUSE
Sandveld. Usually in pairs or flocks at waterholes. More ochre and heavily speckled than other sandgrouse. Female with yellow face and throat, male grey-blue and more rufous overall.
(Gevlekte sandpatrys) 25 cm

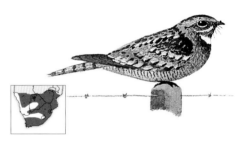

NIGHTJARS
These birds are all heavily mottled, barred and spotted rufous, dark brown, black and white. Can only be specifically identified by call or by wing and tail patterns.
(Naguile) 23-28 cm

NAMAQUA SANDGROUSE
Desert. Longer, pointed tail than other sandgrouse; female has dense barring all over, apart from throat and underbelly. Both sexes have ochre heads and flock at waterholes mainly in morning.
(Kelkiewyn) 28 cm

SPOTTED CREEPER
Broad-leaved woodland. Slender, down-curved bill. Upperparts dark brown heavily spotted white; underparts white, finely scalloped brown.
(Boomkruiper) 15 cm

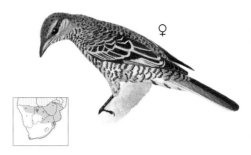

CHESTNUT-BACKED FINCHLARK (female)
Bare areas in grassland. Bill white; legs grey. Crown, nape and upperparts dappled dusky and black; hindcollar white; carpal region chestnut; wing feathers edged white; breast white dappled black; belly black. (Rooiruglewerik) 12 cm

BLACK CUCKOOSHRIKE (female)
Woodland. Gape orange. Above dull olive-brown; wings and tail black; all feathers edged yellow; below white heavily barred black. (Swartkatakoeroe) 22 cm

Non-br.

BLACK-EARED FINCHLARK (female)
Scrublands. Bill and legs white. Upperparts dappled dusky; ear coverts rufous; wings rufous dappled black, pale feather edges; below white streaked black. (Swartoorlewerik) 12-13 cm

EUROPEAN STARLING (non-breeding)
Suburbs. Bill black; legs dark red. Above light brown heavily spotted tawny; wing feathers edged tawny; below greenish-black spotted white. (Europese spreeu) 20-22 cm

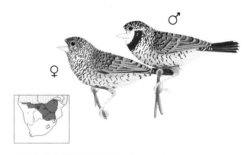

GREY-BACKED FINCHLARK (female)
Scrublands and desert. Bill and legs white. Crown dusky; upperparts greyish; all feathers broadly edged white; breast streaked black; belly black. (Grysruglewerik) 12-13 cm

CUT-THROAT FINCH (female)
Dry woodland. Bill and legs white. Head and breast white but well barred black, above rufous barred black, feather edges paler, below white, washed rufous. (Bandkeelvink) 12 cm

birds with
collars and breast-bands

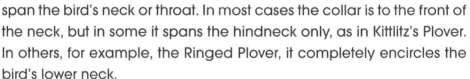

Capped Wheatear

Collars or bands are found in many bird species and are excellent recognition features. Collars, as the term suggests, refer to bands of colour that span the bird's neck or throat. In most cases the collar is to the front of the neck, but in some it spans the hindneck only, as in Kittlitz's Plover. In others, for example, the Ringed Plover, it completely encircles the bird's lower neck.

The term 'breast-band' is applied to bands of colour, often black, that span the bird's breast or chest. Breast-bands may number as many as three, as in the Three-banded Plover, although a single band is most common. Some birds have a wide breast-band, for example, the Bokmakierie, and these are usually called 'gorgets'.

In a few species the breast-band is found only in the male bird during the breeding season and fades or disappears completely during the non-breeding season, an example being the Black-chested Prinia.

BROOD PARASITES

These are birds that lay their eggs in the nest of an unrelated species and take no part in raising their own young. While cuckoos are well known for this behaviour, within our region there are other species that practice brood parasitism. These are the honeyguides, the whydahs and related widow-finches, and the Cuckoo Finch. Most of our cuckoos are summer visitors that parasitise a range of other species according to their preferences. The common Red-chested Cuckoo favours the robin group, while the equally common Diederik Cuckoo prefers weavers and bishops. In both of these species the cuckoo egg normally hatches before those of the host, and the chick ejects the eggs of its foster siblings. Young honeyguides also hatch early and are initially equipped with a sharp bill-hook which is used to break the eggs of its host or to kill the chicks. In contrast, the whydahs and widow-finches parasitise mostly waxbills and other small finches. The parasite's chicks resemble those of the host in several ways, and grow up in harmony with them. The Cuckoo Finch, a parasitic weaver, usually parasitises cisticolas and prinias and, as far as is known, the chick does not deliberately dispose of its foster siblings.

The birds you will find in this chapter

African Marsh Harrier **268**
African Mourning Dove **269**
African Pied Wagtail **272**
Alpine Swift **270**
Banded Martin **270**
Bar-throated Apalis **272**
Black-chested Prinia **273**
Bokmakierie **274**
Bronze-winged Courser **267**
Burnt-necked Eremomela **273**
Cape Batis **273**
Cape Turtle Dove **269**
Cape Wagtail **272**
Capped Wheatear **272**
Caspian Plover **266**
Chestnut-banded Plover **266**
Chin-spot Batis **274**
Collared Palmthrush **274**
(Common) Ringed Plover **266**
Crowned Plover **267**
Cut-throat Finch **275**
Double-banded Courser **267**
Double-banded Sandgrouse **268**
European Bee-eater **270**
(European) Sand Martin **270**
European Swallow **269**
Gorgeous Bush Shrike **274**
Greater Double-collared
  Sunbird **275**
Kittlitz's Plover **266**
Kori Bustard **268**
Lesser (Southern)
  Double-collared Sunbird **274**
Little Bee-eater **270**
Long-tailed Wagtail **271**
Long-toed Plover **267**
Marico Sunbird **275**
Mocking Chat (male) **272**
Namaqua Sandgrouse **268**
Orange-breasted Sunbird **275**
Orange-throated Longclaw **271**
Osprey **268**
Painted Snipe **266**
Pied Kingfisher **271**
Pririt Batis **273**

Red-chested Cuckoo **269**
Red-collared Widow **275**
Red-eyed Dove **269**
Rudd's Apalis **272**
Ruddy Turnstone **267**
Rufous-eared Warbler **273**
Swallow-tailed Bee-eater **270**
Three-banded Courser **267**
Three-banded Plover **266**
White-throated Swallow **269**
Yellow-breasted Apalis **273**
Yellow-throated Longclaw **271**
Yellow-throated Sandgrouse **268**

Chin-spot Batis

(COMMON) RINGED PLOVER

Inland shorelines. The black gorget extends as a narrow hindcollar parallel with the extension of the white throat. (Ringnekstrandkiewiet) 18 cm

PAINTED SNIPE

Swamps. In both sexes the white underparts extend as a white band, bordered black, over the bird's mantle. (Goudsnip) 28-32 cm

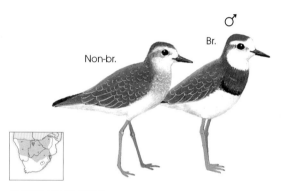

THREE-BANDED PLOVER

Inland shorelines. Two black and one white band on upper breast, the upper black-and-white bands encircling the neck. (Driebandstrandkiewiet) 18 cm

CASPIAN PLOVER

Dry plains. The male in breeding plumage has a wide rufous gorget, bordered black below; throat and below white. (Asiatiese strandkiewiet) 21-23 cm

CHESTNUT-BANDED PLOVER

Coastal sandflats. The chestnut collar of the male is paler in the female, grey in the immature; underparts white. (Rooibandstrandkiewiet) 15 cm

KITTLITZ'S PLOVER

Inland shorelines. The black mask and ear coverts extend as a black hindcollar parallel with the extension of its white eyebrows. (Geelborsstrandkiewiet) 16 cm

RUDDY TURNSTONE

Coastal shorelines. In breeding plumage the black facial and mantle markings extend as a breast-band; less distinct in non-breeding plumage. (Steenloper) 22 cm

BRONZE-WINGED COURSER

Broad-leaved woodland. The light brown throat is separated from the white underparts by a narrow black breast-band. (Bronsvlerkdrawwertjie) 25 cm

LONG-TOED PLOVER

Floodplains. The black nape extends to the breast to form a very wide breast-patch or gorget. (Witvlerkkiewiet) 30 cm

DOUBLE-BANDED COURSER

Dry grasslands. Two narrow black breast-bands on white underparts. (Dubbelbanddrawwertjie) 22 cm

CROWNED PLOVER

Dry grasslands. The light brown upperparts and breast terminate in a black band across the lower breast; a white head-band encircles the black cap. (Kroonkiewiet) 30 cm

THREE-BANDED COURSER

Dry woodland. The white throat has a chestnut V-shaped collar; the upper breast has a dark brown breast-band extending to the shoulders, and a chestnut lower breast-band. (Driebanddrawwertjie) 28 cm

KORI BUSTARD
Dry woodland and grasslands. The greyish neck of this huge bird is separated from its upper breast by a broken black band.
(Gompou) 135 cm

DOUBLE-BANDED SANDGROUSE
Broad-leaved woodland. The male has black-and-white bands on its forehead and breast.
(Dubbelbandsandpatrys) 25 cm

Imm.

AFRICAN MARSH HARRIER (immature)
Marshes. Young birds are dark brown with a diagnostic broad white breast-band.
(Afrikaanse vleivalk) 44-49 cm

NAMAQUA SANDGROUSE
Desert. The male's lower breast has a white breast-band bordered below by a rufous one.
(Kelkiewyn) 28 cm

OSPREY
Lagoons and inland waters. Adults have white underparts with a broad, broken, light brown breast-band.
(Visvalk) 55-63 cm

YELLOW-THROATED SANDGROUSE
Kalahari. The male's yellow throat is bordered by a black collar.
(Geelkeelsandpatrys) 30 cm

AFRICAN MOURNING DOVE
Riverine woodland. A grey-headed, yellow-eyed dove with a black hindcollar.
(Rooioogtortelduif) 30 cm

RED-CHESTED CUCKOO
Woodland. A grey cuckoo with a broad, dull orange band on the upper breast.
(Piet-my-vrou) 28 cm

RED-EYED DOVE
Woodland. A large, pink-breasted dove with red eyes and a broad hindcollar.
(Grootringduif) 33-36 cm

WHITE-THROATED SWALLOW
Wetlands. Clear white underparts with a black breast-band.
(Witkeelswael) 17 cm

CAPE TURTLE DOVE
Widespread. A grey dove with black eyes and a black hindcollar.
(Gewone tortelduif) 28 cm

EUROPEAN SWALLOW
Widespread. Dull orange chin bordered below by a broad black collar.
(Europese swael) 18 cm

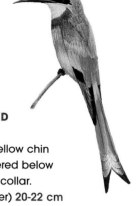

SWALLOW-TAILED BEE-EATER
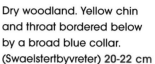
Dry woodland. Yellow chin and throat bordered below by a broad blue collar.
(Swaelstertbyvreter) 20-22 cm

(EUROPEAN) SAND MARTIN
Estuaries. Small. Brown above; white below with a narrow brown breast-band.
(Europese oewerswael) 12 cm

LITTLE BEE-EATER
Riverine bush. Yellow throat separated from rufous underparts by a V-shaped black band on upper breast.
(Kleinbyvreter) 17 cm

BANDED MARTIN
Inland waters. Large. Dark brown above; white below with a broad, dark brown breast-band.
(Gebande oewerswael) 17 cm

EUROPEAN BEE-EATER
Widespread. Blue forehead and underparts; yellow throat bordered below by a small black collar.
(Europese byvreter) 25-29 cm

ALPINE SWIFT
Mountains. Large, dark brown swift with white underparts; dark brown breast-band and vent.
(Witpenswindswael) 22 cm

PIED KINGFISHER
Wetlands. Male has a double black
breast-band, the upper one broad,
the lower one narrow. Female has a
single broad breast-band with a gap
in the centre.
(Bontvisvanger) 28-29 cm

YELLOW-THROATED LONGCLAW
Grasslands. Yellow below, chin to
vent, with a black gorget extending
from the gape.
(Geelkeelkalkoentjie) 20 cm

ORANGE-THROATED LONGCLAW
Grasslands. The orange throat is
separated from the yellow underparts
by a black border ending in a V-shape
on the lower neck.
(Oranjekeelkalkoentjie) 20 cm

LONG-TAILED WAGTAIL
Mountain streams. Very long tail; below
white with a narrow black breast-band.
(Bergkwikkie) 19-20 cm

CAPE WAGTAIL
Wetlands and gardens. Greyish wagtail with white throat and upper breast; black breast-band. (Gewone kwikkie) 18 cm

CAPPED WHEATEAR
Burnt fields and short grass. Broad black gorget extending from the ear coverts. Throat and lower breast white. (Hoëveldskaapwagter) 18 cm

AFRICAN PIED WAGTAIL
Lowland rivers. Above black and white; below white with a broad black breast-band. (Bontkwikkie) 20 cm

BAR-THROATED APALIS
Forests and woodland. Grey above; white or yellow below; all races have a black collar. (Bandkeelkleinjantjie) 12-13 cm

MOCKING CHAT (male)
Rocky habitats. The black breast and rufous belly are separated by a white breast-band. (Dassievoël) 20-23 cm

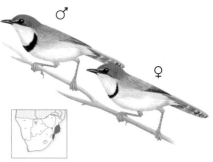

RUDD'S APALIS
Coastal bush. Grey cap; green upperparts; white below with black collar. (Ruddse kleinjantjie) 10-12 cm

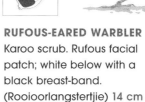

YELLOW-BREASTED APALIS
Bushveld. Below white with yellow breast; lower breast may have a small black breast-bar, often absent. (Geelborskleinjantjie) 10-12 cm

RUFOUS-EARED WARBLER
Karoo scrub. Rufous facial patch; white below with a black breast-band. (Rooioorlangstertjie) 14 cm

BURNT-NECKED EREMOMELA
Woodland. Grey above; creamy below with a small brown throat-bar, often absent. (Bruinkeelbossanger) 12 cm

PRIRIT BATIS
Dry thornveld. The male is grey above and white below, with a broad black breast-band. (Priritbosbontrokkie) 12 cm

BLACK-CHESTED PRINIA
Dry thornveld. White below when breeding, with a black breast-band; underparts yellow in non-breeding plumage. (Swartbandlangstertjie) 13-15 cm

CAPE BATIS
Forest fringes. Male has a broad black breast-band and rufous flanks. Female has rufous throat, flanks and breast-band. (Kaapse bosbontrokkie) 12-13 cm

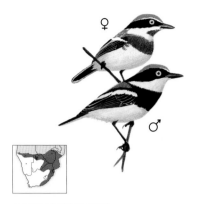

CHIN-SPOT BATIS
Woodland. Male is white below with a broad black breast-band. Female is white below with a rufous chin-spot and broad rufous breast-band. (Witliesbosbontrokkie) 12-13 cm

BOKMAKIERIE
Bush and suburbia. Grey cap and mantle; olive-green wings; below yellow with a black gorget. (Bokmakierie) 23 cm

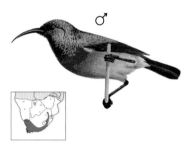

COLLARED PALM-THRUSH
Palm savanna. Russet brown head, back and tail; pale eye; grey neck with distinctive black-bordered cream throat patch. (Palmmôrelyster) 19 cm

LESSER (SOUTHERN) DOUBLE-COLLARED SUNBIRD (male)
Lowland bush. Glossy-green above, extending around neck; blue and narrow red breast-band; belly greyish. (Kleinrooibandsuikerbekkie) 12,5 cm

GORGEOUS BUSH SHRIKE
Bushveld and forest fringes. Scarlet throat, black gorget and yellow underparts. (Konkoit) 20 cm

RED-COLLARED WIDOW (male)
Grassy bushveld. When breeding, the all-black, long-tailed male has a red collar.
(Rooikeelflap) 40 cm

GREATER DOUBLE-COLLARED SUNBIRD (male)
Montane bush. Glossy-green above, extending around neck; blue and broad red breast-band.
(Grootrooibandsuikerbekkie) 14 cm

MARICO SUNBIRD
Bushveld. Glossy-green above, extending around neck; lower breast has purple and ruby-red breast-band; belly black.
(Maricosuikerbekkie) 13-14 cm

CUT-THROAT FINCH (male)
Broad-leaved woodland. The white-billed, scaly-looking male has a broad red collar.
(Bandkeelvink) 12 cm

ORANGE-BREASTED SUNBIRD (male)
Fynbos. Head, mantle and throat green; upper breast has purple breast-band; underparts orange.
(Oranjeborssuikerbekkie) 15 cm

birds with
crests and
head-plumes

Striped Cuckoo

Crests are extended feathers, stiff or floppy, on the crowns of some birds. They may be more or less permanent tufts, as in some bulbuls and flycatchers, while in others, such as the African Hoopoe, they can be erect or lowered. In several birds the crest is only raised in alarm or in display. A good example of its use in display can be seen in the Red-crested Korhaan, which erects its crest only in courtship.

The (African) Crowned Eagle has a lateral crest formed by raising its rear crown feathers in agitation or in conflict situations, giving the eagle a formidable appearance.

Head-plumes are mostly long and floppy and extend from the rear of the crown, as in the Secretarybird and the Kori Bustard, but in a few cases they are short and fairly stiff, as in the Grey Crowned Crane.

African Hoopoe

KESTRELS

Kestrels are a group of small falcons. They share certain characteristics of their larger cousins in that they have pointed wings and build no nest of their own. However, they feed on small rodents, reptiles and small birds caught mostly on the ground, or on flying insects caught on the wing. The summer-visiting Lesser and Red-footed kestrels are gregarious and hunt in flocks over grasslands, catching especially grasshoppers and flying termites. The resident kestrels mostly hunt from a roadside post or wire, making short aerial forays to catch their prey on the ground before returning with it to feed on their perch. The flight of the kestrel is graceful, with much hovering. The kestrels and the falcons have greatly increased their feeding and breeding ranges in southern Africa through man's provision of roadside perches, especially Eskom's pylons (towers) where crows and other birds of prey build their nests, which in turn, are used by the falcons and kestrels.

The birds you will find in this chapter

(African) Crowned Eagle 281
African Cuckoo Hawk 282
African Hoopoe 284
(African) Paradise Flycatcher 285
(African) Red-eyed Bulbul 285
Bank Cormorant 278
Black Egret 278
Black-crowned Night Heron 279
Black-eyed Bulbul 285
Black-headed Heron 279
Blue-mantled (Crested)
  Flycatcher 285
Cardinal Woodpecker 284
Crested Barbet 284
Crested Francolin 280
Crested Guineafowl 281
Crowned Cormorant 278
Giant Kingfisher 284
Great Crested Grebe 280
Great Spotted Cuckoo 283
(Grey) Crowned Crane 280
Grey Heron 279
Gymnogene 282

Jacobin Cuckoo 283
Knysna Lourie 282
Kori Bustard 280
Little Egret 279
Long-crested Eagle 281
Martial Eagle 281
Osprey 282
Pied Kingfisher 284
Purple Heron 279
Purple-crested Lourie 282
Red-crested Korhaan 280
Red-faced Mousebird 283
Reed Cormorant 278
Rufous-naped Lark 284
Secretarybird 281
Slaty Egret 278
Speckled Mousebird 283
Squacco Heron 278
Stark's Lark 285
Striped Cuckoo 283
White Helmet Shrike 285
White-backed Mousebird 283

(African) Crowned Eagle

BANK CORMORANT
Coastal. Large black cormorant
with a small permanent crest
just forward of its yellow eyes.
(Bankduiker) 75 cm

SQUACCO HERON
Inland waters. Breeding plumage has
dark plumes extending from the
rear-crown, which rest on the nape.
(Ralreier) 43 cm

CROWNED CORMORANT
Coastal. Small black cormorant
with permanent crest; yellow
eyes and lower mandible.
(Kuifkopduiker) 54 cm

REED CORMORANT
Inland and coastal waters.
Male has a small crest on its
forehead; bill yellow; eyes red.
(Rietduiker) 60 cm

BLACK EGRET
Inland waters. Long grey
plumes hanging freely from
the rear-crown; feet yellow.
(Swartreier) 66 cm

SLATY EGRET
Inland waters. Slate-grey with
long plumes hanging freely
from the rear-crown; throat
rufous; legs and feet yellow.
(Rooikeelreier) 60 cm

PURPLE HERON
Inland waters. Grey above
with rufous neck; black
cap extending to two
plumes from the rear-crown.
(Rooireier) 89 cm

BLACK-CROWNED NIGHT HERON
Inland waters. Black crown and back
with two long, white plumes extending
from the rear-crown; white below;
wings grey.
(Gewone nagreier) 64 cm

LITTLE EGRET
Inland waters. Entirely white
with long, free-hanging plumes
extending from the rear-crown;
feet yellow.
(Kleinwitreier) 64 cm

BLACK-HEADED HERON
Grasslands. Grey heron with
black hood and rear-neck;
two plumes extending
from rear-crown.
(Swartkopreier) 97 cm

GREY HERON
Inland waters. Grey above; white head
and neck; black brow extending as
two plumes from the rear-crown.
(Bloureier) 100 cm

GREAT CRESTED GREBE
Inland waters. In breeding plumage the black crown extends backward as two pointed crests that can be fanned. (Kuifkopdobbertjie) 50 cm

(GREY) CROWNED CRANE
Reedbeds and estuaries. Mostly grey bird with black crown and a stiff, permanent fan-shaped golden crest. (Mahem) 105 cm

RED-CRESTED KORHAAN
Woodland. Rufous crest not normally visible, erect from nape in courtship; above brown with creamy arrow shapes. (Boskorhaan) 53 cm

CRESTED FRANCOLIN
Bushveld. Rufous above; dark crown feathers raised in alarm; tail is held raised. (Bospatrys) 32 cm

KORI BUSTARD
Woodland and grasslands. Huge bird with blackish plumes extending from rear-crown. (Gompou) 135 cm

Imm.

(AFRICAN) CROWNED EAGLE
Forests. When excited the entire rear-crown is raised; eyes yellow; gape and feet orange.
(Kroonarend) 80-90 cm

CRESTED GUINEAFOWL
Riverine forests. Neck and crown black; crown feathers elongated to form a floppy crest; bill white; body black with small blue spots.
(Kuifkoptarentaal) 50 cm

SECRETARYBIRD
Grasslands. Large grey and black bird with long, black and grey nape feathers; facial skin orange.
(Sekretarisvoël) 125-150 cm

MARTIAL EAGLE
Woodland. Does not normally appear crested but loose rear-crown feathers tend to form a crest when lifted by wind.
(Breëkoparend) 78-83 cm

LONG-CRESTED EAGLE
Wooded valleys. Dark brown eagle with long, upstanding crest; unmistakable. Eyes and gape pale yellow.
(Langkuifarend) 53-58 cm

OSPREY
Lagoons and large dams. Loose rear-crown feathers can be raised; head and below white; yellow eyes on dark mask.
(Visvalk) 55-63 cm

KNYSNA LOURIE
Forests. The green, white-edged crest is a permanent feature, and is longer in northern races.
(Knysnaloerie) 47 cm

GYMNOGENE
Wooded habitats. At all ages the nape feathers are raised to form a ruff when excited.
(Kaalwangvalk) 60-66 cm

AFRICAN CUCKOO HAWK
Riverine forests. Small, backward-projecting crest at the rear-crown at all ages.
(Koekoekvalk) 40 cm

PURPLE-CRESTED LOURIE
Riverine woodland. Purple-blue crest is a permanent feature; green head; eye-ring red; bill black.
(Bloukuifloerie) 47 cm

SPECKLED MOUSEBIRD
Bush and suburbia.
Permanent loose crest
on head; over all brownish;
bill black above; white below.
(Gevlekte muisvoël) 30-35 cm

STRIPED CUCKOO
Woodland. Black above; head
with backward-projecting crest;
below white; throat and breast
spotted black.
(Gestreepte nuwejaarsvoël) 38-40 cm

JACOBIN CUCKOO
Woodland. Both colour morphs
have a crest projecting backward
from the black head; white
morph unspotted.
(Bontnuwejaarsvoël) 33-34 cm

WHITE-BACKED MOUSEBIRD
Dry bush and suburbia.
Grey above with upstanding
crest; back white; bill white
with black tip.
(Witkruismuisvoël) 30-34 cm

RED-FACED MOUSEBIRD
Moist woodland and
suburbia. Light brown above
with backward-projecting
crest; mask red; eyes blue.
(Rooiwangmuisvoël) 32-34 cm

GREAT SPOTTED CUCKOO
Savanna. Adult has backward-
projecting crest on its grey
head; upperparts black
spotted white; below white.
(Gevlekte koekoek) 38-40 cm

GIANT KINGFISHER
Rivers. Black head with backward-projecting feathers on rear-crown, crest fully raised only in stress situations. Breast or belly rufous.
(Reusevisvanger) 43-46 cm

CRESTED BARBET
Woodland and suburbia. Yellow, red-speckled head with black, backward-projecting crest; bill cream.
(Kuifkophoutkapper) 23 cm

PIED KINGFISHER
Inland waters. Black-and-white kingfisher; black crown with backward-projecting crest.
(Bontvisvanger) 28-29 cm

CARDINAL WOODPECKER
Woodland. Male with red crown, female with black crown, frequently raised as a crest while feeding.
(Kardinaalspeg) 14-16 cm

AFRICAN HOOPOE
Woodland. Large, rufous crest is normally held flat, but is raised when landing or when alarmed.
(Hoephoep) 27 cm

RUFOUS-NAPED LARK
Grassland with bushes. Rufous crown raised; wings fluttered frequently while singing.
(Rooineklewerik) 18-19 cm

STARK'S LARK
Arid grasslands. A small, pale lark with a crested head imparting a 'peaked' appearance.
(Woestynlewerik) 13 cm

BLUE-MANTLED (CRESTED) FLYCATCHER
Forest edges. Male blue-black above, female brown; both with crested heads, longest in male; below white.
(Bloukuifvlieëvanger) 17-18 cm

WHITE HELMET SHRIKE
Bushveld. Grey crown has stiff forehead feathers that project forward; eyes and eye-rings yellow.
(Withelmlaksman) 20 cm

(AFRICAN) PARADISE FLYCATCHER
Woodland. Blue-grey, permanently crested head in both sexes; blue eye-rings and bill; rufous upperparts.
(Paradysvlieëvanger) 23-41 cm

(AFRICAN) RED-EYED BULBUL
Bush and suburbia. Black head permanently crested; eye-ring red.
(Rooioogtiptol) 19-21 cm

BLACK-EYED BULBUL
Suburbia. The black head is permanently crested; eyes black.
(Swartoogtiptol) 20-22 cm

flight patterns

Wattled Crane

of some larger birds, mainly as seen from below

Small birds are not easy to recognise in flight simply because of their size and rapid movements, but the larger, slower flying birds often soar with their wings firmly outstretched and present good opportunities for study. The larger herons, for example, invariably fly at low altitudes and flap their wings slowly so that, with the aid of binoculars, their details can be seen. Remember that herons, unlike storks and cranes, fly with their necks tucked in. Remember also that the two most common large herons are easily identified in flight. The Grey Heron has entirely grey underwings, while the similar Black-headed Heron has two-tone black and grey underwings. Herons seldom soar, but storks often do, their necks and legs extended.

The larger birds of prey spend much of the day soaring, circling around in rising warm air. Their flight action is moderately slow and usually affords ample time for their wing shape and underwing pattern to be seen. With practise, the technique of focusing binoculars on flying birds will become second nature.

ACCIPITERS IN FLIGHT

The underwings and undertails of most sparrowhawks and goshawks are surprisingly similar, the common arrangement being a confusion of greyish transverse bars on the underwings and four dark bars on the undertail. The entire pattern, together with the barred underbody, is of little help in species identification during the brief glimpse normally presented to an observer by these fast-flying little hawks. In the field it is better to concentrate on seeing the bird's rump and upper tail which is usually possible as the bird banks and turns. Individual rump or tail patterns are the key to certain identification. The Little Sparrowhawk has a white bar on the rump plus two distinctive white spots on the central tail; the Little Banded Goshawk has entirely grey upperparts; the Gabar Goshawk has a bold white rump patch (absent only in the melanistic form); and the Ovambo Sparrowhawk shows white tail feather-shafts when a good view is obtained.

The birds you will find in this chapter

Underwings and bodies that are mostly white

African Spoonbill **288**
Augur Buzzard **289**
Black-breasted Snake Eagle **289**
Black-shouldered Kite **289**
Cattle Egret **288**
Great White Heron **288**
Grey Heron **288**
Little Egret **288**
Sacred Ibis **288**

Black-and-white underwings or bodies

Abdim's Stork **290**
(African) Black Eagle **292**
Bateleur **291**
Black Harrier **292**
Black Stork **290**
Brown Snake Eagle **291**
Cape Gannet **289**
Eastern White Pelican **289**
Greater Flamingo **290**
Jackal Buzzard **292**
Knob-billed Duck **291**
Long-crested Eagle **291**
Marabou Stork **290**
Martial Eagle **292**
Palm-nut Vulture **291**
Saddle-billed Stork **290**
Wattled Crane **291**
White Stork **290**
White-headed Vulture **291**
Yellow-billed Stork **290**

Black-and-grey underwings and bodies

Black-headed Heron **292**
Blue Crane **292**
Dark Chanting Goshawk **293**
Eastern Red-footed Kestrel **293**
(Grey) Crowned Crane **293**
Grey Heron **292**
Gymnogene **293**
Secretarybird **293**
(Southern) Pale Chanting
    Goshawk **293**
Western Red-footed Kestrel **293**

Birds of prey with barred underparts

(African) Crowned Eagle **294**
African Cuckoo Hawk **296**
African Goshawk **296**
Black Sparrowhawk **295**
Eastern Red-footed Kestrel
    (female) **297**
Eurasian Hobby **297**
(European) Honey Buzzard **294**
Gabar Goshawk **295**
Lanner Falcon **296**
Lesser Kestrel **297**
Little Banded Goshawk **295**
Little Sparrowhawk **295**
Montagu's Harrier **296**
Ovambo Sparrowhawk **295**
Peregrine Falcon **297**
Pygmy Falcon **297**
Red-necked Falcon **296**
Rock Kestrel **297**
Rufous-breasted Sparrowhawk **295**
Southern Banded Snake Eagle **294**
Western Banded Snake Eagle **294**

Underwings and bodies that are mostly white

CATTLE EGRET
Look for yellow bill and legs; in summer look for rufous breast. Flies with head tucked in.
(Veereier)

GREY HERON
Yellow bill and legs; grey underwings; slow wing beats. Head tucked in.
(Bloureier)

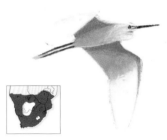

LITTLE EGRET
Look for black bill and legs; yellow feet. Head tucked in.
(Kleinwitreier)

GREAT WHITE HERON
Yellow bill; black legs trailing; head tucked in; slow wing beats.
(Grootwitreier)

AFRICAN SPOONBILL
Spatulate red bill; neck extended; long red legs trailing.
(Lepelaar)

SACRED IBIS
Black head and neck extended; black legs; black trailing edge to wings; red 'armpits'.
(Skoorsteenveër)

BLACK-BREASTED SNAKE EAGLE
Dark brown head and breast; fine brown barring on underwings and tail. Seldom flaps, frequently hovers.
(Swartborsslangarend)

BLACK-SHOULDERED KITE
Black tips to white underwings; often hovers for long periods, glides or flaps fast.
(Blouvalk)

AUGUR BUZZARD
Black edges to wings; female has black head; rufous tail; seldom flaps.
(Witborsjakkalsvoël)

Black-and-white underwings or bodies

EASTERN WHITE PELICAN
Black flight feathers; large yellowish bill; neck tucked in; slow wing beats, often soars.
(Witpelikaan)

CAPE GANNET
Flight feathers and tail black. Flies over the sea and plunges for fish. Crown and nape yellow.
(Witmalgas)

SADDLE-BILLED STORK
White below except for black underwing coverts; black head and neck extended; legs trailing; large red and black bill; wing beats slow.
(Saalbekooievaar)

ABDIM'S STORK
Underwings and tail black; body white extending onto wings; head and neck black, outstretched; bill horn-coloured; trailing legs white; flocks soar. Summer.
(Kleinswartooievaar)

MARABOU STORK
Underwings and tail black; body and 'armpits' white; neck tucked in; large bill horn-coloured; trailing legs whitish. Wing beats slow, may soar.
(Maraboe)

WHITE STORK
Black flight feathers; neck stretched out; bill and trailing legs red; flocks soar. Summer.
(Witooievaar)

YELLOW-BILLED STORK
Flight feathers black; rest of underwings pinkish with narrow, parallel red bars; white head and neck outstretched; trailing legs red. Wing beats slow, soars often.
(Nimmersat)

BLACK STORK
Underwings and tail black; body white; black head and neck stretched out; bill and trailing legs red. Wing beats slow.
(Grootswartooievaar)

GREATER FLAMINGO
Slender white neck stretched out; red legs trailing; wings red and black. Fast-flapping.
(Grootflamink)

WATTLED CRANE
Black body and flight feathers; grey underwings; white head and neck stretched out; black legs extend beyond tail. Flight ponderous. (Lelkraanvoël)

KNOB-BILLED DUCK
Black underwings and tail; bulky, white body with dusky neck and head outstretched; legs do not extend. (Knobbeleend)

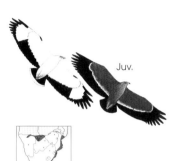

WHITE-HEADED VULTURE
White body with black breast; underwings black with white inner secondaries in the female; tail black; head tucked in. Soars. (Witkopaasvoël)

PALM-NUT VULTURE
Body white; underwings and rounded tail black and white. Flaps slowly, may soar. (Witaasvoël)

BATELEUR
Body black; short tail rufous; underwings white with broad black trailing edge in the male, narrow in the female. Flies fairly low, rocks side to side. (Berghaan)

LONG-CRESTED EAGLE
Body and underwing coverts black; secondaries dusky; conspicuous white 'windows' in outer wings; tail banded black and white. (Langkuifarend)

BROWN SNAKE EAGLE
Body and underwing coverts dark brown; rest of wings whitish; tail well barred dark brown and white. (Bruinslangarend)

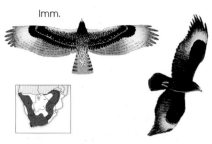

MARTIAL EAGLE
Body white with black breast; underwings dark. In immature, body and underwing coverts white, only tail and flight feathers dark. Soars. (Breëkoparend)

(AFRICAN) BLACK EAGLE
Entirely black below except for white 'windows' at the base of primaries. (Witkruisarend)

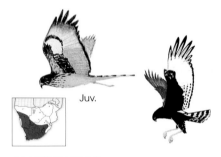

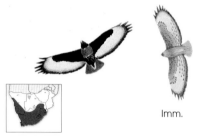

BLACK HARRIER
Body and underwing coverts black; rest of wing white with thin black trailing edge; tail banded black and white. Flies low, may hover briefly. (Witkruisvleiarend)

JACKAL BUZZARD
Underwing coverts black; tips of primaries and trailing edge of wing black; rest of wing white; tail rufous; body black-and-rufous. Soars. (Rooiborsjakkalsvoël)

Black-and-grey underwings and bodies

GREY HERON
Yellow bill and legs; grey underwings; slow wing beats. Head tucked in. (Bloureier)

BLACK-HEADED HERON
Body and underwings grey, except for black flight feathers. (Grey Heron underwings have no black.) Neck tucked in. Wing beats slow. (Swartkopreier)

BLUE CRANE
Entirely grey except for black flight feathers. Flies with neck outstretched and legs trailing. Wing beats slow. (Bloukraanvoël)

SECRETARYBIRD

Body and underwing coverts grey;
flight feathers black; thighs black;
tail grey, terminal bar black.
(Sekretarisvoël)

(GREY) CROWNED CRANE

Body and underwings grey;
flight feathers black. Flies with
neck outstretched and legs trailing.
(Mahem)

GYMNOGENE

Adult grey with black
primaries and trailing
edge; black tail with
single white bar.
Flaps slowly.
(Kaalwangvalk)

(SOUTHERN) PALE CHANTING GOSHAWK

Above and below pale grey,
secondaries whitish, primaries
black, tail barred black-and-
white. Legs red. Usually flies low.
(Bleeksingvalk)

EASTERN RED-FOOTED KESTREL

Male has grey body and undertail with
chestnut vent; underwing coverts white;
flight feathers black. Flight is gentle,
may soar in wheeling flocks.
(Oostelike rooipootvalk)

DARK CHANTING GOSHAWK

Above and below dark grey,
underwing coverts paler,
primaries black, tail barred
black-and-white. Legs red.
(Donkersingvalk)

WESTERN RED-FOOTED KESTREL

Male is entirely dark grey below except for
chestnut vent. Flight is gentle, may soar in
wheeling flocks.
(Westelike rooipootvalk)

Birds of prey with barred underparts

Many of the small raptors, and a few of the larger ones too, have barred underbodies, underwings and undertails. Heavy barring is a difficult feature to see in a small, fast-flying bird since the barring cannot be properly distinguished. Many barred raptors, especially the sparrowhawks and goshawks, look confusingly similar, leaving you with the tantalising memory of an all-too-brief encounter. The best plan is rather to look for other, unique features of the flying bird and disregard the barring initially. The following notes are designed to draw attention to other important features that are worth watching for.

WESTERN BANDED SNAKE EAGLE
Body and underwing coverts grey; rest of wings white, well barred black; undertail white with single, broad black band (a second band is almost obscured by the undertail coverts). Soars. (Enkelbandslangarend)

SOUTHERN BANDED SNAKE EAGLE
Breast and underwing coverts grey; rest of wings well barred black; undertail banded black-and-white. Soars. (Dubbelbandslangarend)

(AFRICAN) CROWNED EAGLE
Body darkish; underwing coverts rufous; rest of wings white with two narrow black bars and broad black trailing edge; tail with three dark bands. (Kroonarend)

(EUROPEAN) HONEY BUZZARD
A large raptor; body colour pale, dark or streaked. Underwings well barred plus dark carpal patches; undertail with two dark bands near the vent, plus one at the tip. Soars. (Wespedief)

RUFOUS-BREASTED SPARROWHAWK

Body and underwing coverts rufous; rest of underwings and tail well barred; soft parts yellow. Flight rapid. (Rooiborssperwer)

OVAMBO SPARROWHAWK

Below well barred; above grey; dark tail with three pale bands, each band intersected with white feather shafts. (Ovambosperwer)

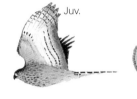

Juv.

LITTLE SPARROWHAWK

White throat, rest of underparts well barred rufous. Above grey, two conspicuous white spots on the upper tail. Soft parts yellow. Flight rapid. (Kleinsperwer)

BLACK SPARROWHAWK

Large sparrowhawk; body black-and-white or mostly black; underwings and tail white, well barred dark; eyes and legs yellow. (Swartsperwer)

LITTLE BANDED GOSHAWK

All underparts well banded rufous; above plain grey. (Gebande sperwer)

GABAR GOSHAWK

Breast grey; rest of underparts well barred; cere and legs red; eyes ruby-red; above grey with broad white rump. Flight rapid. (Witkruissperwer)

AFRICAN GOSHAWK
Well barred rufous below; eyes and legs yellow. Above grey (male) or brown (female); two white spots on upper tail denote a male. Flight rapid unless in high morning display flight.
(Afrikaanse sperwer)

AFRICAN CUCKOO HAWK
Pale grey throat; rest of body and underwing coverts barred rufous; rest of wings barred brown; tail banded brown and white. Flies leisurely with slow wing beats.
(Koekoevalk)

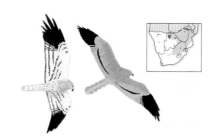

MONTAGU'S HARRIER
Grey head and breast; belly white, streaked brown; underwings white with brown barring; primaries black; above grey with black primaries and thin black wing-bars. Flies low and slowly.
(Blouvleivalk)

LANNER FALCON
Body and underwing coverts lightly washed rufous; wings closely barred grey; undertail barred grey and white. Fast wing-flaps followed by brief glides; tail often spread.
(Edelvalk)

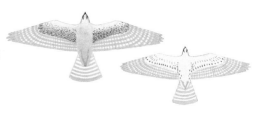

RED-NECKED FALCON
Below white; flanks and underwing coverts washed rufous; all except throat closely barred black; tail with a broad, black subterminal band. Flight rapid.
(Rooinekvalk)

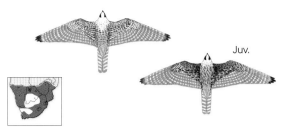

Juv.

PEREGRINE FALCON
Throat and upper breast white; rest of body and underwing coverts very pale rufous, closely barred black; tail well banded black. Fast wing-flaps followed by glides. (Swerfvalk)

EURASIAN HOBBY
Body and underwing coverts washed rufous; thighs chestnut; underparts (except throat) heavily streaked and barred black. Flight rapid or leisurely. Summer. (Europese boomvalk)

♂

♀

PYGMY FALCON
Very small (robin-sized) falcon. Body and underwing coverts white; underwings and tail black with dense white barring and banding. Flight rapid. (Dwergvalk)

ROCK KESTREL
Below body rufous; rest white; flight feathers lightly barred grey; tail with broad, black subterminal band. Often hovers. (Rooivalk)

♂

♀

♀

LESSER KESTREL
Male has pale rufous body; underwings white; tail white with single, broad black terminal band. Female has entire underparts lightly streaked and barred black; tail with three narrow and one broad band. Small flocks wheel about in a leisurely manner. Summer. (Kleinrooivalk)

EASTERN RED-FOOTED KESTREL (female)
Body, tail and underwings white, streaked and barred black; flight feathers much darker. Flocks of both sexes wheel about in a leisurely manner. Summer. (Oostelike rooipootvalk)

Glossary

Band
A horizontal stripe of colour, as in tail-band.

Cap
The top of the head above the eyes.

Cere
The soft base of the beak in parrots, pigeons and birds of prey.

Coverts
The feathers that cover the ears, wings, etc.

Crown
The topmost part of the head.

Culmen
The top ridge of the bird's upper mandible.

Eye-stripe
A band of colour, often black, in front of and behind the eye.

Gape
The corner of the mouth where the mandibles are hinged.

Gular region
The sides of the throat.

Hood
The colouring of the top of the head when it extends to below the eyes.

Lores
The area between the eye and the beak.

Mandibles
The upper and lower jaws of a bird.

Mantle
The upper back adjacent to the lower back.

Moustacial streak
A line of colour extending from the bird's gape.

Nape
The back of the head.

Pectoral region
The sides of the upper breast.

Primaries
The major flight feathers on the outer part of the wing.

Rectrices
Tail feathers; rectrix in the singular.

Remiges
The primary flight feathers; remix in the singular.

Secondaries
The second most important flight feathers lying between the primary feathers and the body.

Streak
A vertical mark, longer than a spot.

Underwing coverts
The contour feathers covering the forward part of a bird's wing.

Thighs
The feathers covering a bird's upper legs.

Vent
The feathered region covering the bird's anus.

Afrikaans index

Aasvoël, baard- 249, 261
Aasvoël, Egiptiese 291
Aasvoël, krans- 221, 249
Aasvoël, monnik- 136, 221
Aasvoël, swart- 67, 137, 221
Aasvoël, wit- 67, 291
Aasvoël, witkop- 67, 137, 221, 291
Aasvoël, witrug- 221, 249
Arend, breëkop- 68, 101, 224, 250, 281, 292
Arend, bruin- 223
Arend, bruinslang- 222, 291
Arend, dubbelbandslang- 87, 294
Arend, dwerg- 222
Arend, enkelbandslang- 87, 294
Arend, gevlekte 222
Arend, grootjag- 68, 223, 250
Arend, kleinjag- 223
Arend, kroon- 198, 224, 261, 281, 294
Arend, langkuif- 51, 223, 281, 291
Arend, roof- 249
Arend, steppe- 223, 250
Arend, swartborsslang- 68, 222, 289
Arend, vis- 198, 224
Arend, witkruisvlei- 51, 292
Berghaan 51, 137, 291
Bleshoender 50, 133
Bokmakierie 96, 167, 183, 274
Bontrokkie, gewone 207
Boomkruiper 262
Bosbontrokkie, beloog- 75, 143, 274
Bosbontrokkie, Kaapse 209, 273
Bosbontrokkie, Mosambiek- 75
Bosbontrokkie, pririt- 75, 273

Bosbontrokkie, witlies- 75, 209, 274
Boskraai, gewone 71, 113
Boskrapper 233
Bosmusikant 168, 241
Breëbek 232
Bromvoël 53, 141
Byvanger, klein- 53
Byvanger, mikstert- 53
Byvreter, blouwang- 110, 180
Byvreter, Europese 110, 160, 270
Byvreter, klein- 160, 180, 270
Byvreter, olyf- 180
Byvreter, rooibors- 109, 119
Byvreter, rooikeel- 119, 180
Byvreter, swaelstert- 109, 160, 180, 270
Dassievoël 56, 207, 272
Diederikkie 139, 179
Dikkop 260
Dikkop, water- 255
Dobbertjie, klein- 195, 217
Dobbertjie, kuifkop- 218, 280
Dobbertjie, swartnek- 217
Draaihals 205
Drawwertjie, bloukop- 198
Drawwertjie, bronsvlerk- 248, 267
Drawwertjie, drieband- 267
Drawwertjie, dubbelband- 267
Drawwertjie, trek- 198, 248
Duif, geelbekbos- 227
Duif, gewone tortel- 90, 269
Duif, grootring- 138, 269
Duif, krans- 118, 139, 202
Duif, papegaai- 139, 177
Duif, rooioogtortel- 138, 269

Duif, tuin- 177
Duifie, groenvlek- 177
Duifie, kaneel- 202
Duifie, Namakwa- 138, 251
Duifie, rooibors 90
Duifie, witbors- 227
Duiker, bank- 48, 278
Duiker, kuifkop- 48, 278
Duiker, riet- 48, 216, 278
Duiker, trek- 48
Duiker, witbors- 63, 216
Eend, bloubek- 104, 195, 217
Eend, bruin- 217
Eend, fluit- 245
Eend, geelbek- 158, 176, 259
Eend, gevlekte 104, 258
Eend, Kaapse slop- 104, 176, 258
Eend, knobbel- 66, 104, 291
Eend, koper- 84, 195
Eend, nonnetjie- 195
Eend, rooibek- 133, 258
Eend, swart- 217
Eend, teel- 176, 258
Eend, witrug- 258
Elsie, bont- 66
Elsie, rooipoot- 66, 135
Fisant, bosveld- 136, 220
Fisant, Kaapse 220
Fisant, Natalse- 136, 220, 261
Fisant, rooibek- 135, 249
Fisant, rooikeel- 136, 220
Flamink, groot- 101, 118, 290
Flamink, klein- 118, 132
Flap, geelrug- 59, 171

Flap, Kaapse 59, 171
Flap, kortstert- 58, 123
Flap, langstert- 59, 124
Flap, rooikeel- 58, 124, 275
Flap, witvlerk- 59, 171
Fret, dikbek- 79
Fret, gewone 79
Fret, rooirug- 79, 212
Gans, dwerg- 148, 176
Gans, kol- 195
Glasogie, geel- 168
Glasogie, Kaapse 168, 184
Hadeda 244
Hamerkop 216
Heuningvoël, dunbek- 97, 166
Heuningvoël, skerpbek- 232
Heuningwyser, gevlekte 97, 166
Heuningwyser, groot- 162, 232
Heuningwyser, klein- 232
Hoephoep 204, 284
Houtkapper, bont- 72, 120, 161
Houtkapper, groen- 180
Houtkapper, kuifkop- 120, 161, 284
Houtkapper, rooikop- 120
Houtkapper, witoor- 72, 231
Hyliota, Mashona- 74, 166
Ibis, glans- 176, 216
Ibis, kalkoen- 104, 132
Jakkalsvoël, bos- 224
Jakkalsvoël, bruin- 224
Jakkalsvoël, rooibors- 199, 225, 250, 292
Jakkalsvoël, witbors 68, 225, 289
Janfrederik, gewone 151
Janfrederik, Heuglinse 152
Janfrederik, lawaaimaker- 152
Janfrederik, Natal- 152
Janfrederik, witkeel- 151
Janfrederik, witkol- 164
Jangroentjie 183
Kakelaar, gewone 53, 113, 141
Kakelaar, pers- 53
Kakelaar, swartbek- 53, 113, 189
Kalkoentjie, geelkeel- 162, 271
Kalkoentjie, oranjekeel- 150, 162, 271
Kalkoentjie, rooikeel- 271
Kalkoentjie, rooskeel- 122
Kanarie, berg- 173
Kanarie, bergpietjie- 173, 241
Kanarie, dikbek- 172, 185
Kanarie, geel- 172, 185
Kanarie, geelbors- 173
Kanarie, geeloog- 172
Kanarie, gestreepte 185
Kanarie, Kaapse 172
Kanarie, streepkop- 97
Kanarie, swartkop- 79, 213
Kanarie, swartoor- 79, 245
Kanarie, witkeel- 173
Kanarie, witvlerk- 97
Kapokvoël, grys- 95, 152
Kapokvoël, Kaapse 165
Katakoeroe, blou- 92
Katakoeroe, swart- 54, 163, 263
Katakoeroe, witbors- 92
Katlagter, pylvlek- 234
Katlagter, wit- 74
Katlagter, witkruis- 234
Kelkiewyn 262, 268
Kemphaan 259
Kiewiet, bont- 66, 85

Kiewiet, grootswartvlerk- 85, 219
Kiewiet, kleinswartvlerk- 85, 219
Kiewiet, kroon- 134, 247, 267
Kiewiet, lel- 158, 247
Kiewiet, witkop- 85, 158, 248
Kiewiet, witvlerk- 66, 134, 247, 267
Klappertjie, laeveld- 252
Kleinjantjie, bandkeel- 165, 272
Kleinjantjie, geelbors- 165, 182, 273
Kleinjantjie, Ruddse 182, 272
Knoet 247
Koekoek, dikbek- 69
Koekoek, gevlekte 69, 283
Koekoek, swart- 52
Koester, geelbors- 162
Kolpensie, groen- 126, 171, 185
Kolpensie, rooikeel- 126
Kolpensie, rooskeel- 73, 126
Konkoit 122, 167, 182, 274
Korhaan, blou- 86, 105
Korhaan, bos- 280
Korhaan, langbeen- 248
Korhaan, swart- 67, 135
Korhaan, vaal- 204
Korhaan, woestyn- 248
Koringvoël 241
Kraai, huis- 55, 93
Kraai, swart- 55, 113
Kraai, witbors- 72
Kraai, withals- 55
Kraanvoël, blou- 86, 105, 292
Kraanvoël, lel- 86, 135, 291
Kwartel, Afrikaanse 260
Kwartel, bont- 198
Kwartelkoning 196, 245
Kwêkwêvoël, groenrug- 182
Kwêkwêvoël, grysrug- 95
Kwelea, rooibek- 144
Kwelea, rooikop- 123
Kwêvoël 91
Kwikkie, berg- 92, 271
Kwikkie, bont- 72, 272
Kwikkie, geel- 162
Kwikkie, gewone 92, 272
Laksman, bontrok- 76, 210
Laksman, fiskaal- 76
Laksman, grys- 96
Laksman, kortstert- 77
Laksman, kremetart- 254
Laksman, langstert- 56, 76
Laksman, olyfbos- 182
Laksman, oranjeborsbos- 152, 167
Laksman, rooibors- 122
Laksman, rooirug- 96, 210
Laksman, stekelkophelm- 57
Laksman, swarthelm- 57, 143
Laksman, swartoogbos- 153
Laksman, withelm- 78, 285
Langstertjie, bruinsy- 236
Langstertjie, gevlekte 166, 238
Langstertjie, Karoo- 238
Langstertjie, Namakwa- 238
Langstertjie, rooioor- 209, 273
Langstertjie, swartband- 238, 273
Langtoon, groot- 197
Lepelaar 101, 132, 288
Lewerik, Barlowse 205, 252
Lewerik, donker- 232
Lewerik, duin- 252
Lewerik, grysrug- 263

Lewerik, Karoo- 205
Lewerik, Karoo langbek- 252
Lewerik, Namib- 253
Lewerik, pienkbek- 206
Lewerik, rooi- 205
Lewerik, rooikop- 252
Lewerik, rooinek- 205, 252, 284
Lewerik, rooirug- 72, 206, 263
Lewerik, sabota- 252
Lewerik, swartoor- 72, 263
Lewerik, Vaalrivier- 232
Lewerik, vlakte- 206
Lewerik, woestyn- 253, 285
Loerie, bloukuif- 106, 119, 139, 188, 282
Loerie, bos- 119, 179
Loerie, Knysna- 106, 119, 139, 179, 282
Lyster, Angolaklip 93, 206
Lyster, bruin- 150, 234
Lyster, gevlekte 235
Lyster, Kaapse berg- 207
Lyster, Kaapse klip- 93, 207
Lyster, korttoonklip- 93, 151, 206
Lyster, langtoonklip- 93, 151, 207
Lyster, Natal- 235
Lyster, olyf- 150, 234
Lyster, oranje- 150, 234
Lyster, oranjeborsberg- 151
Lyster, palmmôre- 208, 245, 274
Lyster, rooibek- 150, 234
Lyster, swartberg- 56
Mahem 86, 280, 293
Makou, wilde- 49, 66, 132, 176, 217
Malgas, wit- 62, 156, 289
Maraboe 64, 84, 290
Mees, acaciagrys- 73, 93
Mees, gewone swart- 55, 73
Mees, miombogrys- 73
Mees, Ovamboswart- 55, 73
Mees, swartkop- 73
Meeu, gryskop- 82, 130
Meeu, kelp- 62
Meeu, Hartlaubse 82, 100, 130
Meeu, swartrug- 62, 130, 156
Meitjie 179
Melba, geelrug- 125, 144
Melba, gewone 124, 144, 185
Mooimeisie 159, 179
Mossie, gewone 78, 97, 212
Mossie, groot- 212
Mossie, gryskop- 97, 211
Mossie, huis- 211
Muisvoël, gevlekte 251, 283
Muisvoël, rooiwang- 140, 251, 283
Muisvoël, witkruis- 92, 283
Naguile 262
Neddikkie 94, 237
Neushoringvoël, Bradfieldse 150, 231
Neushoringvoël, geelbek- 71, 160
Neushoringvoël, gekroonde 71, 141, 231
Neushoringvoël, grys- 231
Neushoringvoël, Monteirose 141, 231
Neushoringvoël, rooibek- 71, 141
Nikator, geelvlek- 163
Nimmersat 65, 131, 157, 290
Nuwejaarsvoël, bont- 52, 69, 283
Nuwejaarsvoël, gestreepte 69, 283
Ooievaar, grootswart- 64, 131, 290
Ooievaar, kleinswart- 65, 290
Ooievaar, oopbek- 49
Ooievaar, saalbek- 64, 131, 157, 290

Ooievaar, wit- 64, 131, 290
Ooievaar, wolnek- 65, 216
Papegaai, bloupens- 106, 159, 227
Papegaai, bosveld- 106, 159, 178, 227
Papegaai, bruinkop- 178, 227
Papegaai, groot- 178
Papegaai, ringnek- 178
Parkiet, Niassa- 118, 139, 178
Parkiet, rooiwang- 118, 178
Patrys, berg- 260
Patrys, bos- 135, 198, 280
Patrys, Kalahari- 260
Patrys, laeveld- 261
Patrys, rooivlerk- 261
Pelikaan, klein- 83, 156
Pelikaan, wit- 100, 156, 289
Piek, bont- 74
Piek, swart- 56, 235
Pietjiekanarie, Kaapse 173, 241
Piet-my-vrou 91, 269
Pikkewyn, bril- 62
Pou, gom- 248, 268, 280
Reier, blou- 84, 279, 288, 292
Reier, dwergriet- 83
Reier, geelbekwit- 100, 157
Reier, gewone nag- 63, 83, 279
Reier, groenrug- 83
Reier, grootriet- 258
Reier, grootwit- 100, 157, 288
Reier, kleinwit- 100, 157, 279, 288
Reier, ral- 244, 278
Reier, reuse- 84, 194
Reier, rooi- 244, 279
Reier, rooikeel- 49, 83, 278
Reier, rooipens- 49, 194
Reier, swart- 49, 157, 278
Reier, swartkop- 84, 279, 292
Reier, vee- 100, 288
Reier, witrugnag- 194
Renostervoël, geelbek- 143, 240
Renostervoël, rooibek- 143, 240
Riethaan, gestreepte 245
Riethaan, groot- 85, 218
Riethaan, grootkoning- 105, 133,
    177, 188
Riethaan, klein- 196
Riethaan, kleinkoning- 105, 133, 177
Riethaan, swart- 50, 134, 158
Rooiassie 126, 145, 153, 171
Rooibekkie, koning- 79, 145
Rooibekkie, pylstert- 145
Rotsvoël 209
Ruiter, bos- 218
Ruiter, gewone 218
Ruiter, groenpoot- 246
Ruiter, moeras- 246
Ruiter, terek- 247
Saadvretertjie, rooirug- 125
Saadvretertjie, rooistert- 125
Sandpatrys, dubbelband- 262, 268
Sandpatrys, geelkeel- 262, 268
Sandpatrys, gevlekte 202, 262
Sanger, bruinkeelbos- 236, 273
Sanger, donkerwangbos- 166, 182
Sanger, gebande 237
Sanger, geel- 165
Sanger, geelkeel- 166
Sanger, geelpensbos- 166, 236
Sanger, hof- 167
Sanger, kaneelbors- 208, 237

Sanger, rooiborsruigte- 232
Sanger, Stierlingse 237
Sanger, tuin- 236
Sanger, Kaapse vlei- 232
Sekretarisvoël 87, 281, 293
Skaapwagter, hoëveld- 74, 272
Skoorsteenveër 65, 288
Slanghalsvoël 194, 244
Slangverklikker 236
Sneeubal 76
Snip, Afrikaanse 259
Snip, goud- 196, 266
Spegte 181
Speg, baard- 121
Speg, Bennettse 121
Speg, goudstert- 121
Speg, grond- 120
Speg, gryskop- 120
Speg, kardinaal- 121, 284
Speg, Knysna- 121
Spekvreter, gewone 235
Spekvreter, Herero- 253
Spekvreter, Karoo- 94, 253
Spekvreter, vlakte- 235
Spekvreter, woestyn- 253
Sperwer, Afrikaanse 88, 225, 296
Sperwer, gebande 88, 199, 295
Sperwer, klein- 87, 199, 295
Sperwer, Ovambo- 88, 199, 295
Sperwer, rooibors- 199, 250, 295
Sperwer, swart- 52, 68, 295
Sperwer, witkruis- 52, 88, 137, 295
Spookvoël 96, 153, 267, 183
Spotvoël 165
Spreeu, bleekvlerk- 57
Spreeu, Europese 57, 189, 263
Spreeu, groot-blouoorglans- 114, 190
Spreeu, grootglans- 114, 190
Spreeu, Indiese 240
Spreeu, klein-blouoorglans- 114, 190
Spreeu, kleinglans- 115
Spreeu, langstertglans- 114, 189
Spreeu, lel- 101
Spreeu, rooivlerk- 57
Spreeu, spitsstertglans- 115
Spreeu, witbors- 189
Spreeu, witgat- 57, 78, 240
Sprinkaanvoël, rooivlerk- 219
Sprinkaanvoël, swartvlerk- 219
Sprinkaanvoël, withals- 219
Steenloper 148, 158, 197, 259, 267
Sterretjie, Arktiese 63, 82, 131
Sterretjie, geelbek- 156
Sterretjie, gewone 63, 82, 130
Sterretjie, groot- 62, 82
Sterretjie, kuifkop- 148
Sterretjie, reuse- 62, 82, 130
Sterretjie, witbaard- 63, 82, 131
Sterretjie, witvlerk- 63
Strandkiewiet, Asiatiese 197, 245, 266
Strandkiewiet, drieband- 134, 218, 266
Strandkiewiet, geelbors- 246, 266
Strandkiewiet, grys- 259
Strandkiewiet, ringnek- 148, 246, 266
Strandkiewiet, rooiband- 197, 245, 266
Strandkiewiet, vaal- 246
Strandloper, klein- 247
Streepkoppie, geel- 173
Streepkoppie, klip- 213
Streepkoppie, rooirug- 153, 173

Streepkoppie, rooivlerk- 213
Streepkoppie, vaal- 255
Suikerbekkie, blou- 191
Suikerbekkie, geelpens- 168, 184, 190
Suikerbekkie, grootrooiband- 122,
    183, 254, 275
Suikerbekkie, grys- 96
Suikerbekkie, kleinrooiband- 122,
    183, 254, 274
Suikerbekkie, kortbek- 168, 183
Suikerbekkie, Marico- 123, 184,
    255, 275
Suikerbekkie, Namakwa 78
Suikerbekkie, olyf- 184
Suikerbekkie, oranjebors- 153, 184, 275
Suikerbekkie, purperband- 184, 255
Suikerbekkie, rooikeel- 123
Suikerbekkie, rooikeel- 58
Suikerbekkie, swart- 58, 191, 255
Suikerbekkie, witpens- 115
Swael, Afrikaanse oewer- 230
Swael, blou- 108
Swael, draadstert- 108, 149
Swael, Europese 108, 269
Swael, Europese oewer- 230, 270
Swael, familie- 108
Swael, gebande oewer- 230, 270
Swael, grootstreep- 107, 149
Swael, gryskruis- 109
Swael, huis- 107
Swael, kleinstreep- 107, 149
Swael, krans- 230
Swael, moskee- 107
Swael, pêrelbors- 109
Swael, rooibors- 107
Swael, swartsaagvlerk- 54
Swael, witkeel- 108, 269
Swie, suidelike- 127, 171, 185
Sysie, gewone blou- 115
Sysie, grys- 97, 127
Sysie, koningblou- 115, 145, 191, 212
Sysie, rooibek- 126, 145
Sysie, swartwang- 127
Tarentaal, gewone 51, 86, 105, 136
Tarentaal, kuifkop- 51, 105, 281
Tinker, geelbles- 150, 161
Tinker, groen- 181
Tinker, rooibles- 120, 161
Tinker, swartbles- 161
Tinktinkie, bosveld- 234
Tinktinkie, grysrug- 92, 196
Tinktinkie, rooiwang- 237
Tiptol, Kaapse 164, 233
Tiptol, rooibek- 142, 233
Tiptol, rooioog- 142, 164, 233, 285
Tiptol, swartoog- 164, 233, 285
Tjagra, grysbors- 210
Tjagra, rooivlerk- 211
Tjagra, swartkroon- 211
Tjeriktik, bosveld- 94, 208
Tjeriktik, grys- 94
Tobie, swart- 50, 135
Troupant, Europese 112
Troupant, geelbek- 112, 160, 188
Troupant, gewone 112, 188
Troupant, groot- 112, 188, 204
Troupant, knopstert- 112
Uil, bos- 228
Uil, gebande 229
Uil, gevlekte oor- 229

Uil, gras- 228
Uil, Kaapse oor- 148, 228
Uil, nonnetjie 91, 250
Uil, reuse-oor- 91
Uil, skops- 91, 229, 250, 258
Uil, vis- 204, 229
Uil, vlei- 228
Uil, witkol- 228
Uil, witwang- 91, 148
Valk, Afrikaanse boom- 201
Valk, akkedis- 87
Valk, bleeksing- 88, 293
Valk, blou- 87, 101, 289
Valk, blouvlei- 89
Valk, Dickinsonse 89, 226, 293
Valk, donkersing- 88, 137, 293
Valk, dwerg- 89, 200, 297
Valk, edel- 89, 200, 296
Valk, Europese boom- 201, 297
Valk, grootrooi- 201
Valk, kaalwang- 89, 251, 282, 293
Valk, kleinrooi- 90, 201, 297
Valk, koekoek- 200, 226, 251, 282, 296
Valk, oostelike rooipoot- 90, 138, 202, 293, 297
Valk, roet- 293
Valk, rooi- 297
Valk, rooinek- 200, 296
Valk, swerf- 297
Valk, taita- 200
Valk, vis- 69, 226, 268, 282
Valk, vlermuis- 52, 226
Valk, westelike rooipoot- 90, 138, 202, 293
Versamelvoël 255
Vink, bandkeel- 127, 263, 275
Vink, gewone paradys- 59
Vink, goudgeel- 170
Vink, kleingeel- 170
Vink, koekoek- 172
Vink, rooi- 124

Vink, rooikop- 127
Vink, swartkeelgeel- 170
Vink, vuurkop- 124
Vinkie, blou- 59, 125
Vinkie, gewone kwartel- 144
Vinkie, staalblou- 145
Visvanger, blou- 111, 149
Visvanger, bont- 70, 271, 284
Visvanger, bosveld- 110, 140
Visvanger, bruinkop- 110, 140
Visvanger, dwerg- 111, 140
Visvanger, gestreepte 71, 111
Visvanger, gryskop- 110, 140, 204
Visvanger, gryskop- 92
Visvanger, kuifkop- 111, 140, 149
Visvanger, reuse- 70, 204, 284
Vleikuiken, gevlekte 196
Vleikuiken, rooibors- 196
Vleiloerie, gewone 203
Vleiloerie, groen- 159
Vleiloerie, groot- 203
Vleiloerie, Senegal- 203
Vleiloerie, swart- 203
Vleiloerie, witbrou- 203
Vleivalk, Afrikaanse 225, 268
Vleivalk, blou- 89, 296
Vleivalk, witbors- 89, 101, 289
Vleivalk, witkruis- 52, 69, 292
Vlieëvanger, blougrys- 95
Vlieëvanger, bloukuif- 239, 285
Vlieëvanger, donker- 238
Vlieëvanger, Europese 239
Vlieëvanger, fee- 95
Vlieëvanger, fiskaal- 75
Vlieëvanger, groot- 239
Vlieëvanger, Marico- 239
Vlieëvanger, muiskleur- 239
Vlieëvanger, paradys- 95, 113, 210, 285
Vlieëvanger, rooistert- 152, 167
Vlieëvanger, swart- 54
Vlieëvanger, waaierstert- 95
Volstruis 67, 220

Vuurvinkie, bruin- 125
Vuurvinkie, Jamesonse 126
Vuurvinkie, Kaapse 126
Vuurvinkie, rooibek- 125, 255
Wagter, berg- 56, 74, 94, 235
Wagter, bergklip- 75, 253
Waterfiskaal, moeras- 77
Waterfiskaal, suidelike- 77
Waterfiskaal, tropiese- 77
Waterhoender 50
Waterhoender, klein- 50, 134
Waterploeër 62, 130
Watertrapper 132, 216
Wespedief 225, 294
Wewer, bontrug- 170
Wewer, bril- 169
Wewer, bruinkeel- 169
Wewer, buffel- 58, 143, 240
Wewer, dikbek- 58, 241
Wewer, geel- 169
Wewer, goud- 169
Wewer, Kaapse 169
Wewer, rooikop- 123, 144, 170
Wielewaal, Afrikaanse 142, 163
Wielewaal, Europese 142, 163
Wielewaal, groenkop- 181
Wielewaal, swartkop- 142, 163
Willie, geelbors- 164
Willie, gewone 181
Willie, streepwang- 181
Windswael, horus- 70
Windswael, klein- 54, 70
Windswael, palm 230
Windswael, witkruis- 54, 70
Windswael, witpens- 270
Wipstert, baard- 254
Wipstert, gestreepte 208, 254
Wipstert, Kalahari- 208, 254
Wou, geelbek- 159, 222
Woudapie 244
Wulp, groot- 260
Wulp, klein- 260

English index

Apalis, Bar-throated 165, 272
Apalis, Rudd's 182, 272
Apalis, Yellow-breasted 165, 182, 273
Avocet, (Pied) 66
Babbler, Arrow-marked 234
Babbler, Hartlaub's 234
Babbler, Pied (Southern) 74
Babbler, White-rumped, Southern see Babbler, Hartlaub's
Barbet, Black-collared 120
Barbet, Crested 120, 161, 284
Barbet, Green 180
Barbet, Pied, Acacia 72, 120, 161
Barbet, White-eared 72, 231
Bateleur 51, 137, 291
Batis, Cape 209, 273
Batis, Chin-spot 75, 209, 274
Batis, Mozambique 75
Batis, Pririt 75, 273
Bee-eater, Blue-cheeked 110, 180
Bee-eater, Carmine (Southern) 109, 119

Bee-eater, European 110, 160, 270
Bee-eater, Little 160, 180, 270
Bee-eater, Olive 180
Bee-eater, Swallow-tailed 109, 160, 180, 270
Bee-eater, White-fronted 119, 180
Bishop, Fire-crowned 124
Bishop, Golden 170
Bishop, Red (Southern) 124
Bittern (Great) 258
Bittern, Dwarf 83
Bittern, Little 244
Blackcap, Bush 142, 233
Bokmakierie 96, 167, 183, 274
Boubou, Crimson-breasted 122
Boubou, Southern 77
Boubou, Swamp 77
Boubou, Tropical 77
Broadbill, African 232
Brubru 76, 210
Bulbul, Black-eyed 164, 233, 285
Bulbul, Cape 164, 233

Bulbul, Red-eyed (African) 142, 164, 233, 285
Bulbul, Sombre 181
Bulbul, Stripe-cheeked 181
Bulbul, Terrestrial 233
Bulbul, Yellow-bellied 164
Bunting, Cabanis's 173
Bunting, Cape 213
Bunting, Golden-breasted 153, 173
Bunting, Lark-like 255
Bunting, Rock 213
Bustard, Kori 248, 268, 280
Buzzard, Augur 68, 225, 289
Buzzard, Forest 224
Buzzard, Honey (European) 225, 294
Buzzard, Jackal 199, 225, 250, 292
Buzzard, Lizard 87
Buzzard, Steppe 224
Canary (or Seedeater), Black-eared 79, 245
Canary, Black-headed 79, 213
Canary, Black-throated 173

Canary, Bully 172, 185
Canary, Cape 172
Canary, Forest 185
Canary, Lemon-breasted 173
Canary, Protea 97
Canary, Streaky-headed 97
Canary, White-throated 173
Canary, Yellow 172, 185
Canary, Yellow-eyed 172
Chat, Ant-eating (Southern) 56, 235
Chat, Arnot's 74
Chat, Boulder 56
Chat, Buff-streaked 75, 253
Chat, Familiar 235
Chat, Herero 253
Chat, Karoo 94, 253
Chat, Mocking 56, 207, 272
Chat, Mountain 56, 74, 94, 235
Chat, Sickle-winged 235
Chat, Tractrac 253
Cisticola, Grey-backed 92, 196
Cisticola, Rattling 234
Cisticola, Red-faced 237
Coot, Red-knobbed 50, 133
Cormorant, Bank 48, 278
Cormorant, Cape 48
Cormorant, Crowned 48, 278
Cormorant, Reed 48, 216, 278
Cormorant, White-breasted 63, 216
Corncrake 196, 245
Coucal, Black 203
Coucal, Burchell's 203
Coucal, Coppery-tailed 203
Coucal, Green 159
Coucal, Senegal 203
Coucal, White-browed 203
Courser, Bronze-winged 248, 267
Courser, Burchell's 198
Courser, Double-banded 267
Courser, Temminck's 198, 248
Courser, Three-banded 267
Crake, Black 50, 134, 158
Crake, Striped 245
Crane, Blue 86, 105, 292
Crane, Crowned (Grey) 86, 280, 293
Crane, Wattled 86, 135, 291
Creeper, Spotted 262
Crow, Black 55, 113
Crow, House 55, 93
Crow, Pied 72
Cuckoo, Black 52
Cuckoo, Diederik 139, 179
Cuckoo, Emerald, African 159, 179
Cuckoo, Spotted, Great 69, 283
Cuckoo, Jacobin 52, 69, 283
Cuckoo, Klaas's 179
Cuckoo, Red-chested 91, 269
Cuckoo, Striped 69, 283
Cuckoo, Thick-billed 69
Cuckooshrike, Black 54, 163, 263
Cuckooshrike, Grey 92
Cuckooshrike, White-breasted 92
Curlew (Eurasian) 260
Dabchick 195, 217
Darter, African 194, 244
Dikkop, Spotted 260
Dikkop (or Thick-knee), Water 255
Dove, Cinnamon 202
Dove, Laughing 90
Dove, Mourning, African 138, 269

Dove, Namaqua 138, 251
Dove, Red-eyed 138, 269
Dove, Tambourine 227
Dove, Turtle, Cape 90, 269
Dove, Wood-, Emerald-spotted 177
Drongo, Fork-tailed 53
Drongo, Square-tailed 53
Duck, Black, African 217
Duck, Fulvous 245
Duck, Knob-billed 66, 104, 291
Duck, Maccoa 104, 195, 217
Duck, White-backed 258
Duck, White-faced 195
Duck, Yellow-billed 158, 176, 259
Eagle, Black (African) 51, 292
Eagle, Booted 222
Eagle, Crowned (African) 198, 224, 261, 281, 294
Eagle, Fish, African 198, 224
Eagle, Hawk, African 68, 223, 250
Eagle, Spotted, Lesser 222
Eagle, Long-crested 51, 223, 281, 291
Eagle, Martial 68, 101, 224, 250, 281, 292
Eagle, Snake, Black-breasted 68, 222, 289
Eagle, Snake, Brown 222, 291
Eagle, Snake, Southern Banded 87, 294
Eagle, Snake, Western Banded 87, 294
Eagle, Steppe 223, 250
Eagle, Tawny 249
Eagle, Wahlberg's 223
Egret, Black 49, 157, 278
Egret, Cattle 100, 288
Egret, Little 100, 157, 279, 288
Egret, Slaty 49, 83, 278
Egret, Yellow-billed 100, 157
Eremomela, Burnt-necked 236, 273
Eremomela, Yellow-bellied 166, 236
Falcon, Lanner 89, 200, 296
Falcon, Peregrine 297
Falcon, Pygmy 89, 200, 297
Falcon, Red-necked 200, 296
Falcon, Sooty 293
Falcon, Taita 200
Finch, Cuckoo 172
Finch, Cut-throat 127, 263, 275
Finch, Melba 124, 144, 185
Finch, Quail (African) 144
Finch, Red-headed 127
Finchlark, Black-eared 72, 263
Finchlark, Chestnut-backed 72, 206, 263
Finchlark, Grey-backed 263
Finfoot, African 132, 216
Firefinch, Blue-billed 126
Firefinch, Brown 125
Firefinch, Jameson's 126
Firefinch, Red-billed 125, 255
Flamingo, Greater 101, 118, 290
Flamingo, Lesser 118, 132
Flufftail, Buff-spotted 196
Flufftail, Red-chested 196
Flycatcher, Black (Southern) 54
Flycatcher, Blue-grey 95
Flycatcher, Blue-mantled (Crested) 239, 285
Flycatcher, Chat 239

Flycatcher, Dusky (African) 238
Flycatcher, Fairy 95
Flycatcher, Fan-tailed 95
Flycatcher, Fiscal 75
Flycatcher, Marico 239
Flycatcher, Pallid 239
Flycatcher, Paradise (African) 95, 113, 210, 285
Flycatcher, Spotted 239
Francolin, Cape 220
Francolin, Crested 135, 198, 280
Francolin, Grey-winged 260
Francolin, Natal 136, 220, 261
Francolin, Orange River 260
Francolin, Red-billed 135, 249
Francolin, Red-necked 136, 220
Francolin, Red-wing 261
Francolin, Shelley's 261
Francolin, Swainson's 136, 220
Gallinule, Purple 105, 133, 177, 188
Gannet, Cape 62, 156, 289
Goose, Egyptian 195
Goose, Pygmy, African 148, 176
Goose, Spur-winged 49, 66, 132, 176, 217
Goshawk, African 88, 225, 296
Goshawk, Chanting, Dark 88, 137, 293
Goshawk, Chanting, Pale (Southern) 88, 293
Goshawk, Gabar 52, 88, 137, 295
Goshawk, Little Banded 88, 199, 295
Grebe, Black-necked 217
Grebe, Great Crested 218 280
Greenshank (Common) 246
Guineafowl, Crested 51, 105, 281
Guineafowl, Helmeted 51, 86, 105, 136
Gull, Grey-headed 82, 130
Gull, Hartlaub's 82, 100, 130
Gull, Cape 62, 130, 156
Gymnogene 89, 251, 282, 293
Hamerkop 216
Harrier, Black 52, 69, 292
Harrier, Marsh, African 268, 225
Harrier, Montagu's 89, 296
Hawk, Bat 52, 226
Hawk, Cuckoo (African) 200, 226, 251, 282, 296
Helmet Shrike, Chestnut-fronted 57
Helmet Shrike, Red-billed 57, 143
Helmet Shrike, White 78, 285
Heron, Black-headed 84, 279, 292
Heron, Goliath 84, 194
Heron, White, Great 100, 157, 288
Heron, Green-backed 83
Heron, Grey 84, 279, 288, 292
Heron, Night, Black-crowned 63, 83, 279
Heron, Night, White-backed 194
Heron, Purple 244, 279
Heron, Rufous-bellied 49, 194
Heron, Squacco 244, 278
Hobby, African 201
Hobby, Eurasian 201, 297
Honeybird, Green-backed see Honeybird, Slender-billed
Honeybird, Sharp-billed 232
Honeybird, Slender-billed (or Green-backed) 97, 166
Honeyguide, Greater 162, 232

Honeyguide, Lesser 232
Honeyguide, Scaly-throated 97, 166
Hoopoe, African 204, 284
Hornbill, Crowned 71, 141, 231
Hornbill, Grey, African 231
Hornbill, Ground, Southern 53, 141
Hornbill, Monteiro's 141, 231
Hornbill, Red-billed 71, 141
Hornbill, Southern Yellow-billed 71, 160
Hornbill, Trumpeter 71, 113
Ibis, Bald, Southern 104, 132
Ibis, Glossy 176, 216
Ibis, Hadeda 244
Ibis, Sacred 65, 288
Jacana, African 197
Kestrel, Dickinson's 89, 226, 293
Kestrel, Greater 201
Kestrel, Lesser 90, 201, 297
Kestrel, Red-footed, Eastern 90, 138, 202, 293, 297
Kestrel, Red-footed, Western 90, 138, 202, 293
Kestrel, Rock 90, 201, 297
Kingfisher, Brown-hooded 110, 140
Kingfisher, Giant 70, 204, 284
Kingfisher, Grey-headed 92, 110, 140, 204
Kingfisher, Half-collared 111, 149
Kingfisher, Malachite 111, 140, 149
Kingfisher, Pied 70, 271, 284
Kingfisher, Pygmy, African 111, 140
Kingfisher, Striped 71, 111
Kingfisher, Woodland 110, 140
Kite, Black-shouldered 87, 101, 289
Kite, Yellow-billed 159, 222
Knot (Red) 247
Korhaan, Black, Southern 67, 135
Korhaan, Black-bellied 248
Korhaan, Blue 86, 105
Korhaan, Karoo 204
Korhaan, Red-crested 280
Korhaan, Rüppell's 248
Lark, Barlow's 205, 252
Lark, Botha's 232
Lark, Dune 252
Lark, Dusky 232
Lark, Flappet 252
Lark, Gray's 253
Lark, Karoo 205
Larks, Long-billed 252
Lark, Pink-billed 206
Lark, Red 205
Lark, Red-capped 252
Lark, Rufous-naped 205, 252, 284
Lark, Sabota 252
Lark, Spike-heeled 206
Lark, Stark's 253, 285
Longclaw, Orange-throated 150, 162, 271
Longclaw, Yellow-throated 162, 271
Lourie, Grey 91
Lourie, Knysna 106, 119, 139, 179, 282
Lourie, Purple-crested 106, 119, 139, 188, 282
Lovebird, Lilian's 118, 139, 178
Lovebird, Rosy-faced 118, 178
Mannikin, Bronze 79
Mannikin, Pied 79
Mannikin, Red-backed 79, 212
Martin, Banded 230, 270

Martin, Brown-throated 230
Martin, House (Common) 109
Martin, Rock 230
Martin, Sand, European 230, 270
Moorhen 50
Moorhen, Lesser 50, 134
Mousebird, Red-faced 140, 251, 283
Mousebird, Speckled 251, 283
Mousebird, White-backed 92, 283
Myna, Indian 240
Neddicky (S and SE race) 94, 237
Nicator, Yellow-spotted 163
Nightjars 262
Oriole, Black-headed (Eastern) 142, 163
Oriole, Golden, African 142, 163
Oriole, Golden, Eurasian 142, 163
Osprey 69, 226, 268, 282
Ostrich (Common) 67, 220
Owl, Barn 91, 250
Owl, Barred, African 228
Owl, Eagle, Cape 148, 228
Owl, Eagle, Giant 91
Owl, Eagle, Spotted 229
Owl, Grass, African 228
Owl, Marsh 228
Owl, Pearl-spotted 228
Owl, Scops, African 91, 229, 250, 258
Owl, White-faced Scops 91, 148
Owl, Wood, African 228
Oxpecker, Red-billed 143, 240
Oxpecker, Yellow-billed 143, 240
Oystercatcher, Black, African 50, 135
Palm-Thrush, Collared 208, 245, 274
Paradise-Whydah (Eastern) 59
Parakeet, Rose-ringed 178
Parrot, Brown-headed 178, 227
Parrot, Cape 178
Parrot, Meyer's 106, 159, 178, 227
Parrot, Rüppell's 106, 159, 227
Pelican, Pink-backed 83, 156
Pelican, White, Eastern 100, 156, 289
Penguin, African 62
Pigeon, Feral 177
Pigeon, Green, African 139, 177
Pigeon, Rameron 227
Pigeon, Rock 118, 139, 202
Plover, Blacksmith 66, 85
Plover, Black-winged 85, 219
Plover, Black-winged, Lesser 85, 219
Plover, Caspian 197, 245, 266
Plover, Chestnut-banded 197, 245, 266
Plover, Crowned 134, 247, 267
Plover, Grey 259
Plover, Kittlitz's 246, 266
Plover, Long-toed 66, 134, 247, 267
Plover, Ringed (Common) 148, 246, 266
Plover, Three-banded 134, 218, 266
Plover, Wattled (African) 158, 247
Plover, White-crowned 85, 158, 248
Plover, White-fronted 246
Pochard, Southern 217
Pratincole, Black-winged 219
Pratincole, Red-winged 219
Pratincole, Rock 219
Prinia, Black-chested 238, 273
Prinia, Karoo 238
Prinia, Saffron 166, 238
Prinia, Tawny-flanked 236
Puffback 76

Pytilia, Golden-backed 125, 144
Quail, Common 260
Quail, Harlequin 198
Quelea, Red-billed 144
Quelea, Red-headed 123
Rail, African 85, 218
Raven, White-necked 55
Robin, Bearded 254
Robin, Cape 151
Robin, Chorister 152
Robin, Heuglin's 152
Robin, Kalahari 208, 254
Robin, Karoo 236
Robin, Natal 152
Robin, Starred 164
Robin, Scrub, White-browed 208, 254
Robin, White-throated 151
Rock-jumper, Cape 207
Rock-jumper, Orange-breasted 151
Rockrunner 209
Roller, Broad-billed 112, 160, 188
Roller, European 112
Roller, Lilac-breasted 112, 188
Roller, Purple 112, 188, 204
Roller, Racket-tailed 112
Ruff 259
Sandgrouse, Burchell's 202, 262
Sandgrouse, Double-banded 262, 268
Sandgrouse, Namaqua 262, 268
Sandgrouse, Yellow-throated 262, 268
Sandpiper, Common 218
Sandpiper, Marsh 246
Sandpiper, Terek 247
Sandpiper, Wood 218
Saw-wing, Black 54
Scimitarbill (Common) 53, 113, 189
Secretarybird 87, 281, 293
Seedeater, Black-eared see Canary, Black-eared
Seedeater, Protea see Canary, Protea
Shelduck, South African 84, 195
Shoveller, Cape 104, 176, 258
Shrike, Bush, Black-fronted 153
Shrike, Bush, Gorgeous 122, 167, 182, 274
Shrike, Bush, Grey-headed 96, 153, 167, 183
Shrike, Bush, Olive 182
Shrike, Bush, Orange-breasted 152, 167
Shrike, Fiscal 76
Shrike, Grey, Lesser 96
Shrike, Long-tailed 56, 76
Shrike, Red-backed 96, 210
Shrike, White-crowned (Southern) 254
Shrike, Helmet, White 78
Shrike, White-tailed 77
Siskin, Cape 173, 241
Siskin, Drakensberg 173, 241
Skimmer, African 62, 130
Snipe, African 259
Snipe, Painted 196, 266
Sparrow, Cape 78, 97, 212
Sparrow, Great 212
Sparrow, House 211
Sparrow, Grey-headed, Southern 97, 211
Sparrowhawk, Black 52, 68, 295
Sparrowhawk, Little 87, 199, 295
Sparrowhawk, Ovambo 88, 199, 295
Sparrowhawk, Rufous-breasted 199, 250, 295
Sparrow-weaver, White-browed 241

Spoonbill, African 101, 132, 288
Starling, European 57, 189, 263
Starling, Glossy, Blue-eared, Greater 114, 190
Starling, Glossy, Blue-eared, Lesser 114, 190
Starling, Glossy, Burchell's 114, 190
Starling, Glossy, Cape 115
Starling, Glossy, Long-tailed 114, 189
Starling, Pale-winged 57
Starling, Pied (African) 57, 78, 240
Starling, Plum-coloured 189
Starling, Red-winged 57
Starling, Wattled 101
Stilt, Black-winged 66, 135
Stint, Little 247
Stonechat, African 207
Stork, Abdim's 65, 290
Stork, Black 64, 131, 290
Stork, Marabou 64, 84, 290
Stork, Open-billed 49
Stork, Saddle-billed 64, 131, 157, 290
Stork, White 64, 131, 290
Stork, Woolly-necked 65, 216
Stork, Yellow-billed 65, 131, 157, 290
Sunbird, Black 58, 191, 255
Sunbird, Collared 168, 183
Sunbird, Double-collared, Greater 122, 183, 254, 275
Sunbird, Double-collared, (Southern), Lesser 122, 183, 254, 274
Sunbird, Dusky 78
Sunbird, Grey 96
Sunbird, Malachite 183
Sunbird, Marico 123, 184, 255, 275
Sunbird, Olive, Eastern 184
Sunbird, Orange-breasted 153, 184, 275
Sunbird, Purple-banded 184, 255
Sunbird, Scarlet-chested 58, 123
Sunbird, Violet-backed (Western) 191
Sunbird, White-bellied 115
Sunbird, Yellow-bellied 168, 184, 190
Swallow, Blue 108
Swallow, European 108, 269
Swallow, Grey-rumped 109
Swallow, Mosque 107
Swallow, Pearl-breasted 109
Swallow, Red-breasted 107
Swallow, Cliff, South African 108
Swallow, Striped, Greater 107, 149
Swallow, Striped, Lesser 107, 149
Swallow, White-throated 108, 269
Swallow, Wire-tailed 108, 149
Swift, Alpine 270
Swift, Horus 70
Swift, Little 54, 70
Swift, Palm, African 230
Swift, White-rumped 54, 70

Tchagra, Black-crowned 211
Tchagra, Southern 210
Tchagra, Three-streaked 211
Teal, Cape 176, 258
Teal, Hottentot 104, 258
Teal, Red-billed 133, 258
Tern, Arctic 63, 82, 131
Tern, Caspian 62, 82, 130
Tern, Common 63, 82, 130
Tern, Crested, Lesser 148
Tern Sandwich 62
Tern, Swift 156
Tern, Whiskered 63, 82, 131
Tern, White-winged 63
Thick-knee, Water see Dikkop, Water
Thrush, Groundscraper 235
Thrush, Karoo (or Sombre) 150, 234
Thrush, Kurrichane 150, 234
Thrush, Olive 150, 234
Thrush, Rock, Cape 93, 207
Thrush, Rock, Miombo 93, 206
Thrush, Rock, Sentinel 93, 151, 207
Thrush, Rock, Short-toed 93, 151, 206
Thrush, Sombre see Thrush, Karoo
Thrush, Spotted 235
Tinkerbird, Golden-rumped 161
Tinkerbird, Green 181
Tinkerbird, Red-fronted 120, 161
Tinkerbird, Yellow-fronted 150, 161
Tit, Ashy 73, 93
Tit, Carp's 55, 73
Tit, Black, Southern 55, 73
Tit, Grey, Northern 73
Tit, Penduline, African see Tit, Penduline, Grey
Tit, Penduline, Cape 165
Tit, Penduline, Grey (or African) 95, 152
Tit, Rufous-bellied 73
Titbabbler 94, 208
Titbabbler, Layard's 94
Trogon, Narina 119, 179
Turnstone, Ruddy 148, 158, 197, 259, 267
Twinspot, Pink-throated 126
Twinspot, Red-throated 126
Vulture, Bearded 249, 261
Vulture, Egyptian 291
Vulture (Griffon), Cape 221, 249
Vulture, Hooded 136, 221
Vulture, Lappet-faced 67, 137, 137
Vulture, Palm-nut 67, 291
Vulture, White-backed (African) 221, 249
Vulture, White-headed 67, 137, 221, 291

Wagtail, Pied, African 72, 272
Wagtail, Cape 92, 272
Wagtail, Long-tailed 92, 271
Wagtail, Yellow 162
Warbler, Barred 236
Warbler, Barred, Stierling's 237
Warbler, Bleating, Grey-backed

(or Camaroptera) 95
Warbler, Cinnamon-breasted 208, 237
Warbler, Garden 236
Warbler, Icterine 165
Warbler, Namaqua 238
Warbler, Rufous-eared 209, 273
Warbler, Sedge, African 232
Warbler, Victorin's 232
Warbler, Willow 167
Warbler, Yellow 165
Warbler, Yellow-throated (Woodland) 166
Waxbill, Black-cheeked 127
Waxbill, Blue 115
Waxbill, Common 126, 145
Waxbill, Grey 97, 127
Waxbill, Orange-breasted 126, 145, 153, 171
Waxbill, Swee 127, 171, 185
Waxbill, Violet-eared 115, 145, 191, 212
Weaver, Brown-throated (Southern) 169
Weaver, Cape 169
Weaver, Forest 168, 241
Weaver, Golden (Large) 169
Weaver, Masked (Southern) 170
Weaver, Masked, Lesser 170
Weaver, Red-billed Buffalo 58, 143, 240
Weaver, Red-headed 123, 144, 170
Weaver, Sociable 255
Weaver, Spectacled 169
Weaver, Spotted-backed 170
Weaver, Thick-billed 58, 241
Weaver, Yellow 169
Wheatear, Capped 74, 272
Whimbrel (Common) 260
White-eye, Cape 168, 184
White-eye, Yellow (African) 168
Whydah, Pin-tailed 79, 145
Whydah, Shaft-tailed 145
Widow Finch, Steel-blue 145
Widow Finch, Black 59, 125
Widow, Long-tailed 59, 124
Widow, Red-collared 58, 124, 275
Widow, Red-shouldered 58, 123
Widow, White-winged 59, 171
Widow, Yellow-backed 59, 171
Widow, Yellow-rumped 59, 171
Wood Hoopoe, Red-billed 53, 113, 141
Wood Hoopoe, Violet, Southern 53
Woodpecker, Bearded 121
Woodpecker, Bennett's 121
Woodpecker, Cardinal 121, 284
Woodpecker, Golden-tailed 121
Woodpecker, Ground 120
Woodpecker, Knysna 121
Woodpecker, Olive 120
Woodpeckers 181
Wryneck, Red-throated 205